Rebels
at
Rock Island

Rebels at Rock Island

The Story of a Civil War Prison

Benton McAdams

NORTHERN ILLINOIS

UNIVERSITY

PRESS

DeKalb 2000

Library of Congress Cataloging-in-Publication Data

McAdams, Benton.

    Rebels at Rock Island : the story of a Civil War prison / Benton McAdams.

      p.   cm.

    Includes bibliographical references and index.

    ISBN 0-87580-267-2 (alk. paper)

    1. Rock Island Arsenal (Ill.)—History—19th century. 2. United States—History—Civil War,

1861–1865—Prisoners and prisons. 3. United States—Politics and government—1861–1865.

4. Prisoners of war—Illinois—Rock Island—History—19th century. I. Title.

    E616.R6 M38 2000

    973.7'72—dc21   00-037226

To Ian and Alex Marshall

CONTENTS

A C K N O W L E D G M E N T S

I am indebted to a number of people without whose un-stinting help this book would have been impossible. First and fore-most among these is my wife, Vickie. It has often surprised me that wives are so often listed last in sections like this. Without Vickie this project would have proved impossible. She has served as an ex-cellent editor and research assistant, happily poring over nearly in-decipherable records for hours to find a single citation. Throughout the research and writing of this book she cheerfully kept the faith. My gratitude is immeasurable.

David McLaughlin of Philadelphia read early versions of the manuscript and made valuable suggestions. It was his sharp eye that noticed, among other things, my tendency to use parentheses rather more often than necessary. To Frank Crawford of Caledonia, Illinois, my thanks for access to his voluminous files on Illinois in the war. My thanks also to David Noe of Poplar Grove, Illinois, for answering some ordnance questions he probably does not even re-member I asked. Helen Ormsby graciously provided me a copy of part of her ancestor William Dillon's diary, which has proved the best and least emotionally tainted record left by a prisoner.

At the National Archives in Washington, D.C., Michael Musick and Michael Meier provided invaluable assistance on numerous oc-casions. My thanks especially to DeAnne Blanton of the Archives, who selflessly devoted herself to my problems and taught me that you can go fishing without being anywhere near water. Scott Forsythe of the Great Lakes Branch of the National Archives proved very helpful in providing records of the early days of the Rock Island Arsenal.

On the arsenal itself, Ralph Krippner, formerly archivist in the Arsenal's historical office, and Herbert Le Pore, formerly chief of that office, put up with my questions and demands for several days and allowed me to make very free with their copier, saving me countless hours of transcription. Chris Gayman Leinicke of the Arsenal Museum went far beyond the call of duty in helping me gather photographs. Bryan England, who wrote a short history of the prison, provided several suggestions.

For reading the sections on smallpox, pondering various medical conundrums I posed, and providing general moral support, I am indebted to Dr. Jack Welsh. Arlis Enburg of Rock Island, Illinois, put me up during research trips and greased the ways for me on the Island. To her go my heartfelt thanks.

In Springfield, Illinois, Cheryl Schnirring of the Illinois State Historical Library assisted me. Mary Michals of that institution proved a saint; Ms. Michaels gives public service a good name. Cody Wright of the Illinois State Archives was also extremely helpful. Sam Davis Elliot of Chattanooga offered several pieces of worthwhile advice. Bud Parrish, proprietor of Brandy Station Bookshelf, not only provided excerpts from some of his rare books but also came up with a copy of Thomas Berry's memoir when I had all but despaired of it. In Carlisle, Pennsylvania, at the U.S. Army Military History Institute, Pam Cheney put aside her own work to provide fresh copies of some records I had lost in my intricate, not to mention chaotic, file system. Her help was timely and crucial.

Finally, the staff at Rockford Education Center deserves thanks for enduring my owlish ways and omnipresent sarcasm. And my thanks go to the staff of Northern Illinois University Press for guiding me through a process both unfamiliar and aggravating. Most especially I owe a debt to Kevin Butterfield and Martin Johnson. Kevin's attention to detail has resulted in a more readable book, although we will forever disagree on certain uses of the comma. Martin's gentle but unyielding insistence on some structural changes have drastically improved this book, and he has singlehandedly managed to undermine my attitude toward editors.

Despite the help of all these people, any remaining mistakes are mine alone. I'd like to think otherwise, but that, too, would be a mistake.

T he most famous prisoner of Rock Island Barracks, the prison for Confederate soldiers at Rock Island, Illinois, was never actually at the prison. In fact, he never existed at all. He was the creation of Margaret Mitchell who, in her novel *Gone with the Wind,* sent the dashing Ashley Wilkes to Rock Island and there subjected him to unimaginable torments. In doing so, she helped perpetuate a myth, the legend of Rock Island as the "Andersonville of the North." The legend continues to this day: in an April 1999 book review in the *Civil War News,* Rock Island was yet again called the "Andersonville of the North."

The comparison is unjust: the death rate at Andersonville exceeded 30 percent; mortality at Rock Island was 16 percent. Shelter at Andersonville ranged from minimal to nonexistent; not a single prisoner at Rock Island ever slept outside. The citizens of Andersonville held no love for nor offered much aid to the Union prisoners; the citizens of Rock Island sustained the Confederate prisoners without stint.

This is not to deny that there was suffering at Rock Island. But the suffering did not exceed that at other Northern camps and never approached that at Andersonville. Mortality at other Northern prisons, such as Camp Douglas in Chicago and Camp Chase in Ohio, roughly paralleled the death rate at Rock Island. Mortality at Elmira, New York, far exceeded that of any other prison in the North: 24 percent of the prisoners who went to Elmira died there. Despite this, Rock Island has been singled out as a hellhole. Rock

Island deserves censure perhaps; it does not deserve the legend.

In truth, Rock Island Barracks was one of a half dozen major prisons in the North. Twelve thousand prisoners would reside on the Island, and some two thousand of them would die. At times the Barracks ranked second in terms of numbers of men held, exceeded only by the giant camp at Point Lookout, Maryland. Yet Rock Island has never been studied in detail. This seems strange, for several reasons.

Rock Island offers a nearly pristine view of the system Commissary General of Prisoners William Hoffman created and administered. Not only was it one of only three camps created specifically to house prisoners of war (the other two being Johnson's Island, Ohio, and Point Lookout), but it also enjoyed a rare stability of command. From two days after prisoners arrived until the Barracks closed, one man, Adolphus J. Johnson, commanded. What happened at Rock Island was not affected by changing personalities. Parallel to the stability of command was the stability of population. Prisoner exchanges ended before the Barracks opened, so a man who found himself at Rock Island usually remained there.

Rock Island serves as a pattern for a much larger story: what happened at Rock Island during the Civil War happened across a continent. Conversely, what happened across a continent in 1861 also happened at Rock Island. Politics and patriotism, loyalty and treachery, courage and cowardice—all could be found in and around Rock Island during the war. What also happened at Rock Island, both before the war and during it, was money. The River Bend cities, the Iowa and Illinois towns near Rock Island, had been founded for the purpose of acquiring wealth. The greatest conflict this nation has ever endured did not change that purpose. And, although they were not the government's primary concern, financial considerations were quite important at the Barracks because of a device William Hoffman engineered to save money: the prison fund. The fund caused needless suffering at all the Northern camps, and Rock Island is perhaps the most perfect example of the workings of the fund.

The Barracks was located in a community much smaller than that of many camps, which offers a focused view of politics. The Civil War was a political conflict, and its politics are handsomely illustrated by the relationship between the Barracks and the city. Part of the politics of the war concerned blacks, and a black regiment served on the Island. Their experience shows the general attitude of

Northerners toward black troops during the war and demonstrates the role most black regiments were relegated to during the conflict.

Finally, there is the myth. Born in November 1864, in a newspaper duel between Adolphus Johnson, Republican and hidebound commandant of the prison, and a fire-eating Democratic newspaper editor named J. B. Danforth Jr., it was nurtured in after years by bitter veterans who recorded their experiences on the Island. Their tales lost nothing in the telling. If their memories or veracity were questioned, they could point to the columns of the newspaper where Johnson himself had said, if he had his way, he would let the prisoners starve.

In truth, the Barracks was not a pleasant place. But there was suffering enough without the increase added by rhetoric and romance. The prisoners and their advocates who have followed after them ascribe the suffering to intentional policy and inhumane jailers. In truth, there were smallpox and hunger at the prison. But, also in truth, they have been exaggerated. Most of the suffering was not the result of policy and inhumanity but rather of accident, incompetence, and the inability to cope with a war larger than any the nation had ever before endured. Events outran experience, and the prisoners paid the price. And in this respect at least the parallel between Rock Island and Andersonville stands: men died. It is hoped this book will reduce the myth without shrinking the truth.

NOTE ON THE TEXT

Generally speaking, the men who left records on Rock Island fall into one of two groups: men educated and literate, and men so much the opposite that they rendered the phrase "great deal" as "grd dlle." The letters of the latter group are in some cases nearly indecipherable; the letters and records of the former group contain little more than common spelling mistakes. In light of this, the spelling in all quotes has been corrected. For the literate men, this saves them embarrassment for the mistakes we are all heir to. For the nearly illiterate men, it saves the reader huge effort to decipher the words they left behind as well as embarrassment to the writers. Further, this obviates the need for the always irritating and often misused *sic*. In no case has this practice affected meaning.

During the Civil War there remained a vestige of the rule that nouns and pronouns should be capitalized. This has been largely

eliminated. Conversely, during the war Northerners consistently refused to capitalize such terms as "rebel" or "copperhead," nor were
the names of political parties capitalized. This has been changed to
modern usage. The word "island" is capitalized when referring to
Rock Island specifically, and "barracks" when referring to the prison
rather than to a type of building.

Punctuation remains largely as in the originals, save for the insertion of some commas, the deletion of others, and the insertion of a
few periods. These changes were made to improve comprehension.
Finally, no italics have been added to any quote. All emphasis is in
the original documents. These people were emphatic writers.

Several abbreviations are used in the text, both because they
were in common use at the time and because the repetitive
spelling out of the names would be quite distracting. On first use
the terms are given in full; thereafter, in general, the abbreviations
are used. These are:

IC: Invalid Corps

OAK: Order of American Knights

USCT: United States Colored Troops

VRC: Veteran Reserve Corps

Rebels
at
Rock Island

"It is not to be expected that prisoners of war shall uniformly receive the comforts of a camp life."

—*Henry Wager Halleck*

CHAPTER ONE

"That Is the Way You Do Here, Is It?"

In the summer of 1863, Federal Commissary General of Prisoners William Hoffman had a problem. Hoffman was responsible for Confederate prisoners of war, and the number of his wards was growing. Recent Federal victories at Gettysburg and Vicksburg reaped a large harvest of captured Rebels, and an exchange cartel that for nearly a year had kept the Northern prisons relatively empty had broken down. Hoffman needed more prisons. A new camp at Point Lookout, Maryland, would help, but Hoffman needed still more space to house his prisoners.

Hoffman found his space in the River Bend, a reach of the Mississippi River between Iowa and Illinois that flows nearly west for 30 miles. Accidents of geology had left a 14-mile stretch of rapids in this reach, and at the foot of the rapids lay an island three miles long and half a mile wide. Rock Island stood on limestone cliffs that rose 20 feet above the water, and virgin forest topped the cliffs. It was a beautiful place. One early tourist had said it was "the handsomest and most delightful spot of the same size, on the whole globe." Hoffman cared little about the beauty, but he did care about the space. In July 1863 he decided to build a new prison on Rock Island.

Born on 2 December 1807 in New York, Hoffman was the son of an army captain also named William. Hoffman the elder had served in the War of 1812 and had remained in the army. At the time of his son's birth he was a captain. He was also prolific: ten children graced his home. Unfortunately for everyone, he was also poor. The captain had neither prospects nor property; he was "dependent solely upon his pay in the Army." Although Hoffman the elder would rise to the rank of lieutenant colonel before dying in 1845, it was apparent that there would be no education for his children unless the government paid for it. Accordingly, in 1823 Hoffman began lobbying for a place at West Point for his son and namesake. The army was a small club then, and Hoffman wrote directly to Secretary of War John C. Calhoun, and he importuned his military friends, including the founder of the United States Military Academy, Colonel Sylvanus Thayer, to do likewise. The appointment came through in 1825. Hoffman's character had been forged in the furnace of a large and poverty-stricken family. Colonel Enos Cutler, writing to support Hoffman's appointment to the Academy, said he was "direct, manly in his deportment and without taste for dissipation, correct in his habits." Cutler was being kind. As events would demonstrate, Hoffman was narrow, strict, jealous of his prerogatives, and sensitive to slights real or imagined. His encyclopedic knowledge of regulations and his inflexible adherence to the most arcane minutiae of those rules earned him the nickname "Old Huffy." Such traits did not perhaps differentiate him from many officers. What did set him apart was another trait, the result of scrambling in a moneyless household with nine siblings: Hoffman was cheap. His father had scratched for every penny. After being stationed at Fort Smith, Arkansas, where he had rented house, Hoffman the elder dunned the secretary of war for payment. The secretary twice denied reimbursement, but Hoffman persisted, and after his death another of his sons, John, continued to argue with the War Department for years, trying to recoup the few dollars his father had spent. Thus trained, William Hoffman suffered a penury of the soul that would follow him to his grave.[1]

After four unremarkable years Hoffman graduated from West Point in 1829, 18th in a class of 46. His career roughly paralleled that of hundreds of other graduates of those years. Hoffman served in the West and accompanied army chief Winfield Scott to Rock Island for the Black Hawk War. He fought Seminoles in Florida, Sioux in the Dakotas, and Mormons in Utah. During the Mexican War he was again with Scott and received brevets for his conduct at the battles of Contreras and Churubusco.[2]

Hoffman's promotion to lieutenant colonel sent him to Texas just in time to become a prisoner, along with 1,700 other men, when General David Twiggs surrendered that state's installations to the Confederates. The Texans paroled the soldiers and sent them north to await formal exchange. If they could have seen the future they might well have kept Hoffman in Texas, for in the course of events he would cause untold misery for the soldiers of the Confederacy. On returning to Washington he began petitioning the War Department for something to do that would not violate his parole. He was eager, as he later put it, to "take part in the active and arduous services which now engage the army." In the end, it was not the secretary of war who found work for Hoffman but the quartermaster general, Montgomery Meigs.[3]

Meigs had been quartermaster general since a month after the surrender of Fort Sumter. An Academy man and career soldier, he graduated from West Point in 1836, fifth in his class. An engineer, he had been entrusted with building an aqueduct to bring water to Washington, D.C., and with putting a new dome on the Capitol. He had also, like so many others in the army, spent a little time in the River Bend, assisting an engineer named Robert E. Lee in surveying the Rock Island rapids. Meigs was a rigid man, described as "too damned honest." Having spent much time in the nation's capital, Meigs was also an excellent politician, and he exercised his skill in ridding himself of a duty he wanted nothing to do with: caring for prisoners of war. Meigs was saddled with this responsibility because there was no official apparatus to handle prisoners. This war would change that, and Meigs realized it long before anyone else. Perhaps the fire-eyed farm boys of Illinois and the firebreathers in Congress expected a short and happy war, but Montgomery Meigs knew better. Even before the first battle of Bull Run he wrote to the secretary of war: "In the conflict now commenced it is to be expected that the United States will have to take care of large numbers of prisoners of war." Meigs urged some arrangement be made for the expected flood of prisoners.[4]

Even without caring for prisoners Meigs had plenty to do. He and his department were responsible for equipping an army that a few weeks before had not existed. By the end of 1861 Illinois alone had put 60,000 men in the field, and every state signed up men in a recruiting frenzy. All these men had to be clothed and sheltered; to do this there had to be depots and warehouses, contracts and transportation. Before 1865 more than two million men donned federal uniforms. Meigs had to provide for every man. And he had to provide wagons and ambulances and animals for them.

Thus burdened, Meigs sought to rid himself of the prisoner problem. Even before First Bull Run he wrote to the secretary of war: "I respectfully recommend that some person be designated as commissary of prisoners, and charged with the care of the prisoners." Meigs repeated his recommendation on 29 August 1861, and he also recommended that a prison be built on one of the islands off Sandusky, Ohio. On 3 October Meigs wrote again to the War Department. He had received permission to build the camp, and he now proposed Hoffman, "an officer of rank and experience," as the commissary of prisoners. Not only did Hoffman have experience, Meigs pointed out, but Hoffman's parole would allow him to do little else. On 7 October 1861, Meigs received word that Hoffman had been appointed commissary general of prisoners. In a gross misjudgment, Meigs told Hoffman that his appointment would "alleviate the hardship of confinement to these erring men."[5]

Hoffman was behind from the day he took office. There were already prisoners and no system to care for them. They were sent willy-nilly to any place that could house them. Camp Chase in Ohio held prisoners by October 1861, as did Fort McHenry in Baltimore, Fortress Monroe outside Washington, and Governor's Island in New York. Hoffman's first official task was to investigate the Ohio islands on which Meigs wanted to put a prison. By 22 October he had returned from Ohio. It is not surprising that he confirmed his superior's recommendation of Johnson's Island for the prisoners' depot—Hoffman, like Meigs, had a finely tuned sense of office politics. He included detailed estimates of the cost, and his sharp eye was already apparent when he noted, "It would lessen the cost somewhat to put two or three of these buildings together and if they could be built two stories high it would still more diminish the cost." Hoffman thought $30,000 would build the whole camp. Meigs approved the scheme, and in his reply to Hoffman he exhibited his own parsimony: "In all that is done the strictest economy consistent with security and proper welfare of the prisoners must be observed."[6]

While Hoffman devoted himself to building the depot at Johnson's Island, Ohio, every other officer in the army devoted himself to ignoring Hoffman. Generals sent prisoners where they liked, effected exchanges, and created prisons. In short, every commander acted as if his prisoners belonged to him. In the early days of the war the number of prisoners involved was relatively small. But everything changed on 16 February 1862. On that day Brigadier General Ulysses S. Grant captured Fort Donelson in Tennessee, along with some 12,000 prisoners. Grant had no intention of exchanging anyone. He immediately began shipping the Confederates north. A mad scramble ensued while governors and generals tried to find places to keep them. Governor Oliver Morton of Indiana offered space for 3,000; Major General Henry Halleck used training camps at Chicago and Springfield, Illinois, for thousands more, ignoring Governor Richard Yates's protest that Springfield contained "many secessionists." Adjutant General H. Price of Iowa also offered to keep 3,000 men at Camp McClellan, on the bluffs above Davenport, Iowa. Price was careful to note how cheaply he could keep the prisoners: sixteen cents a day each. Halleck declined the offer. Hoffman probably would not have declined it, but Hoffman was in the dark. The prisoners were being shipped and housed without reference to him. For example, Illinois's Adjutant General Allen Fuller wrote Halleck asking what sort of discipline should be imposed on the prisoners, because he, Fuller, needed to instruct the camp commandants. This communication should have gone to Hoffman, but Fuller was probably unaware that Hoffman even existed.[7]

As Grant inundated the North with prisoners and others made decisions that rightly belonged to Hoffman, on 24 February 1862 Hoffman was proudly notifying Meigs that the Johnson's Island camp could receive "500 or 600." Meigs, unimpressed and suddenly awake to his own responsibilities, immediately sent Hoffman to inspect the places the Donelson prisoners had been sent. In the dark he might have been, but Hoffman knew why. On 7 December 1861 he had written the adjutant general at the War Department: "The offices and duties of commissary general of prisoners are not familiar to the service and I therefore respectfully request . . . that those who are in charge of prisoners of war . . . may be notified that I have been appointed to that office and that any directions I may give in relation to prisoners may be complied with."[8]

He received no reply to this, and when the flood of Donelson prisoners illustrated just how powerless he was, he wrote again, this time to Meigs: "My office is not known to the generals, and any information I have about the movements of prisoners I pick up from the newspapers." Hoffman also suggested that the charge of all prisoners be given to one man. This fitted Meigs's ideas—as long as that one man was not Montgmery Meigs. Meigs pulled a few political levers, and on 17 June 1862 Federal Adjutant General Lorenzo Thomas issued General Order No. 67, which gave Hoffman complete control of Confederate prisoners and the apparatus necessary for keeping them. And, doubtless a relief to Meigs, the commissary general of prisoners was removed from the Quartermaster Department and made directly responsible to Secretary of War Edwin Stanton.[9]

Order 67 created an empire for Hoffman. Given his own domain, Hoffman's character began to assert itself. During the early days of his tenure his correspondence showed some concern for humanity. For example, in inspecting a camp at Lafayette, Indiana, he noted that 700 prisoners were being kept in a pork house, and he wanted them out. An inspection of Camp Randall in Wisconsin found things "in a very unsatisfactory condition." The prisoners were dying in droves, and a six-month supply of medicinal liquor had been consumed in five days. He told the commissary of subsistence at Camp Morton to "purchase . . . any articles necessary for the health or comfort of the sick." But lying beneath this concern lurked obsession, and it showed itself in the very letters that expressed concern for the prisoners. The obsession was money.[10] In the same letter in which he railed about the poor care at Camp Randall, Hoffman mentioned that some empty horse stables in Chicago could hold 2,000 prisoners. Similarly, in ordering an expansion of Camp Chase in Columbus, Ohio, he admitted that his plan would result in insufficient ventilation, but he ordered it done anyway. Hoffman even told one commandant to issue sheets only to those who really needed them: "There are very many sick who can very well do without sheets."[11]

This struggle between humanitarian and pecuniary concerns was decided by Order 67. Freed of any constraint save Stanton's, who generally left him alone, Hoffman's concern with money gained the upper hand. As the war continued his correspondence contained fewer mentions of suffering or its relief, and more and more demands for economy. He had already accepted unfit clothing sold to Meigs by "fraud of inspectors and dealers," because it was free. After pondering the clothing problem for a while, he decided the prisoners had too much of it, and he forbade the issue of socks and underwear during summer months. He ordered the sutlers who provided incidentals to the prisoners taxed. And he insisted on the use of a contraption called a Farmer boiler for prisoners' messes, because regular cooking pots consumed too much fuel.[12]

All these measures saved money, but it was small change. The jewel in Hoffman's financial crown was the prison fund. While inspecting Camp Morton near Indianapolis, Hoffman discovered something not at all to his liking: the bread, like the rest of the ration, was contracted with civilian merchants. The ration called for 22 ounces of bread, but the contract bakers returned only 20 ounces of baked bread for each 22 ounces of flour; some evil magic was consuming 10 percent of the bread ration. To eliminate the waste, Hoffman thought the prison should bake its own bread and recover those lost two ounces. Within weeks Hoffman expanded his idea: he decided the prisoners could do with less food. On 7 March 1862, he wrote Colonel James Mulligan, commandant at Camp Douglas in Chicago: "The regular issue is larger than necessary for men living quietly in camp, and by judiciously withholding some part of it to be sold to the commissary, a fund may be created with which many articles needful to the prisoners may be purchased, and thus save expense to the government." Thousands of men would reap a bitter harvest from this idea.[13]

The idea was based on the post funds of the old army, as well as Hoffman's discovery that he was paying for two ounces of flour he never received. In 1861 and 1862 the entire ration was only 12 or 15 cents in most places; at Camp Douglas it was 10.85 cents. What could those two ounces of flour be worth in the larger scheme of things? Not much, perhaps, but Hoffman was not interested in larger schemes—he was interested in the cost of two ounces of flour, and the prison fund quickly grew to rule his life. By May 1862, the fund at Camp Morton held $2,400. Other camps had similar balances. The commandants used the money to buy such things as combs, brooms, cooking utensils, and tobacco.[14]

Later Hoffman would insist that his authority for creating the fund rested in General Order No. 67. The order did say that he would "direct the manner in which all funds arising from the saving of rations at prison hospitals, or otherwise, shall be accounted for." But Hoffman created the fund three months before Order 67 was issued. He also insisted that the purpose of the fund was to "make the prisoners as comfortable as circumstances will admit." And, at least in the beginning, he wanted the money spent: "We want to use the camp fund as fast as it accumulates," he told the quartermaster in Indianapolis. But as time went on the rising balances worked a strange power on Hoffman. Despite his statements to the contrary, the accumulation of money became the main object of the fund. Woe betide the commandant who misspent a penny or lost a voucher: not only would he hear about it in unmistakable terms, but he would have to make good the loss from his own pocket. So important did Hoffman consider the subject that for a time he kept letters relating to the fund in a special file, separate from all other correspondence.[15]

Although ration cuts provided the bulk of the money, Hoffman was not one to overlook a penny. When the Confederate John Hunt Morgan escaped from the Ohio Penitentiary in 1863, he left behind his gold watch. Learning of this, Hoffman ordered the watch sold for the benefit of the fund. Effects of some deceased prisoners were also sold and the proceeds added to the growing fund. Not satisfied with the contributions from Confederate prisoners, Hoffman applied the system to the parole camps, which held Federal troops who had been paroled by the Confederates but not yet officially exchanged. Hoffman cut their rations by nearly a third. When a member of Congress complained, Hoffman told him the cut had Stanton's approval. He also told the commandant at Camp Douglas, "The amount of the reduction is left to your discretion." And whenever anyone, prisoner or parolee, broke the rules, Hoffman suggested that the commandant "stop one-third to one-half the rations of all in the block," if no culprit could be found.[16]

The result of Hoffman's desire to curb waste was misery. The concept was sound—few men need 4,000 calories a day—but the execution was abysmal. Hoffman left the precise nature of the ration reductions to his commandants, and given the pressure he exerted to increase the balances, it is not surprising that they went too far. At Camp Douglas, for example, the ration cut almost immediately produced scurvy. Although the vegetables were restored, it took four months to conquer the disease. Commandants who liked their jobs were quick to curry favor with Hoffman. George Sangster, in charge of Camp Parole near Annapolis, proudly reported that he worked his clerks 15 hours a day and that "the whole work of my department has not cost the government one cent." When the subsistence commissary in St. Louis suggested even further ration cuts Hoffman apparently approved, because a few months later an inspector complained that the diet was insufficient. The insufficient diet had produced a prison fund of $4,000, wrung from a population of only 250 prisoners. On the other hand, Hoffman's concern with frugality did not apply to his own staff. He restricted the pay of clerks at one camp to 40 cents a day for head clerks and a quarter a day for assistants. At the same time, 13 of his own clerks earned $100 or more per month, for doing the same work the 40-cent men did. The double standard bothered Hoffman not a whit. He went on about the business of squeezing money from his camps.[17]

Neither Meigs nor Stanton bothered Hoffman, either. Indeed, on at least one occasion, Hoffman chided the secretary of war, himself an autocrat of fearsome fame, about a lot of overcoats a commandant in St. Louis had requested. Instead of issuing a rebuke or dismissal, however, Stanton immediately did Hoffman's bidding and sent the coats. Meigs constantly deferred to Hoffman's judgment in matters of construction, long after Hoffman stopped reporting to the quartermaster general. Thus supported, Hoffman constructed a prison system that would eventually house a quarter of a million Confederates as well as thousands of guards and civilian employees. He would control two dozen prisons scattered from New York Harbor to St. Louis and New Orleans, and his control would be absolute. During the 1864 Atlanta campaign, Confederate John Bell Hood proposed an exchange of prisoners, to which Union General William Sherman agreed, but only if the prisoners had not yet reached Nashville—after that, the prisoners belonged to Hoffman. And his own needs notwithstanding, it was Hoffman's "great desire to be governed by the strictest economy in all cases."[18]

Governed by this desire, Hoffman soldiered on. After an initial jump, the balance in the fund probably disappointed him. On 22 July 1862, shortly after the institution of the fund, an exchange cartel was established between the Confederacy and the United States. The cartel provided that prisoners captured by either side would sign paroles not to take up arms until exchanged; they were then released to their own army (it was men thus paroled who occupied Hoffman's parole camps). Agents of exchange for both sides kept records of captured men and from time to time declared the prisoners exchanged. Men not paroled were confined by the capturing army until an exchange was agreed to by the agents, whereupon they were transported to either City Point, Virginia, or Vicksburg, Mississippi, and returned to their own armies.

Almost immediately the prisons began emptying. Some 3,200 Confederates left the North in July 1862. Another thousand left in August, and in September the prisons were nearly emptied as 10,000 men took the cars and boats to the exchange points. Confederate prisoners who had no desire to return South were simply released after signing an oath swearing they would support the Federal government. Nearly 4,000 men whose ardor for rebellion had cooled signed the allegiance oath and were turned loose in the North.[19]

Empty prisons meant no money for the fund, but Hoffman need not have worried. As the war continued the prisons filled again. The cartel agents bickered over numbers and conditions; their correspondence has aptly and mildly been termed "vituperative." The Confederate agent for the cartel, Assistant Secretary of War Robert Ould, interpreted the rules to suit himself, causing Hoffman to describe him as being "utterly reckless of integrity." When Ould made trouble, the exchanges halted. Also, after a few months it occurred to the federal judge advocate general, Joseph Holt, that releasing prisoners on oath was bad business: every man thus released was one less man for exchange, and that in turn meant one more Union soldier condemned to remain in Southern prisons. Once Holt came to this realization, the North began to refuse exchange. The prisoners began to accumulate in the camps through the spring of 1863. On 19 July 1863, Hoffman informed exchange agent W. H. Ludlow that there would be no more exchanges "until there is a better understanding in relation to the cartel and a more rigid adherence to its stipulations on the part of the Rebel authorities."[20]

To make room for the expected flood of prisoners, Stanton and Hoffman had already decided to build a new camp. After some equivocation, Hoffman decided on Rock Island. It was an easy choice: Rock Island was both a rail and shipping head, so transport would be cheap. Coal fields lay nearby, and timber covered the Island itself, so fuel and lumber would be cheap. More to the point, the Island itself was free. The government still held title to most of it, and could doubtless regain title to the rest. There would be no ground rents at Rock Island, and economy overcame Hoffman's fear of sympathizers. On 14 July 1863, Montgomery Meigs wrote to Captain Charles A. Reynolds of the Quartermaster Department: "You will proceed at once to Rock Island, Ill., and take charge of the construction of a depot for prisoners of war."[21]

Captain Charles Reynolds was a career soldier, one of the few career men who had not attended West Point. He had volunteered as a private during the Mexican War and had been discharged in 1848. But military life had a hold on him, and in March 1855 Reynolds accepted an appointment as second lieutenant in the 9th Infantry. He had been promoted to captain a few months before the war began, and in November 1862 he was given the temporary rank of lieutenant colonel so that he could hold the post of quartermaster in Ulysses Grant's Department of Tennessee. Although a Chicago paper called Reynolds "one of the best quartermasters in the service," Grant did not share that opinion. In April 1863, he relieved Reynolds, perhaps because of some creative accounting he had employed in the matter of a load of cotton. A captain once again, Reynolds was in Washington when he got the call to proceed to the River Bend.[22]

Although he could not know it, Reynolds was actually proceeding into a lion's den of Democratic politics and commercial avarice, and the chief lion was a newspaperman named Joseph Baker Danforth, Jr. Danforth had descended into the happy commercial maelstrom of Rock Island in 1851. Danforth was a Vermont native, and it was no accident that he came to the River Bend: his father had been one of the first settlers in the area. To spare others the mouthful of his name, Danforth the younger went all his life by his initials: J. B. But that was all he spared anyone. J. B. was a fire-eater, who understood money, power, and prestige, and who wanted as much of all three as he could get. He began by starting a hardware store in partnership with a man named Lee; they advertised with the unusual, not to mention incomprehensible, slogan, "A nimble pie is better than a slow dime."[23]

The hardware store was a false start. For one thing, J. B. apparently had a difficult time keeping his hands out of the till. For another, he detested merchant princes and always held himself to be a champion of the working man, a friend "of those who find it difficult to live." Besides, selling nails would not lead to power and influence. Danforth knew what would: journalism. This was not another false start. Danforth had been bred to the trade, and before coming west he had been partner and manager of the Montpelier *Patriot* in Vermont. In a world generally free of restraint, journalists were the most unrestrained of all. The concept of libel was either completely unknown or cheerfully ignored by everyone. Not even taking a man's money obliged Danforth to any consideration of the

advertiser. When a phrenologist came to town and placed an advertisement, J. B. noted: "O'Leary continues to feel the bumps of such
heads as are green enough to submit to the operation, and the
humbugging goes on swimmingly. See his advertisement."[24]

In November 1852, J. B. bought into the Rock Island *Republican*.
In his inaugural column he said he would "go quietly about the duties of my station." It was his first case of editorial license in the
west; J. B. was anything but quiet. The *Republican* took on all com-
ers. He castigated local businessmen who did not support commercial growth, designating them "claw-suckers," because they sat on
their money and sucked their claws. Nor did he ignore his fellow
editors: in reply to one he said that "we set the writer of that sentence down as an ass. He could not comprehend an idea if it were as
big as an ear of corn and fastened on to his nose." Even his own
subscribers felt J. B.'s whip: "[U]nless they pay before long," he
warned them, "we shall . . . [send] an invitation by Mr. Cobb." Mr.
Cobb was the town marshal.[25]

As is often the case when a man speaks his mind, Danforth made
enemies. His partner in the hardware venture, Lee, accused him of
larceny after an auditor named Holmes Hakes discovered shortages,
and J. B. found himself before a grand jury. However, the law at the
time stipulated that between partners there could be no larceny. J. B.
could not be, and was not, indicted. Hakes the auditor was another
enemy. In May 1853, he attacked Danforth and inflicted "a severe
wound in our back." In 1855 a citizen named Ira Wilkinson, dissat-
isfied with J. B.'s editorial treatment of him, attacked him with a
cane, and Danforth retaliated with a knife. This time he suffered a
break of "one of the small bones of our hand . . . and a slight scratch
in the face." Wilkinson escaped by Danforth's chivalrous restraint:
"[W]e could easily have killed him, we did not strike hard."[26]

Despite these tribulations, J. B. spoke his mind, and his mind was
full of politics. Danforth was a Democrat to the bone: he hated the
Maine (temperance) laws, Know-Nothings, Whigs, and anything in
the least tainted with centrism. When the Whig party came apart
and a new party rose from the ashes, it called itself the Republican
Party. This was too much for J. B. On 15 December 1855 he led his
paper with a pronouncement: "It is well known . . . such men as
Seward . . . Chase, [and] Sumner, are ranging themselves in battle ar-
ray against the democracy, under the misapplied name of 'Republicans.'—This has led us to regard the name 'Republican' as an inap-

propriate one for our paper. . . it has been disgraced by self-appropriated association with a party advocating principles subversive of our government." The name Danforth selected was the *Argus,* and he apparently chose well: the paper still publishes under that name.[27]

Both the paper and its editor thrived. In addition to the *Argus,* the *Union* also published in Rock Island. The *Union* was as rabidly Republican as Danforth was Democratic, and across the river in Davenport two other major papers published, the *Gazette* and the *Democrat,* Republican and Democratic organs respectively. Other papers came and went, including some in German, which served the large immigrant population. For a few cents a day the citizens could treat themselves to a political smorgasbord.

J. B. lived on the Island for a time, having been appointed government caretaker. Some of his duties he took seriously, for example, vandalism. He reported that "some thoughtless or ill-bred people are in the habit of defacing the public buildings on this Island, breaking windows and tearing down fences," and he threatened legal measures. Some other duties he took less seriously, especially if their neglect lined his pocket. It was illegal to cut wood from the Island, but J. B. overlooked the law if the woodcutters paid him. In one case, when the local lumberjack refused to pay up, Danforth shot the man's horse, which action immediately brought an offer of $1.00 for the wood. Such license with his duties brought an attempt to relieve him, but J. B. weathered the storm. In fact, U.S. Senator James Shields returned the papers with the endorsement that he was "glad to be informed that J. B. D. makes so good an officer."[28] J. B. disappeared from Rock Island for a time in the late 1850s, having engineered himself an appointment as purser in the U.S. Navy. He was soon on the coast of Africa, from whence he sent back long letters about the dark continent, which included his opinions on servitude. The blacks in Sierra Leone, said J. B., "have all the evils and none of the benefits of slavery." Also, to his horror, Danforth discovered racial intermarriage in Africa.[29]

By 1861 Danforth had returned to the helm of his paper, and his city was a thriving river town. It had not always been so. In 1832 the early settlers and the army had chased the Sauk warrior Black Hawk out of the River Bend in the last Indian war east of the Mississippi. But despite the white settlers' having the land to themselves, the area developed slowly, mostly because of the river. The Mississippi River was truly the Father of Waters, and in the River

Bend it was a stern parent. The Upper Rapids, a 14-mile reach of rocks, began at the foot of the Island. Steamboats could traverse the rapids only in times of high water and under the hands of the most skilled pilots. But the shrewd citizens of the River Bend turned their greatest tribulation into their greatest asset. Who thought of it is not recorded, but someone unloaded a boat, carted its goods past the rapids, and then put them on another boat. Rock Island was born, by the accident of a river full of rocks. From a sleepy, swampy village of a half dozen dwellings in 1838, Rock Island burgeoned into a small city. Warehouses sprang up along the river front; shipyards and foundries, chandleries and hotels rose from the swamp. The entire area thrived. George Davenport, the city's founder, crossed the water to Iowa and founded another city, which bears his name. At the upper end of the Island an enterprising citizen named D. B. Sears noted that a dam across the slough would produce power. He forthwith built the dam and instantly another town sprang up, called Moline.[30]

The citizens of the River Bend were in it for themselves and made no bones about it, as one young immigrant discovered pretty quickly. When he first arrived, J. M. Burrows toured the area. On taking the ferry to Davenport, Burrows made a discovery: "As soon as we left the shore the old gentleman [ferry owner John Wilson] began to collect his fares. I noticed that each passenger paid twenty-five cents. I tendered my quarter, when I was informed my fare was fifty cents. I demurred, of course, and was surprised to be told that for citizens the fare was twenty-five cents, but for strangers it was fifty cents. I replied 'oh! That is the way you do here, is it?'"[31]

It was indeed. By the mid-1850s, 3,000 people called Rock Island home, and as many as a dozen boats a day docked at the levee. Runners hawked their hotels, and stevedores toted bags between boat and wagon, everyone happily gouging the customers for all the market would bear. In 1854 the telegraph brought the world to Rock Island, and the railroad also came to the River Bend, greatly increasing commerce. Further growth came in 1856, with the completion of a bridge across the Father of Waters, the only one between the headwaters and the Gulf of Mexico. Rock Island thrived. At least, it thrived until the newly formed Confederacy fired on a Federal fort named Sumter.

The coming of the war momentarily distracted the citizens. Like a popping wine cork, the bombardment of Fort Sumter released the pent-up emotions of generations, and before the echoes died a hot madness for war lay on the nation. The horrors were yet to come, and in the spring of 1861 there was only glamour. From the state capital of Springfield, a Rock Island citizen reported, "The enthusiasm in the capital is beyond any description—everybody is in favor of the most extensive and vigorous preparations to defend the government."[32]

For J. B., defending the government was the only excuse for going to war. In recent years there has been a great deal of argument over whether slavery was the root cause of the war, but in Danforth's eyes there was no argument. Slavery was perhaps the manifestation, but not the cause itself: "The plausible question, 'Are you for freedom or are you for slavery?' is not the real issue. The real question is 'Are you for the constitution or against it?' If you are for the constitution, then you are for the existence of the union under that constitution just as it stands, with slavery existing, just as our fathers found it." The most rabid Georgia secessionist could not have put the case more succinctly.[33]

The question of slavery aside, there was the Union to preserve, and the war fever infected even the Democratic lair of the River Bend. Within five days of Major Robert Anderson's surrender of Fort Sumter, recruiting started for a company of volunteers, and within a week it had elected officers and been accepted for service by Governor Yates. The women of the town turned out flags to present to the company. At a citizens' meeting a man named Robinson, gripped by a paroxysm of patriotism, promised to support the families of every man who volunteered from the city's third ward. Thousands of people gathered to see the company off. Danforth wrote an article covering the ceremonies and exhorted the citizens to support the soldiers with "the sympathy, the prayers, and the cash of our people." And so they did. The women immediately turned out several hundred havelocks and sent them to Springfield. More than 400 blankets were collected and shipped to the shivering soldiers. When the paymaster failed in his duty, a subscription raised money for the troops and their families, Robinson having apparently forgotten his promise.[34]

J. B. filled his columns with the war. He took a paternal if not interfering interest in every man the county sent off to battle, and he took up the cause for his subscribers' interests, as when he wrote Illinois Adjutant General Allen Fuller demanding to know the whereabouts of the 51st Illinois, because anxious wives and mothers wanted to know where their men were. But supporting the troops was not the same as supporting the war; nor was the war a quick three-month excursion of flag waving and brave words. It turned out to be something far different. As the citizens learned, men die in war. The war ground on without end; the casualty lists mounted. And besides the blood there was the effect on business to consider. Despite the adage, war was not good business for Rock Island.[35]

Things had turned sour almost the minute Anderson surrendered Fort Sumter. Napoleon Buford, one of whose many interests was a bank, had a great deal of his capital in Southern bonds, and when Fort Sumter fell his bank promptly failed. Buford made good his debts by liquidating other property and then left for the front. Prices began to rise. By 1864, flour that in 1861 had been $3.50 a barrel rose to $11.00; sugar quadrupled in price; cotton sheeting went from ten to seventy-five cents a yard. In the late 1850s as many as a dozen boats a day docked at the levee. By 1863, half that many was a cause for rejoicing.[36]

Blood and lack of business wore heavily on the citizens. In 1863 Napoleon Buford's cousin Charles, another of the ubiquitous Bufords, complained, "Great God! When will this bloody war be over! Is the whole country from Canada to the Gulf to be involved in one universal ruin?" J. B. had also had enough by 1863. The war was a machination of abolitionists and Republicans, and badly mismanaged besides. He lambasted the administration at every opportunity: "A white man is not of much consequence, now, in the estimation of the shoddy patriots and loyal leaguers. It is all nigger."[37]

In short, J. B. had become a Copperhead, one of those who opposed the war and in some cases actively supported the South. They earned their name by the habit of wearing the liberty head cut from a copper penny. In the eyes of Republicans and War Democrats, "Every Democrat who did not openly and actively support the administration and the war was labeled a venomous Copperhead, at once a southern sympathizer and a traitor to the union." In Egypt, as the southern part of the state was called, the Copperhead press went so far as to advise men to fight for the Confederacy.[38]

Although Danforth did not suggest the River Bend don the gray of rebeldom, he lost no opportunity to point out the administration's myriad faults. Indeed, in May 1863, as part of his masthead he began running a screed called "Our Copperhead Platform." This

called for the war to be "prosecuted with the utmost vigor," but
only until terms could be achieved "by which the whole union can
be preserved." He overlooked the fact that the elimination of slavery might be one of those terms. The platform repeatedly mentioned the supremacy of the Constitution, and J. B. also threw in
that he was opposed to the "indolent and imbecile management of
the war." But after a few weeks Danforth changed his title to "Our
Union Platform." Apparently, naming himself a Copperhead in
print daily was a little much even for him.[39]

Still, despite all the political and commercial turmoil the war
caused, there was hope. The government had at last decided to do
something with Rock Island. The Island had been vacant since
1836, when the government closed a fort it had previously maintained there. Over the years there had been threats to sell the Island
to private interests. The most notable had been in 1854, when dam-
builder Sears inveigled a senator to introduce a bill to sell the Island. The railroad supported the scheme, because it already had a
right-of-way and wanted more. Led by Danforth, all the major
newspapers in the area howled against the sale—one of the very few
times when all the editors agreed on anything. As J. B. said, "[S]hall
we sit quietly down and permit a gigantic railroad monopoly to
take these advantages of our land?"[40]

The idea of an armory on the Island was an old one. Napoleon
Buford had suggested it as early as 1851. In 1861 the citizens sent
an official appeal to Congress, pleading for the establishment of an
arsenal on Rock Island. Not satisfied with this, they also sent a delegation to Washington to press their claim. Unfortunately, the war
broke out while the citizens were in the capital, and other matters
occupied the congressmen. The Island remained largely idle. Its
only government use was the boarding of some horses, which was
worth $24 a day to the contractor and not much at all to the rest of
the community. The current caretaker, T. J. Pickett, might have
rented some houses to private individuals, but this, too, failed to
benefit anyone—except, of course, Mr. Pickett.[41]

But the congressmen had been listening, and on 11 July 1862,
they appropriated $100,000 for an arsenal on Rock Island. Having
done their duty, the congressmen, as J. B. would have said, sat
down and sucked their claws: a year later nothing had been done.
Danforth demanded that Congressman Elihu Washburne get to the
bottom of things. Washburne caused James Ripley, head of the

Ordnance Department, to reply soothingly: "The preparation of proper plans . . . is in progress." However, this was not good enough, especially in light of the fact that the people of Davenport, Rock Island's bitter rival across the river, had decided that the Island actually belonged to them and had sent their own committee to Washington. The Illinois citizens instantly sent another delegation to prevent this corruption of geography.[42]

In the midst of all this consternation J. B. allowed the Davenport papers to scoop him on the prison story. He can perhaps be forgiven—he was a very busy man. Besides acting as paterfamilias to every Rock Island soldier, he also had to address crowds of Irishmen who gathered under his window, remind people to pen their hogs, and worry that the river was lower than it had ever been before. And in his idle moments he conducted a bitter feud with the editor of the *Union*.

In 1863 the *Union* was purchased by Colonel Myron Barnes, late of the 37th Illinois. Barnes had been cashiered after "causing and joining a mutiny," which he fomented in part by loudly announcing that he "didn't give a damn" about his district commander's orders. It was only natural that when denied the opportunities of a military career a man so outspoken should go into journalism. Barnes bought the paper on 27 May 1863, and Danforth wished him "every success in his undertaking." But within a week J. B. was noting "the extreme silliness and ignorance of the *Union*." This opening salvo began a battle of ink that lasted the rest of the war. Barnes intimated that if "Danforth had his just deserts the major portion of his life would have been spent in the penitentiary, and his own much-abused wife would say Amen." Danforth returned fire with the story of "Buzzard Barnes, the Blanket Thief," who stole into one of his own soldier's tents and attacked the man's wife, to "satisfy his beastly passions."[43] Given this feud and his many other heavy responsibilities, it is small wonder that J. B. allowed the Davenport papers to scoop him on the biggest story of the war, so far as the River Bend was concerned: a quartermaster captain was coming to build a prison. Once he did hear of it, however, Danforth wasted no time in getting the story into print ahead of Barnes:

> "Better late than never."—but it really is very strange that the administration should not have discovered that Uncle Sam owned 700 or 800 acres of land on this Island, and that its isolated position, its high

grounds . . . its pure and soft running water, its plentiful supply of wood, and all free of charge, and also the low price at which provisions can be obtained here, all point to this place as the most suitable in the west for a military post, a hospital, and a camp for Rebel prisoners. . . . [A] camp should have been established there, two years ago, for Rebel prisoners, instead of paying a high ground rent at Chicago.[44]

When Captain Reynolds arrived at the end of July 1863, blissfully unaware of what awaited him, he overshot his mark by about 1,300 yards and came to rest in Davenport. In view of the recent Iowa intrigues with respect to the Island, this was a serious mistake. Barnes mentioned this, but said "we don't consider it any of our business where Captain Reynolds stops." J. B. immediately took this as an opportunity to attack Barnes, proclaiming among other things that Barnes had abused Reynolds "like a pickpocket." J. B. also attacked the Davenporters who buzzed around Reynolds for contracts the minute he arrived, calling them "a most ravenous set of one-horse shoddy patriots, who will stick to Uncle Sam as long as he has a dollar in his pocket—and desert him as soon as the last dollar is gone." J. B. had reason to be smug. On his arrival, Reynolds had instructed his clerk to place advertisements for lumber. The hapless clerk inquired at the Burtis House in Davenport and was told by Mr. Burtis, a Democrat, that Rock Island had only one paper—the *Argus*. Danforth got the ads, and Barnes went hungry.[45]

The editor's smugness was about to be shattered, however, and both J. B. and the innocent Reynolds were about to receive a political education. On 7 August 1863, only a few days after Reynolds arrived, Meigs sent him a copy of the *Union*, which some stout Republican in the River Bend had sent to Edwin Stanton, and which asked why Reynolds advertised in disloyal papers, that is, the *Argus*. Stanton was properly abhorred by the idea of one of his quartermasters advertising in disloyal papers and demanded an explanation. Meigs in turn told Reynolds, "Great care should be taken by officers not to expose themselves to the charge of employing disloyal papers or persons." Reynolds had already noted in his advertisements that "proposals from disloyal parties will not be considered," but Meigs's letter prompted him to stop advertising in the Democratic papers, and he also annulled some contracts already let, on the ground of disloyalty. Danforth took umbrage at this, although not against Reynolds personally: "He [Reynolds] must support the war for the purpose of destroying slavery or he is a Copperhead and a rebel sympathizer. Such are the orders from Washington."[46]

J. B. spent the late summer and autumn of 1863 happily lashing everyone around him. Because Reynolds could no longer advertise in his paper and his usefulness was otherwise played out, Danforth began whipping the captain regularly for such sins as dealing with Davenporters and locating the Barracks on the north shore of the Island, much too close to the one-horse shoddy patriots across the river. Barnes suffered almost daily. Even Burtis, who had done J. B. the favor of getting him advertising revenue, felt the sting: J. B. pointed out to his readers that the Burtis House caused "a terrible stench" in Davenport, by reason of its privies.[47]

The advertisement that prompted the letter to Stanton about disloyal papers had called for "One million, eight hundred and sixty-one thousand, seven hundred and forty feet of lumber." Two firms, one each in Rock Island and Davenport, split the contract. Reynolds advertised for mechanics and began hiring them. When the lumber arrived the barracks began to go up. Eventually Reynolds completed the construction of a compound described a few months later by a medical inspector: "The prison barracks are 84 in number, each intended to accommodate 120 men. They are arranged in blocks of 7 each, fronting on streets 100 feet wide, with two main avenues, 130 feet wide, intersecting the camp in the center." The barracks had two doors, twelve windows, and 2 ventilators along the roof ridge; the buildings were 100 by 22 feet, with 18 feet partitioned off for a kitchen, which was furnished with a 40-gallon cauldron and kitchen and table furniture. The large sleeping room, which occupied most of the building, had two coal stoves, and the kitchen held a third.[48]

The barracks stood within a plank fence 1,250 by 878 feet; the stockade ran parallel to and fronted the main channel of the river, thus facing Davenport. There was a parapet four feet below the top of the fence, and sentry boxes on the parapet. There were two gates, at the east and west faces of the stockade. Outside the compound a small village sprang up: guards' quarters, officers' quarters, administrative buildings. The construction of these ancillary buildings would continue through most of the prison's history.[49]

Reynolds was working under pressure, not just from Danforth and the other editors, but from Meigs, who pestered his captain by both letter and telegraph. On 12 August he informed Reynolds,

"The barracks for prisoners at Rock Island should be put up in the roughest and cheapest manner. Mere shanties, with no fine work about them." Two days later he wrote: "It is reported here that there is much finer work intended than is necessary. Very rough work only is needed; light frames and sheds." Meigs also unburdened himself of his opinions on the value of contracts over day labor, the former being much cheaper. Then there was trouble over the stoves—Hoffman wanted his Farmer boilers, and this precipitated a small blizzard of correspondence. In the end Reynolds's contractors could not get the boilers. Hoffman doubtless brooded over the waste regular stoves would cause.[50]

By the third week in September all 84 barracks were under roof, and Danforth predicted that the prison would be completed in two weeks. A month later he was saying much the same thing. Things moved too slowly. Some of the delay, however, must be laid at the doors of Danforth and the other citizens: it seems they had decided to build a bridge to the Island.[51] The idea may originally have been Danforth's. In June 1863, he wrote: "Our citizens ought to take instant and energetic measures to build a double track carriage bridge . . . to the Island of Rock Island. No time is to be lost, if we wish to secure to our city and county the benefits of the arsenal." Both the city council and the county board of supervisors passed resolutions to do this very thing, but they fell to haggling over costs, and nothing was done. News of the Barracks, however, put matters in a different light. The Ordnance Department may have been sucking its claws, but the Quartermaster Department and William Hoffman were doing no such thing, and the Barracks promised money for all. Bailey Davenport, Rock Island City's mayor and son of founder George Davenport, immediately offered to donate $500 for the bridge. Noting another deficiency in the town, in the same breath he offered two acres of land to anyone who would build a distillery.[52]

By the middle of August contracts had been let for $13,500. The citizens, their pockets emptied by the war, were eager to reap the financial benefits the Island was about to confer on them. Realizing that the Rebels would need "dry goods, liquors, cigars, stationery, newspapers," J. B. worked his pencil to a nubbin calculating that from the prisoners themselves the city stood to make $10,000 a month, and perhaps as much as $20,000, with "the exercise of ordinary courtesy and civility to the officers." Such a windfall could not be slowed by waiting for the ferry—instant access was required. The citizens pitched in with a will and began to construct the bridge. Unfortunately, they did not trouble themselves to mention their plans to the government, and they instantly ran afoul of the man who had finally arrived to build the arsenal: Major Charles Kingsbury.[53]

Kingsbury was an ordnance officer. He had served at nearly every armory and arsenal in the nation since graduating second in the 1840 class of West Point. Shortly after the war began he was appointed superintendent of the all-important arsenal at Harpers Ferry, Virginia. Kingsbury's tenure lasted just long enough to arrange to burn the armory's $1.2 million worth of arms to prevent their capture; in less than two days he was jobless. After serving in western Virginia and on the Peninsula as George McClellan's chief of ordnance, he served in special assignments until 27 July 1863, when someone decided he was just the man to build the Rock Island Arsenal.[54]

He was not, however, the man to get along with the citizens in the River Bend. During the war many West Pointers looked down on their volunteer counterparts. Kingsbury was not so narrow: he looked down on everybody. When assisting Brigadier General George Cullum in compiling biographies of all Academy graduates, Kingsbury could not be bothered with names. He referred to his comrades only by their graduation numbers. In his final report on leaving the Army of the Potomac, Kingsbury sternly lectured his superiors about the "inadequate appreciation of the magnitude of the . . . conflict." At one point during his stay on the Island, he would icily admonish the chief of ordnance about misaddressed and unstamped mail sent to the Arsenal. His absolute conviction of his own superiority, combined with a rather thin skin, assured the major a difficult time in Rock Island. Complicating the problem was the organization of the War Department: although both the Arsenal and the prison were located on the same island, Kingsbury had no authority over the Barracks, nor did the prison commandant have any authority over the Arsenal. The two installations coexisted, not always peaceably.[55]

On his arrival Kingsbury did just as Reynolds had: he passed through Rock Island City and on to Davenport, where he registered at what Danforth, who knew a black kettle when he saw one, called a "sesech hotel." Kingsbury immediately set to work. According to J. B., the first thing Kingsbury did was hire worthless Iowans as chief clerks and foremen. He spent all his time "throwing everything into the hands of Davenport people." When J. B. and another citizen tried to see him about his policy of "injur[ing] Rock Island and benefit[ing] Davenport as much as possible," he snubbed them.[56]

Almost immediately Kingsbury noticed that someone was building a bridge to the Island and that the someone was neither him nor Reynolds nor anyone else connected with the government. He wrote to James Ripley, the chief of ordnance: "I learn that a bridge is being built from Rock Island City to the Island and so far as I know without authority from the government." The problem was turned over to the Quartermaster Department, and Meigs telegraphed Reynolds that he should not "permit the construction of a bridge to Rock Island without proper authority, which, it is believed, has not been given." However, when Bailey Davenport wrote to Meigs demanding to know what was going on, Meigs blithely replied that his department had not stopped construction and suggested that the citizens talk to the Ordnance Bureau. The government tossed the ball from department to department while construction continued unabated, and seemingly by inertia alone the bridge was permitted. By 17 September 1863, teams crossed the bridge daily. A few days later, baiting the Iowans, Danforth suggested that if they did not like it they should "send a regiment of soldiers here to remove the bridge by force."[57]

Despite his arrogance, Kingsbury had both intelligence and experience, and he instantly recognized what Rock Island was: the greatest natural arsenal "between the Alleghenies and the Rocky Mountains." He thought the entire Island should be brought under government control, that the cessions to dam-builder Sears and the Davenport family should be revoked. He also suggested that no payment would be necessary, because "the advantages already received from these grants, have more than compensated for any labor or improvements the parties have added thereto." Kingsbury wanted quick action, especially with respect to the Davenport property. This quarter-section ran across the narrow axis of the Island, almost cutting in half the government lands. And, in the two weeks since his arrival, citizens had applied to put up both a private dwelling and a saloon. The major envisioned "a congregation of such establishments that must become a perpetual nuisance." This would never do, and Kingsbury set himself to acquire the land.[58]

He ran squarely into the Davenports. Kingsbury's first offer was an exchange of the Davenport property for land near the upper end of the Island. He painted a pretty picture of a mechanics' village where the arsenal workers would live "convenient to their work," on lots owned by the Davenports. But Kingsbury, like so many others, failed to realize with whom he was dealing. George Davenport had single-handedly founded two cities in the River Bend and had done so through the allure and power of commerce. His children had inherited his acumen: they would not trade, but they would sell. Kingsbury had several appraisals made, which averaged around $50 an acre. The Davenports demanded $600 an acre. Although Kingsbury got the use of the land in a few weeks, it required years to get ownership, and it took both Edwin Stanton and Congress to achieve the takeover. In the end, the government paid not $600 an acre, but $800. George Davenport had raised no fools.[59]

While dickering with the Davenports, Kingsbury also dealt with the railroad. The Chicago and Rock Island line had a right-of-way across the lower end of the Island, but the boundaries were vague and seemed too expansive to suit the major. He could not even site the Arsenal, because he had no idea where the railroad's lands were. Complicating the issue was a switch the road was installing to service the Barracks. Kingsbury told the superintendent that, although he had no "wish to interfere with any arrangements that may be necessary for the efficient operation of the road," he intended to fence off a proper right-of-way. The road's agent in Rock Island immediately began holding Arsenal shipments in Rock Island City instead of sending them on to the Island. When Kingsbury complained, which he was quick to do, the agent innocently told him that the freight had not been paid and that when it was he would deliver. Only when the major threatened a visitation from the War Department did the railroad give in.[60]

Nothing went well for the major. While he dealt with the Davenports and the railroad, he himself suffered a visitation from the Internal Revenue Department, which demanded $2.26 he swore he had already paid. Eventually, he gave up and paid it again. And throughout these tribulations Captain Reynolds busied himself felling trees "without reason or necessity" and otherwise annoying the major.[61]

All the turmoil slowed construction of the Barracks. Although all the buildings were under roof by October 1863, much work remained. Still, Reynolds was ahead of Kingsbury, who managed to break ground for the Arsenal the first week of September 1863 but who then sat down and sucked his claws so fervently that Danforth complained "at the present rate of progress the people will die before the walls are erected."[62]

Despite disappointments in the Arsenal's construction, however, Danforth was a happy man. He had recently hit on a new term of opprobrium for his abolitionist competitor and had taken to calling Barnes's paper the *Disunion*. Kingsbury provided grist for Danforth's vengeful mill, and, perhaps most important, the Barracks was going to make everyone rich. The bridge had been completed, and grasping that the government seemed unwilling or unable to stop them, the citizens pressed their advantage and ran a road almost to the gates of the Barracks, although Kingsbury did manage to force them to use a circuitous route.

That was a small price to pay, however, and the Barracks disgorged floods of greenbacks to the eager businessmen of the River Bend. In November 1863, a Rock Island firm, Chamberlain, Reynolds, & Co., got half the lumber contract. C. L. Merrill, digger of wells, was sinking shafts inside the new compound. In a couple of months, J. Keiser & Co. would be awarded the contract to furnish bread at $2.75 per hundredweight. Dimock & Gould provided buckets and other wooden goods. Merchant John Burgh struck a deal with Captain Reynolds to erect a store on the island to supply the laborers. All this flowed simply from construction—the prisoners and their imagined fortunes had not yet arrived. The prospects were so good that some leading citizens thought a new bank was needed to handle all the wealth, and in October the First National Bank was organized, with J. M. Buford as cashier. True, Rock Island lost some of the business. A Davenport firm got half the lumber contract and another provided the hardware. A firm in Geneseo, Illinois, a few miles east of Rock Island, won the beef concession with a bid of three and one-half cents a pound. Being shrewd and frugal men, the beef contractors immediately brought in a drove of hogs and penned them near the slaughterhouse, proposing to fatten them on the entrails of the slaughtered cattle. Waste not, want not.[63]

In the third year of the war, the government also wanted to curb waste, at least in the matter of manpower. On 28 April 1863, the

War Department issued General Order No. 105, which established the Invalid Corps, or the IC. This corps was to consist of sick or wounded men unfit for combat but who could still perform rear-area duty, thus freeing hale men for the killing fields. The order also specified that men would be accepted only if they were "meritorious and deserving." Quickly realizing that there would be problems of interpretation in the matter of who was fit, the War Department issued a second order, outlining the disabilities that qualified and disqualified a man for service. For example, a man could enter the IC who suffered almost any disability involving his left arm—even if he did not have one he could enlist. Incontinence was acceptable, as were rheumatism, hernia, and myopia. On the other hand, blindness disqualified a man, as did "manifest imbecility or insanity." The "solitary vice" (masturbation) disqualified, but only if "practiced to a degree to have materially enfeebled the constitution." Finally, "habitual or confirmed intemperance" would keep a man out of the corps.[64]

There was little inducement to join the corps; eligible men had already suffered to a greater or lesser degree, nor did enlistment entitle them to any bounty or pension. Also, their enlistments were for three years, and time served in prior regiments did not count. Further, the men detested the uniform—it made them feel like second-class citizens. As Provost Marshal General James Fry noted in a report at the end of the war, the name of the corps itself caused "bitter prejudice . . . which made the title Invalid Corps a burden." What Fry failed to note is why the name caused prejudice—IC was the acronym Meigs's quartermasters used to denote equipment that had been "Inspected, Condemned." Adding to the insult, the men themselves were called Invalids. Despite these problems, more than 60,000 men eventually served in the corps. Only about 5,000 actually enlisted, however; most were simply transferred, with or without their consent, from their original regiments. Waste not, want not.[65]

The case of Fletcher Galloway, a guard at Rock Island, is typical. A resident of Dixon, Illinois, Galloway enlisted in the 13th Illinois in May 1861. A farmer by trade, he was described as a "powerful man." Galloway saw action at Chickasaw Bayou, Arkansas Post, and the siege of Vicksburg. Between engagements he also saw a good deal of action at the hospital: diarrhea and peritonitis sent him to the surgeon, as did a head wound from a bayonet incurred not in battle but "during a fracas with one of his comrades." Galloway also found time to commit some minor infraction: during one hospital sojourn his pay was docked $10.00 to cover a fine levied by a court-martial.[66]

In September 1863, as a result of "incipient consumption" Galloway was mustered out of his regiment and into the IC. The transfer did not improve Fletcher's health. Sent home on a 30-day leave in 1864, he came down with rheumatism and was unable to travel until long after his leave expired. When he started back to his post the provosts arrested him because his pass was expired, and he was returned under guard. Galloway escaped punishment this time but was later court-martialed again and fined $2.00 for going to town without permission. On the whole, the Invalid Corps contained men who had little use for authority, discipline, or sobriety—so little use, in fact, that, by the end of December 1863, 14 of them were confined in the Island's guardhouse.[67]

The unpleasant task of commanding these troops fell to Colonel Adolphus J. Johnson of Newark, New Jersey. Johnson was a balding, gaunt, stern-faced Swede, who at 5'11" was taller than most men in those days. Before the war he had been both a barber and a hatter. He enlisted in the three-month 1st New Jersey in 1861, and by September he commanded the three-year 8th New Jersey. During the battle of Williamsburg in May 1862, a bullet entered his side just above the hip, traveled around his body, and exited the other side. A. J., as he signed his name, was done with fighting. His brigade commander said that the loss of his services "is a very serious one in so far as the future service of the brigade is concerned." Johnson's troops probably did not share the commander's opinion, because Adolphus Johnson was a strict disciplinarian, humorless, and devoted to blind and rigid adherence to regulations. He was, in fact, much like William Hoffman. After five months' recuperation Johnson returned to his regiment. He saw no further combat, which was a mercy—his wound had never healed. In March 1863, Johnson finally gave up and resigned. Miraculously, the ulcer above his hip began to heal, and although minor damage to his spine caused weakness and aching in his legs for the rest of his life, Johnson improved enough that, in July 1863, he accepted a major's appointment in the IC. Johnson spent a short apprenticeship at Camp Chase in Ohio, where he commanded 11 companies. On 25 September, he was promoted to colonel. On 10 October, ten of his companies were consolidated into the 4th Regiment, and a few weeks later, a company or two at a time, they began the trip to Rock Island.[68]

The first guards arrived on 17 November 1863, the same day William Hoffman, on a tour of the west, also arrived. He pronounced all of Reynolds's work satisfactory, except that two more guards' barracks were needed. He suggested the troops could put up the buildings themselves to save construction costs. On a tight schedule, Hoffman left town the same day he arrived. Had he had more time, he might have noticed certain other aspects of the construction.[69]

Those other aspects immediately impressed themselves on Richard Henry Rush, the post commandant. Rush had graduated from West Point in 1846, along with Stonewall Jackson, George Thomas, and George Pickett. During the war he had led the 6th Pennsylvania Lancers until April 1863, when the rigors of the Chancellorsville campaign "revived a chronic disease contracted while serving in Mexico." His resignation coincided almost to the day with the creation of the Invalid Corps, and Rush found himself head of the corps until October, when he was ordered to Rock Island. On 24 November 1863, Rush issued Post Order No. 1, assuming command of Rock Island Barracks. Order No. 2 placed A. J. Johnson in command of the troops.[70]

Rush took stock of the prison and began worrying. One concern was that, despite Reynolds's October promise to Meigs that the Barracks would be completed in "five or six days," the prison was far from finished, and Rush would have to order workmen to vacate the compound when the prisoners arrived. Moreover, there were problems even with the finished parts. One problem was the arrangement of buildings outside the fence. Despite an earlier warning from Hoffman via Meigs that it was "not advisable . . . to divide the guard in two parts," that was exactly what Reynolds had done. Worse, he had put the enlisted men's quarters east of the compound and the officers' quarters on the west; more than a thousand feet and a prison stockade separated the privates from their officers. This would certainly account for Danforth's observation that the enlisted men were "delighted with their quarters."[71]

Scarcely had he arrived before Rush began a series of long, almost whining letters to Hoffman about the conditions at the Barracks. His first concern was the size of the guard: only six companies had been assigned, and intricate calculations proved to Rush's satisfaction that he needed more. The prison, said Rush, was no more secure "than if it were not on an Island." Rush claimed he needed at least 1,022 men and that even that many would not allow him extended pickets or patrols. Rush was probably right. Besides the compound, there were numerous outbuildings that would have to be guarded, at least at night: some of the Island's former residents had declared that they thought the Barracks an imposition and had promised to burn down the post. Other men would have to be on duty inside the yard, and there were bridges to be guarded. In addition, many of the guards were sick. To properly command the Barracks Rush would need two colonels, two lieutenant colonels, two majors, and a bevy of lesser officers and civilian employees. He needed more buildings, too, and his soldiers, all being "from rural life," had no conception of how to construct them.[72]

In yet another letter Rush complained that he had no idea about the limits of his authority over the Island and the people who, for myriad reasons, came there. Of particular concern in this respect was Major Kingsbury. Rush had tried to introduce himself to the major, but, according to Rush, Kingsbury returned his letter, "not seeming to understand or recognize my being on duty on the Island." Rush also wondered if he could stop trains from running over the Island. The day after these musings Rush discovered even more problems; he once more took his pen in hand. He needed to know who could administer the allegiance oath to prisoners. He needed office furniture, and more maps, and he wanted to use the prison fund to pay for them, even though they were not items "needful to the prisoners." Rush also wrote to Provost Marshal General James Fry, complaining that his troops were "obedient and willing men but entirely without instruction or discipline. They are nearly all Western men, and from rural districts, but few can write, and but one amongst the privates can write well enough for a clerk."[73]

The only person any of this bothered was Rush himself. Reynolds was merely carrying out orders, and the citizens welcomed the profits that floated across the slough to the city. Hoffman certainly showed little concern for Rush's problems. He did agree that the guard should be larger: shortly after his own visit, Hoffman had written the War Department that at least a regiment would be needed on the Island. But apart from this concession Hoffman gave Rush short shrift. The guard would be only a single regiment, not the regiment and a half Rush wanted. Instead, Hoffman was sending 400 revolvers. This firepower would make up any deficit in the number of guards. Besides, Hoffman noted, "The prisoners we have had in our hands heretofore have never shown any great anxiety to escape." Hoffman was mistaken: in October 1863, 61 prisoners escaped from compounds in Illinois alone. Hoffman also refused Rush the constellation of officers he wanted. These matters disposed of, Hoffman turned to the subject closest to his heart: the prison fund. He told Rush, "Your prison fund will accumulate very rapidly and give you abundant means to make all necessary purchases." Asked about a fence across part of the enclosure, Hoffman allowed that "I have large prison funds at other places and I think I will purchase the lumber for the cross fence with it."[74]

When not complaining to Hoffman, Rush busied himself preparing for the arrival of prisoners. On 25 November 1863, Hoffman had intimated, "It is desirable to send immediately to the depot some two or three thousand prisoners of war and though you may not be well prepared to receive them, I must send them there as soon as your force is strong enough to furnish a sufficient guard." The zealous Rush immediately issued a stream of orders. These included long and detailed regulations governing the receipt and daily inspections of prisoners and the composition of the guard, which would be only 100 men, divided into four reliefs—that is, only 25 men on the walls at any one time. He also ordered all the remaining residents out of their shanties and off the Island.[75]

Although his tone smacked heavily of Chicken Little declaring the sky was about to fall, Rush was right to worry. In only a few days he had discerned problems that had either eluded or been ignored by everyone else. Moreover, he had started to correct these problems. Had he remained, perhaps much of the coming horror would have been avoided; unfortunately, Rush did not remain. Within three weeks he would be gone, first to Chicago, and then to command an Invalid Corps brigade in Washington, D.C., and become assistant adjutant general. On 5 December 1863, he left Rock Island, and A. J. Johnson took command.

More than 30 years before, Black Hawk had said that a good spirit lived in the caves under the Island's bluffs, but when the white man came the noise drove him away, and "no doubt a bad spirit has taken his place." In the late autumn of 1863 it certainly did not appear as if an evil spirit had taken up residence. A happy chaos possessed the Island. The citizens Rush complained of still thronged the place. Many had business there—mechanics and laborers for Kingsbury and Reynolds came daily. Some even lived in tents Reynolds had obligingly provided. The factories at the upper end of the Island still turned out their products, and the operatives crossed the dam daily. And, although the inhabitants had been ordered away, only the human ones had obeyed. Some porcine residents had stayed put, and their owners often returned to care for them. On one occasion two women fought over a pig. One woman "drew her revolver and shot the pig, whereupon the other drew her revolver and threatened to shoot the first woman." Barnes reported, "The parties were Irish," as though that explained the entire matter. By the end of November there were also the soldiers to goggle at. Much to Rush's chagrin, Danforth reported there were no restrictions on visiting the Island, and the editor helpfully noted the time and place of the guards' daily dress parade.[76]

When the guards began to arrive, the character of at least some of the visitors changed. Less than two weeks after the guards began arriving, Barnes's *Union* stridently proclaimed that "there will be no room for dirty harlots!" Barnes was wrong. The Island was, it seemed, big enough for everyone: Barracks and Arsenal laborers, merchants, factory operatives, pig owners, soldiers, curiosity seekers, and whores. And, despite appearances, the old warrior had been right: there was an evil spirit on the Island, and it was about to show itself. Prisoners were on their way to Rock Island.[77]

CHAPTER TWO

"They Are Dying Off Very Fast"

On 3 December 1863 Danforth reported: "A train of cars containing Rebel prisoners is expected to arrive at our depot between 4.30 and 5.30 this afternoon. They are probably a portion of the prisoners recently taken at Chattanooga, and others will doubtless follow every few days . . . until the Barracks are full."[1]

Danforth was right. On 24 and 25 November the armies of Ulysses Grant had swept Braxton Bragg's Army of Tennessee from the mountains around Chattanooga in the battles of Lookout Mountain and Missionary Ridge. In the process Grant's men had scooped up more than 6,000 prisoners, 5,000 of whom were on their way to the River Bend. They went by train, generally passing through Nashville and Louisville, on to Indianapolis, Chicago, and Rock Island.[2]

The train actually arrived about four in the afternoon. On board were 466 men from Lookout Mountain, including James Reeves and most of the 34th Mississippi. The prisoners detrained and the citizens stood around gawking, thanks to Danforth's notice of the arrival time. The guards began the laborious process of searching and registering the Rebels. This entailed calling each man four paces to the front so provost guards could relieve him of contraband. An officer serving as the commissary of prisoners recorded the man's name and assigned him to a barrack. A noncommissioned officer and two privates from the guard were assigned to watch over each company. The prisoners were then marched through the gates into the compound, to officially become Rock Island's first prisoners. Once inside, they re-

mained in ranks while the provost marshal read them the prison regulations. Although not stipulated in the rules, some prisoners mentioned that they were searched a second time. Finally, they were released to their quarters. Rock Island Barracks was in business.[3]

Those first prisoners walked into a facility utterly unprepared for
them. When Hoffman notified Rush that prisoners were on the way,
Rush had replied with one of his frenzied telegrams: "Not ready for
any prisoners yet. No quarter-masters property. Not half enough
garrison, no books, blanks, rolls, etc." A week later, when the prisoners were actually on the cars rolling toward the Island, Rush sent
another telegram: "Yours rec'd. Will do what I can for the 5000 prisoners expected. No water yet in prison yard except one well at west
end. Steam forcing engine not yet ready. Weather extremely cold.
No Rebel clothing, blankets, etc. etc. on hand."[4]

Two days later Richard Henry Rush turned command over to A. J.
Johnson. Hoffman told Johnson prisoners were coming "as fast as
the facilities of the railroad will permit." And that was too fast. Two
days after the first prisoners arrived, another 830 men came in; on 9
December, another 1,300; on 11 December, 1,000. Almost all these
men were from the battles around Chattanooga. Danforth reported
that the prisoners were "generally healthy, clean and good-looking
men," but Barnes said they were "dirty, ragged, careworn looking
objects of pity." Federal General Alpheus Williams agreed with
Barnes. Williams, stationed in Tullahoma, Tennessee, observed the
endless trains full of Chattanooga prisoners wending their way toward Illinois and commented: "We have had for a week past a continuous run of Reb. Prisoners, long lines of railroad trains crammed
with them. . . . They are a hard-looking lot of men without overcoats and very short of dirty blankets, marked generally 'U.S.,'
showing that what they have are taken or stolen from us. . . . But
you should see this 'chivalry' to appreciate it. A more dirty, destitute, and diabolical lot of humanities cannot be conceived."[5]

The long trip north did nothing for the appearance or health of
the diabolical humanities. Crammed into the cars for days without
adequate food or water, they suffered weather that grew progres-
sively colder as the trains rolled north. Added to this was the sometimes harsh treatment of the guards. A. J. Cantrell of the 16th Tennessee later remembered that as the train traveled along the shore
of Lake Michigan "the prisoners asked the Federal guards to open
the doors, so they could see the lake. They soon saw enough, as

they were thinly clad, and the cold and icy wind chilled them quickly; so they begged the guards to shut the doors . . . but this was refused. The prisoners then resorted to boxing and piling on each other, like boys, to keep from freezing." Another prisoner, W. C. Dodson, reported that during the trip to the Island the guards "displayed their bravery by forcing us to lie flat on the bottom of box cars, threatening to shoot the first man who raised his hand or head." The conditions in the cars grew so bad that Hoffman berated the quartermasters: "The fact that in transferring prisoners of war from place to place on railroads the arrangements are often so carelessly made or so badly carried out that much delay and much embarrassment are experienced." Hoffman demanded better arrangements. Although his primary motives were keeping to schedules and preventing escapes, he also required that "a vessel of water of proper size be placed in each car."[6]

Such privations were the norm for prisoners going to any prison camp; however, going to Rock Island was the worst trip of all, because it was the longest trip of all. In the winter of 1863 no prison was farther from the front than the Barracks. Indeed, James Reeves and his friends passed within miles of both Camp Morton in Indianapolis and Camp Douglas in Chicago. But those camps were crowded and Rock Island empty, and although Hoffman did consider sending newly captured prisoners to Camp Douglas, and Douglas prisoners to Rock Island, in the end he did not do so. Reshuffling prisoners to spare them an extra day on the cars was a nicety that events did not afford.

While he may have maintained his position that the men were good looking, Danforth quickly revised his opinion of their health. He had little choice—the evidence rolled through town daily. On 8 December he noted that the arriving prisoners had had "scarcely anything to eat, from the time they left Louisville, (Tuesday morning) until their arrival at Joliet, Thursday morning." After considering the matter for a few days, J. B. told his readers that the prisoners "have been accustomed to a milder climate than this; they have suffered much in the service of the Rebel government, and . . . then to be taken prisoners and placed in box cars and transported to this northern region . . . without being allowed to leave the car, and without regular supplies of water and food, is as much as a well man could endure. The result is that very many are now on the sick list, and hundreds more will follow."[7]

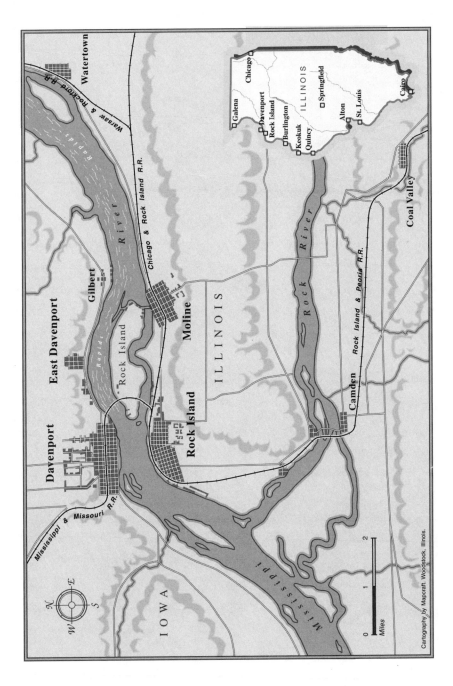

The River Bend in 1861.

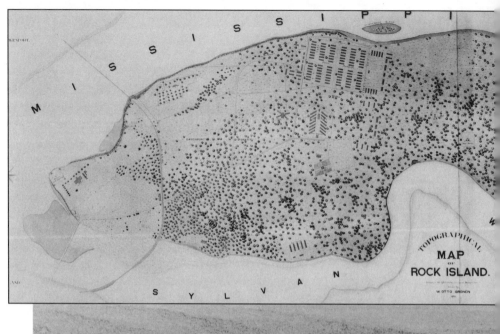

TOPOGRAPHICAL
MAP
OF
ROCK ISLAND.

W OTTO GRONEN

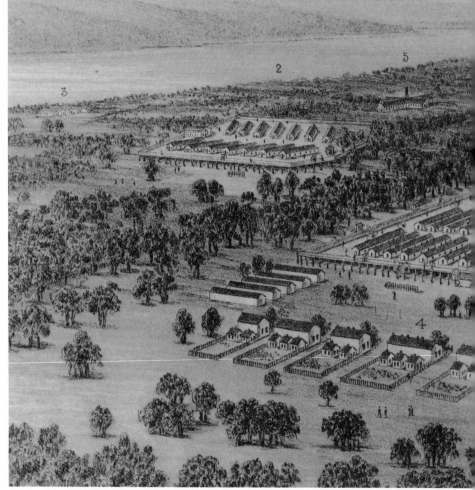

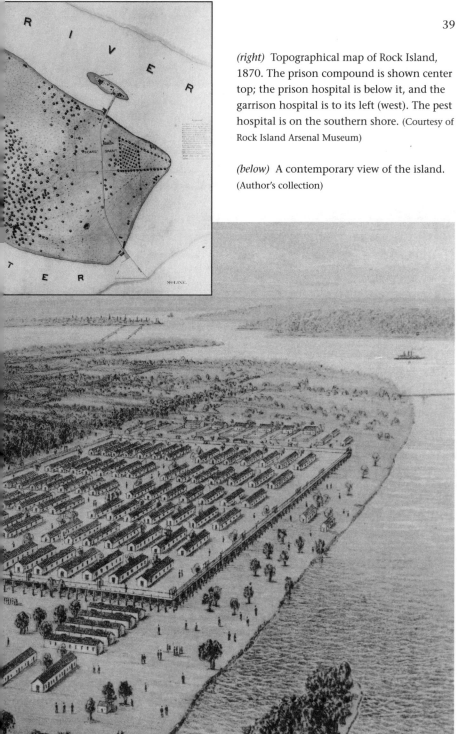

(right) Topographical map of Rock Island, 1870. The prison compound is shown center top; the prison hospital is below it, and the garrison hospital is to its left (west). The pest hospital is on the southern shore. (Courtesy of Rock Island Arsenal Museum)

(below) A contemporary view of the island. (Author's collection)

Commissary General of Prisoners William Hoffman (right) and two unidentified staffers (possibly Captains Lazelle and Freeley) on the steps of Hoffman's office in Washington. (Courtesy of Library of Congress)

"Old Huffy": William Hoffman as a major general. (Author's collection)

Joseph Baker Danforth, Jr., editor, *Rock Island Argus*. (From *Portrait and Biographical Album of Rock Island County* [Chicago: Biographical Publishing Company, 1885])

Captain Charles A. Reynolds, Quartermaster Department, builder of the Rock Island Barracks. (Courtesy of United States Army Military History Institute)

Colonel Adolphus J. Johnson, 4th Veterans Reserve Corps, commandant of Rock
Island Barracks. (Courtesy of United States Army Military History Institute)

44

Prisoners at Chattanooga awaiting transportation to Rock Island, November 1863.
(Author's collection)

Once inside the compound, the prisoners faced new problems. They had been on short rations for months, and as one of the guards, F. A. Jennings, observed: "I tell you they pitch into the hard tack. It takes two to make a shadow." In addition to hearty appetites and stolen blankets, the Rebels brought with them a host of ailments, most prominently pneumonia and diarrhea. A few weeks before, these prisoners had battled men in blue uniforms; now they would battle disease. Moreover, the disease had an extremely powerful ally: the weather. The first prisoners who arrived at the Barracks had been lucky. The weather in the River Bend proved mild for a few days in early December 1863, with temperatures as high as 60 degrees. This was merely a lull, however; a record-breaking winter had already begun.[8]

It had actually begun on 29 August. As J. B. reported, "[V]ery thin ice was discovered on some boards near the railroad track." Both of the following nights hard frosts struck the Midwest, doing "immense damage to the growing crops. On all the low lands the corn is killed outright." The frost extended as far south as Louisville, Kentucky. The frost was only a harbinger; a week later a few flakes of snow fell in the River Bend, and on 22 October two inches blanketed the ground. The thermometer plunged, and before December the river froze at the head of the rapids. Captain Reynolds decided to advertise for 120,000 bushels of coal, to supplement the supplies he had already ordered. And, remembering the tempest that accompanied his first ads, he advertised only in reliable Republican papers.[9]

By 18 December ice closed the river completely, and three days later teams pulling sleighs could cross to the Island. On 29 December an historic storm descended on the Midwest. It began with rain, a steady drizzle that continued for 48 hours. Then the thermometer began to fall and the rain changed to snow. The wind turned to the northwest and howled through the Barracks and the city. The snow fell through New Year's; the temperature dropped to twenty degrees below zero. It was unprecedented. *Harper's Weekly* reported, "[T]he Western newspapers come to us full of the most thrilling accounts of the recent great snow storm in the West, which covered an area of three thousand miles, and was of unparalleled severity." Schools in the River Bend closed for two weeks; trains stopped running; for days the high temperature remained far below zero.[10]

Inside the barracks, the temperature was warmer, but not much. The compound sat on the riverbank, exposed to the full effect of screaming winter winds that quite literally whipped through the barracks. In constructing his "mere shanties," Captain Reynolds had used green lumber, which shrank as time went on. Men huddled around the stoves in vain attempts to keep warm. According to prison diarist William Dillon of the 4th Tennessee, water froze only five feet from the stoves. Frostbitten ears and feet became commonplace. Fortunately, Johnson never rationed coal; the prisoners could burn all they wanted day and night. In fact, when the blizzard made it impossible for him to hire teams to haul coal, Johnson sent troops into town and impressed eleven teams so he could keep his prisoners from freezing. Another problem was a lack of blankets and bedding straw. One of the first inspectors to arrive at the prison echoed Rush's earlier statement: "Blankets and bedding . . . not sufficient—supplies for which requisitions have been made, expected daily." Louisianian J. W. Minnich said that during his entire time on the Island he saw no straw but "only bare bunks, unless someone gathered leaves." Still, being inside was better than being outside, and despite the weather the men had to go out, to use the privies and to collect their rations, a job that could take as long as an hour. Lafayette Rogan of the 34th Mississippi, another prisoner who kept a diary, noted that getting rations "was a cold job . . . some of the detail cried with the pain produced by the cold."[11]

The abysmal weather had one good effect insofar as A. J. Johnson was concerned: it stopped the incessant stream of visitors to the Island. Even though Rush had published Hoffman's order restricting visitors in all the papers, stating, "Visitors to these stations, out of mere curiosity, will in no case be permitted," people continued to throng the Island until the weather accomplished what orders had failed to do. One visitor was Danforth, who managed to make friends with the provost of prisoners and spent afternoons in his office gathering information for his paper. While J. B. warmed himself at Shaffner's stove, Barnes also tried to gain admittance, but as Danforth gleefully reported, the Union's editor was turned back. Indeed, Barnes tried to bluster his way in and "run the guard," and Johnson detailed four men to escort the hapless editor back to the mainland. Had the colonel been able to see into the future he would have sent the Democrat Danforth packing and given the Republican Barnes the run of the Island. But at the time Johnson had another, larger problem to deal with: his prisoners had started dying.[12]

The first to go was James Reeves, who succumbed to pneumonia on 9 December 1863 and who has the dubious honor of occupying grave no. 1 in the Confederate graveyard on the Island. The clerks knew who Reeves was, but they were far less certain about where he was from: to this day his grave stone carries the wrong state and regiment. The next day David Greer, also of the 34th Mississippi, died, also of pneumonia. On the 12th the third man died. The pace picked up: 3 on 13 December, and, in addition to pneumonia, diarrhea made its appearance on the death list. Johnson was about to face a crisis. Before the New Year's blizzard, 86 of his wards died, and the minute the weather turned the death rate jumped. The highest toll for any one day before the storm had been 9; on 5 January 1864, 16 prisoners succumbed. For the whole month of January, 232 prisoners died, triple the number who had died in December. Lafayette Rogan noted in his diary, "Deaths have already occurred from freezing." Even the hospital records support this: "frosted feet" was a common diagnosis in the hospital registers. And when a man died in the barracks, that was usually the only cause of death listed: "died in barracks." Some men did not even make it into the yard. James McGhee of the 8th Tennessee died on the cars—whether of disease or cold remains unknown, because the clerks did not bother to record the cause of death. A few days later another man was found on the cars, tentatively identified as Samuel Kilgore by a Bible found in his pocket. This time, the clerks failed to record the death itself, let alone the cause. Wild rumors raced through the city, recounting tales of the death factory on the Island. The *Union* discounted one that claimed the storm had killed 76 men. Barnes allowed that no more than half a dozen men had died as a result of the weather. A few days later he reported, "There are many people who think that the prisoners on the Island are not properly cared for, but these people are of the Copperhead persuasion." The Copperhead referred to was Danforth, and Barnes's defense of Johnson's administration of the prison withered in the barrage of ink J. B. began hurling at the *Union*, Johnson, and everyone else connected with the war.[13]

Earlier articles, the result of those December afternoons in the provost's office, had been quite complimentary. J. B. had thanked nearly every officer on the Island for "their polite attentions, and for furnishing us with every facility in their power to bestow." He lauded the food and the accommodations and apologized for the wild rumormongering of the *Union*. This was scarcely the sort of thing expected from the man who had for weeks proclaimed him- self a Copperhead at the head of every issue of his paper. But J. B. had only been biding his time. On 27 December he first mentioned deaths on the Island, saying that the reports were "too late for res- cue, and too true for doubt." Less than a week later he wrote:

> There were 10,520 Federal prisoners in Richmond on the 18th in- stant. There were eleven deaths among them on the same day.—*Chicago Journal, Dec. 30th.*
>
> The mortality at Rock Island Barracks for the week ending Dec. 26th, was 42. The number of prisoners was 5,549, or only one half the number at Richmond. This shows a greater mortality at Rock Is- land, according to the number, than at Richmond.[14]

In the same issue, Danforth also published a letter from a citizen who signed himself only as "C," and who happened to agree with J. B.: "[T]hose whose duty it is to attend to the sick, owe the world an explanation of the causes of this shocking mortality. . . . [H]umanity shudders at the thought that possibly [the prisoners'] wholesale death is owing to the insufficiency, the neglect or incom- petency of those who are paid to attend to their health." J. B. oblig- ingly ran this under the bold head "Alarming Mortality Among the Rebel Prisoners." Someone sent that number of the *Argus* to Wash- ington and in response the surgeon general promptly sent an in- spector, Norton Townshend, who told Danforth that he had come in direct response to J. B.'s recent articles.[15]

Townshend arrived in the River Bend on 17 January 1864, after being delayed by "several small railroad disasters." The next day he reported to his superiors, "The statements of the papers were for the most part untrue or greatly exaggerated." Whether Townshend was trying to protect the camp administration or to avoid creating hysteria, this statement simply was not true. Townshend also said there was sufficient bedding straw, a statement contradicted not only by prisoners but by the official correspondence. Although Townshend was apparently blind to the problems themselves, he did put his finger squarely on their source: "Almost all the suffering that has actually occurred has been in consequence of the transportation of prisoners during the extreme cold weather." Town-shend also mentioned, almost in passing, another problem that was beginning to manifest itself: smallpox.[16]

"An acute, highly contagious viral disease, initiated by sudden se-vere constitutional symptoms and characterized by a progressive cu-taneous eruption often resulting in pits and scars." Smallpox had scourged the world for centuries; its extreme contagion struck fear everywhere it appeared. It was called the "prowling spotted beast" in novels, and even the dust-dry, extremely technical *Merck Manual of Diagnosis and Therapy* pays homage to the horror by noting that one form was called "sledgehammer." By 1863 no need remained for smallpox to be a terror. Edward Jenner, an English physician, had discovered vaccination in 1796. As with any new development, there was resistance, but by 1840 Britain provided free vaccination for all infants and by the mid-1850s much of Europe had compul-sory vaccination. It was the beginning of the eradication of the only disease ever rendered extinct. But by the time of the Civil War, more than 60 years after Jenner's discovery, most of America re-mained unvaccinated. A sudden outbreak would send doctors scrambling for vaccine matter, and in the course of events some of that matter, while perhaps inducing immunity, would also produce "large, repulsive-looking, ulcers . . . and many showed no disposi-tion to heal." This phenomenon was called spurious vaccination, and during the Chancellorsville campaign it disabled 5,000 of Robert E. Lee's men. Smallpox mortality varied, depending on the age and general health of the patient and the form of the disease. The sledgehammer variety regularly claimed 60–80 percent of its victims. Even milder forms would have a higher mortality than usual when the patients were soldiers whose immune systems had been weakened by months of hard campaigning in all weathers on short rations and in tattered clothing. By the end of December 1863 there were nearly 6,000 such men at the Barracks. Given the univer-sal fear of smallpox, Danforth's first mention of it was quick and matter-of-fact, almost a throwaway. On 22 December 1863 he noted, "Three cases of small pox have occurred among the prison-ers, and they have been removed to a pest house, erected for that purpose." In fact, J. B. had just announced a crisis.[17]

It is among the most lamentable of facts about the Barracks that the crisis was completely avoidable. The source and cause of the problem can be pinpointed exactly. In Louisville, Kentucky, stood a prison used to hold federal transgressors and Rebels on their way to permanent stations. Rarely did the Rebels remain more than a few days. In October 1863, the Louisville camp was a model prison. An inspector reported that the "cleanliness of men and clothing . . . in by far the best condition I have yet seen." The medical staff was "fully qualified, and . . . strictly discharge their duties." The inspector positively gushed in the last paragraph: "It is exceedingly gratifying to have a report like the present to make, and I have to compliment Captain Pratt [the commandant] most highly for the condition to which he has brought the prison under his command." However, the flood of prisoners from Chattanooga had overwhelmed Captain Pratt. Only two months after the first report, the same inspector, A. M. Clark, found discipline relaxed, the sinks (privies) "filthy, and offensive at a distance." The hospital records were no longer well kept, and the surgeon, while competent, lacked "executive ability." Clark also noted that there had been six cases of smallpox, which had been "promptly sent to the pest house of the general hospital."[18]

When Clark made this second report he did not know that there had been other cases of smallpox and that they had also been promptly sent away—on the cars to Rock Island. The disease made its first appearance at the Barracks on 6 December 1863, only three days after the prisoners arrived. Since the incubation of smallpox is two weeks, it is certain that the disease came from somewhere else. In the blizzard of correspondence engendered by the epidemic, Johnson, his surgeons, and Clark bluntly blamed Louisville. According to Surgeon J. J. Temple, who arrived on 20 December 1863, "Many cases of small pox came here on the cars from Louisville and other sources. They were ordered on the cars at Louisville with the smallpox already broken out, and the surgeon at Louisville knew it at the time." Pratt should have retained all smallpox cases in Louisville. That he did not do so is incontrovertible. He actually sent a telegram ahead of one trainload: "Forward you this evening five hundred and fifty (550) prisoners. Small pox made its appearance here among some of the same lot. It would be well if practicable to quarantine them." Excellent advice, perhaps, but offered far too late. The train in question left Louisville on New Year's Eve 1863, and Pratt had been sending men and smallpox to the River Bend all month long. And when the prisoners arrived at the Barracks, they found the place unprepared for any sickness, let alone anything as virulent as smallpox.[19]

During his November visit, Hoffman had found only a small building, which would later become the post headquarters, fitted up as a hospital. He had not recommended any new construction, telling Rush, "It is intended that as many of the buildings within the enclosure as may be necessary shall be set aside and fitted up for hospital purposes, and it is left for . . . the medical officer to determine which group of buildings will best meet this object." Rush turned the hospital question over to the surgeon in charge when the Barracks opened, ordering him to select two barracks to use as a hospital, and to also "select and designate a suitable building from the shanties left on the Island and have same prepared that it may be used as a 'pest hospital' should any contagious or infectious disease break out." The surgeon, named T. J. Iles, was a Kentuckian who had removed to Davenport some years before the war, and according to one report he was "an old man . . . completely bewildered . . . and without the slightest idea of his duty." Under the bewildered Iles, the situation immediately sank into chaos. Within two weeks, when Surgeon Temple arrived to take over, anarchy reigned:

> Between 700 and 800 sick [were in] various barracks. . . . Five barracks had been set apart as hospitals, and the sick and dying were piled up one above another in three tiers or on double beds. The hospitals as well as barracks were heated by 2 heating stoves—totally insufficient to make the room even indifferently comfortable. . . . The prisoners were but scantily clad, and had not even straw on which to lie, and no blankets, except such tatters as they brought with them. . . . In fact the whole sanitary condition of the prison was so deplorable as to be almost helpless.[20]

A patient at a Confederate hospital in Richmond, Virginia, Felix Formento noted that treatment for smallpox consisted of purgatives, cooling drinks, and nourishing diet, accompanied by eyewashes when the pustules infected the eyelids. There was little such treatment at Rock Island. In December 1863 the aged Iles and two assistants cared for the entire population of 6,000 prisoners.

If medical treatment was lacking, so was prevention. There are two aspects to preventing smallpox: isolation of manifest cases, and vaccination. Captain Pratt in Louisville had negated the value of isolation when he sent infected men north and failed to mention the fact to anyone. And as Surgeon Temple noted, isolation at the Barracks was not practiced even after the epidemic began. To his credit, Johnson tried. When the five barracks Iles had set aside proved utterly insufficient, Johnson commandeered an entire corner of the compound, comprising at least 14 barracks (the records conflict on the actual number), three of which were used for administrative purposes, the remaining eleven as hospitals. Unfortunately, the corner was at the southwest angle of the compound, the "lowest and least salubrious" part of the yard. At some point the colonel also appropriated at least two more barracks along the south fence, to use strictly for smallpox cases. Johnson was also aware of the need for vaccination. Unfortunately, when Temple took over on 20 December 1863, he found vaccine sufficient for only 600 men.[21]

Temple arrived in a frigid butcher's yard. Criticized by A. M. Clark three months later, Temple retorted, "You say the hospital department is horrible as it exists at present; if you had seen it when I first beheld it, you would doubtless have thought it *infernal*." As soon as Temple set foot in the compound, Iles took the opportunity to disappear for two weeks, claiming pneumonia. Although smallpox caught the imagination, it was far from the only problem. The "healthy, clean and good-looking men" Danforth had described in fact suffered a litany of diseases. Diarrhea and pneumonia led the list, but there were cases of typhoid, purpura, rheumatism, bronchitis, tuberculosis, syphilis, inflammation of both the bowels and the brain, congestion of the brain and lungs, softening of the brain, erysipelas—every week the prisoners found new ways to die. One man died of a malady described as "worm in the head," which may have been an infestation of maggots in an open wound. There was also trouble with diagnosis: the disease for which men were admitted was often not the disease of which they died. For example, Thomas Rogers of the 53rd Georgia was admitted for insanity, but he was buried after dying of smallpox. Richard Wright of the 19th Virginia Cavalry went to the hospital for "wounds" but managed to contract typhoid and die of it. And sometimes there simply was no diagnosis. When confronted with vague or bewildering symptoms, Temple several times had the clerks put down "diagnosis undecided," and in the case of George Gibler of the 38th Alabama the record shows only that he "died some time ago." Some complaints the men survived: scald, sciatica, mumps, nephritis and neuralgia, flux, inveterate itch, lumbago, legs and arms broken and sore, bruises, concussions, eczema, chronic gonorrhea, headache, staph, tonsillitis. And all of this chaos was at the beginning of the smallpox epidemic.[22]

Although A. J. Johnson has been condemned for mishandling the epidemic, he was neither inactive nor incompetent. Before leaving Rock Island, Rush had written Provost Marshal General James Fry that Johnson was "fully able to carry on this establishment." Temple seconded that idea, saying that Johnson supported all the surgeon's endeavors with "manly promptitude." Together, Temple and Johnson tried to draw order from the chaos. Johnson sought out vaccine, telegraphing Louisville that vaccine was "urgently needed." The two men appropriated buildings outside the compound and started construction on even more. On Christmas Day they completed contracts with a couple of local surgeons, and Temple found two former doctors among the guards and put them to work. Johnson appealed to the community for hospital supplies and clothing for the smallpox patients. Despite these efforts, it would be a long road back to order. Nor could Johnson devote his full attention to the problems of the sick. His troops also demanded attention.[23]

Colonel Johnson already knew his troops' proclivities. To his chagrin, Danforth quickly discovered them. On 14 December 1863, Danforth reported that a private named Rogers was arrested "for being noisy and drunk and driving ladies from the sidewalk." On being searched, Private Rogers was found "to have a rock in each pocket." Just over a week later J. B. reported that an entire squad invaded one of the hotels, "made a great deal of noise and disturbed the neighborhood, wanted to fight with everybody, and were disagreeable generally." J. B. let no incident pass: every time a man of the Invalid Corps caused trouble in town, the *Argus* reported it in detail. On New Year's Eve a squad of guards invaded a saloon and established a redan of overturned tables. When the authorities tried to arrest them they "commenced throwing chunks of coal at the sheriff" and swore that they "wouldn't be taken alive." It would be an occasion of note some time later for Danforth to remark upon the arrest of Simon Claywell that the private had "managed to keep out of jail for about a month." The authorities on the Island agreed with J. B., at least with respect to Claywell. Johnson would request a dishonorable discharge for Claywell, saying "he is an incorrigibly bad man & a disgrace to the service." If Claywell was worse than his fellows, it was only a matter of degree. None of them seemed much interested in duty, and guarding the prisoners only interfered with their extracurricular activities. As one man remarked to a friend about his wards, "They are dying off very fast. I would not care if they would all die off."[24]

Danforth's reports may have added to Johnson's annoyance, but they told the commandant nothing new. The post's books were full of court-martial proceedings; a court sat every month and pronounced judgment on the miscreants. In March 1864, the court tried 13 men, one of them Fletcher Galloway, who had requested permission to go to town, saying he disliked camp life. His captain had replied sarcastically, "We don't want anyone here who doesn't want to be here." The sarcasm was lost on Galloway, who promptly went to town. Five other men were tried for conduct prejudicial to military discipline, one of whom had delivered himself of the opinion that the officer of the day was "a goddamned shitting pimp." Unfortunately, he had delivered this opinion to the officer himself, who immediately arrested him. Such antics would eventually provoke Johnson to complain: "In organizing the Veteran R Corps it was the intention that none but the most worthy soldiers should be assigned to it. It is now an established fact that from 3 to 5 per cent of its number are the most worthless material that the service has ever been cursed with."[25]

Drunkenness figured large in the court-martial proceedings, as did fighting; men refused to go on guard; they left their posts for hours at a time. If all else failed, the men could entertain themselves by harassing citizens on the bridges or by "robbing and pillaging" gardens and other property. When apprehended, as they often were, their punishments ranged from fines of $1.00 to $4.00, and periods of confinement ranging up to 30 days, part of it on bread and water. Corporal punishments varied from confinement at hard labor for various periods to standing on a barrel, or being "tied up to a tree by his hands for two hours."[26]

Part of the reason for the disorderliness may have been the guards' quarters. Because there were not enough guards' quarters outside the fence, even with two new buildings Hoffman had ordered the previous November, three-quarters of the troops lived in a walled-off section of the yard. Far worse, the laundresses also lived inside the fence, cheek by jowl with the prisoners. The hospital accommodations might also have been a source of discontent. The arrangements for the guards were no better than those for the prisoners. A local lady visited the garrison hospital and found a soldier lying on a thin straw mattress, under which water had run and frozen. As Danforth said: "It is the fault of somebody that these sick people are laid on the floor. We know it is said, in excuse, that iron bedsteads were ordered, but froze up at Keokuk. That excuse won't do."[27]

Complicating matters, the smallpox epidemic continued to rage despite the best efforts of Temple and Johnson. On 24 January 1864, 17 prisoners died, 11 of them of smallpox. Townshend had been either incapable or unwilling to see the chaos during his brief visit, but another inspector was on the way who would not be so lenient. Surgeon A. M. Clark, a volunteer, had been the head surgeon at Union Hotel Hospital in Washington, D.C., in 1862 and 1863, where he got into some trouble. According to Hannah Ropes, the hospital matron, Clark "cared no more for a private than a dog." Ropes described Clark as young and "ignorant of hospital routine, ignorant of life outside of the practice in a country town . . . a weak man with good intentions, but puffed up by the gilding on his shoulder straps."[28]

Clark ignored Ropes's complaint about a steward who was robbing the hospital and the patients. Not to be ignored, she went directly to Edwin Stanton, who had Clark and the steward arrested and confined in Old Capitol Prison. But the war machine needed every man, and after a time Clark found himself free and assigned to William Hoffman as a medical inspector. Hoffman kept him constantly on the move; the minute Clark returned from one trip Hoffman sent him on another. On Christmas Day 1863, Hoffman gave Clark the latest in a long series of assignments: "You will proceed at once to visit the several stations in the West where prisoners of war are held, with a view of ascertaining the present condition of the sick in hospital and in barracks." Hoffman told Clark to make any reforms he thought necessary, and in a statement he would have much cause to regret Hoffman also said that, when hospitals proved necessary, Clark was to "direct them to be built and conveniently fitted up, the expense to be paid out of the prisoners' fund. . . ."[29]

On 3 February 1864 Clark arrived in the River Bend. Within two days he had sized up the situation and started sending long and detailed letters to Johnson, the surgeons, and Hoffman. To Johnson he wrote: "To speak plainly, I was *horrified* to find, on my inspection yesterday, *38* cases of small pox laying in the prison barracks, and in some of which the disease had been in progress for several days. This is utterly inexcusable, and argues gross neglect of duty in some quarter." Clark demanded increased kitchen accommodations, clothing for the sick, a dispensary building, and a dead house. The following day Clark outlined further problems. The sinks concerned him greatly: "These are in a most foul condition. . . . At the rate at which they require to be renewed, all the spare ground within the enclosure will soon become a seething mass of filth." The drainage was poor. The water supply was insufficient even for ordinary needs and "in case of fire would be worse than useless." Clark suggested more wells, filling in the swampy area south of the compound, and a fanciful arrangement of privies suspended over the river. The colonel did not take up Clark's privy plan—the view from the Iowa shore of hundreds of squatting, half-naked Rebels would not have endeared him to the ladies of Davenport.[30]

These things were all minor. The main problem was the hospital, and Clark grasped this firmly: "There are no hospital accommodations provided for the prisoners confined in the camp. . . . The hospital is an absolute necessity, and *must* be provided, whatever may be the way in which the expense is defrayed." In the next paragraph Clark opened a pecuniary Pandora's box, which Johnson would spend months trying to get closed again: "A plan for the proposed hospital has been submitted to me by the present medical officer in charge, which, with some few alterations, I entirely approve. Its estimated cost is $18,000, and it has a capacity of 700 beds. . . . I have to request that its erection be proceeded with *at once*."[31]

Clark also sent a scathing letter to M. K. Moxley, the newest in the line of chief surgeons. He lectured Moxley on the necessity of vaccination, quarantine, and cleanliness. All of this should have been known even by the youngest and most inexperienced doctor, but either Moxley really was ignorant of these things or Clark considered himself the sole repository of all medical knowledge. Having thus pontificated to the men on the Island, Clark unburdened himself to Hoffman:

> I find there has been much remissness on the part of the medical officers of the prison in not taking proper measures to prevent the spread of the small pox. In some cases the proper steps have been suggested,

but not urged with sufficient energy. . . .

A prison hospital is imperatively demanded. A plan for a proposed building . . . has been sent to you by Col. Johnson, which I hope will meet with your approval, as it is I think, the best and certainly as economical as any that can be furnished.[32]

The inspector then entrained for Chicago and Camp Douglas, but in two weeks he was back on the Island to see if his instructions had been followed. And they had been, although not entirely to his satisfaction. The number and severity of smallpox cases was on the decline, and the Barracks was "in admirable order," but on the other hand, Clark noted, "everything is being done slowly." Clark knew where to put the blame: "I find it almost impossible to infuse any degree of energy of action into any of the officers with whom I have to deal. Colonel Johnson appears to possess a sufficiency himself, but does not impart it to his subordinates."[33]

Obviously, conditions in the Barracks were improving. In his second report to Hoffman, Clark was quick to note that the improvements had all been at his order. His correspondence from the Island paints a picture of a camp administration composed entirely of incompetents and sluggards. The tone, if not the wording, of Clark's reports suggests that, had it not been for his timely intervention and masterful action, God alone knows what might have happened at the Barracks. But, as Hannah Ropes had noted, Surgeon Clark was blinded by his epaulets. The correspondence clearly shows that the necessary improvements would have been made even if Clark had never heard of Rock Island. If the doctor's visitations had any value, it was that they speeded up the process a bit. Clark had been right about that: things did move slowly at Rock Island.

Johnson remained silent in the face of Clark's accusations, so Clark took the credit for saving the Island from universal pestilence and decamped again, this time for Nashville. Johnson took the blame and remained on the Island, which was rapidly becoming his own private hell. All the while, Clark's cost estimates for the hospital wended their way toward Washington and William Hoffman.

*F*or Commissary General of Prisoners William Hoffman, 1863 had been a long year. The number of prisoners under his care had grown tremendously: in July 1863, there had been fewer than 12,000 prisoners in Hoffman's system; by New Year's Day 1864, there were 35,000. Hoffman crammed his prisons full, and overfull, and flooded the mails with correspondence to make sure the prisoners were transported, housed, and fed. In all too many cases they were transported dangerously, housed poorly, and fed too little. The system simply could not cope with the flood tide of prisoners, and nowhere was this more apparent than on Rock Island, where the blizzard and smallpox threw into sharp relief the system's inadequacies.

Besides the problems at Rock Island and the other prisons, Hoffman's year had also been filled with incessant bureaucratic battles. Many people, it seemed, failed to understand his importance. For example, field commanders continued to issue orders concerning the prisoners, bypassing his office completely. Even his own commandants thwarted his efforts. At Alton, Illinois, Colonel George Kincaid, in obedience to a departmental order, released 19 prisoners in November 1863. Hoffman promptly chastised Kincaid, who could only reply that he was following orders—which was perhaps true, but they were not Hoffman's orders, and that made all the difference. Hoffman suggested to Edwin Stanton, "It would facilitate the management of affairs of prisoners of war, and lead to a more direct responsibility if the commanders of stations where prisoners are held could be placed under the immediate control of the Com. Gen'l of Pris." Hoffman included the wording of the order he desired, to spare Stanton any trouble.[34]

Hoffman needed direct control over his commandants because they persisted in acting with common sense, without regard to regulations. Lieutenant Colonel George Sangster at Annapolis issued clothing to two citizen prisoners, for which he had no authority, eliciting rebuke from Hoffman: "The sympathies of an officer for those who are in want do not justify him in using the public property to alleviate those wants." Col. A. A. Stevens, commanding at Camp Morton in Indianapolis, also sinned in the matter of clothing, causing Hoffman to explain, "As long as a prisoner has clothing upon him, however much torn, you must issue nothing to him." Then there was the matter of the Farmer boilers. The commandant at Camp Douglas in Chicago, apparently unaware of Hoffman's fascination with the contraptions, baldly stated, "We have tried the Farmer boilers and they are a failure." This instantly brought down Hoffman's wrath: "The Farmer boilers are in use in several camps . . . and are found to be the most convenient mode of cooking, and if they have failed at Camp Douglas it is because those who used them did not want to succeed." As Hoffman pointed out to Stanton, fuel cost money—$10,000 per month at one camp. He insisted on the boilers so that he might "remedy this great evil."[35]

His office and furnishings also perturbed Hoffman. In June 1863, he wrote to the quartermaster in Washington about his office being "quite too small to furnish the necessary accommodations for the duties I have to perform." One of the problems deriving from his cramped quarters was that "my table and papers are covered with dust all the time." Once Hoffman had a more suitable office, the stationery proved inadequate: "It is of a very inferior quality and unfit for the use of the office. . . . The red ink and the steel pens are of the poorest description."[36]

In this crown of thorns lay a single rose: the prison fund. All the two ounces of flour were adding up. But even here Hoffman had to exercise eagle-eyed vigilance. As he told George Sangster at Annapolis, "The number of clerks at your Hd. Qrs. has always been unnecessarily large . . . in the month of October there were *twenty-two* men employed in the Subs[sistence] Dpt. And for this extraordinary number of men there can have been no necessity." To offset such losses, Hoffman continually tinkered with the rations, which formed the bulk of the savings in any case. On Christmas Eve 1863, he wrote his commandants to cut the molasses ration from four quarts per 100 men to one quart. What the prisoners thought of this Yuletide present is not recorded.[37]

Of course Hoffman did authorize expenditures from the funds, sometimes large ones. In the beginning, the commandants purchased such things as stoves, brooms, kitchen utensils, towels, and combs, all of which met the requirement that prison funds be spent for the benefit of the prisoners. But as time went on other items found their way into the fund's books: iron doors, leg irons, handcuffs, and padlocks, among other things. When John M. Schofield, department commander in Missouri, tried to put a stop to such expenditures, Hoffman fired off a barbed missive telling Schofield only he had the right to decide what was and was not proper disbursement of the funds. When the comptroller of the currency tried to direct where the prison funds should be deposited, Hoffman quickly responded that the funds were not public money and his commandants could deposit the money anywhere it pleased them. Despite such inroads as 22 clerks' salaries at Annapolis and the purchase of vegetables to prevent scurvy, Hoffman's stewardship of the prison fund paid fine dividends. By March 1864, roughly two years after instituting the fund, he had a balance of $135,262.35. But his peace was about to be shattered.[38]

When Surgeon Clark's reports and Reynolds's hospital plans arrived, Hoffman noted that the cost was $1,800. Because the Quartermaster Department was going to pay much of that, Hoffman raised no objection. Unfortunately, William Hoffman was the only man in the world who saw the $1,800 figure—everyone else saw $18,000. Clark had reported to Colonel Johnson an estimate of $18,000, and Johnson had reported to Hoffman $18,000; but Hoffman, deep in the grip of his own penury, saw $1,800. And, serene in his ignorance, he authorized payment. A few weeks later Johnson forwarded Clark's reports, and one of them contained the fatal figure, which this time Hoffman noted accurately: $18,000. He reacted instantly and without a trace of serenity.[39]

First, he reined in his profligate inspector. On 9 March 1864, Hoffman telegraphed Clark that there would be no improvements without specific and prior approval from Hoffman. Clark, who understood politics and had no wish to come again to the attention of Edwin Stanton, made a quick and obsequious reply: "Your instructions shall be obeyed." Hoffman then turned to Johnson, telling him that the hospital arrangements were "much more extensive than I thought them to be." Hoffman ordered the work stopped "at that point where a sufficiency of room has been provided for an average number of sick, and no work in the finishing will be done that is not absolutely necessary." Two weeks later Hoffman had not heard from Johnson and wrote again, saying, "I wish the work as far as practicable stopped where it is until you can be further instructed." Hoffman then gathered up the voluminous correspondence relating to the hospital and sent it to Stanton, along with a letter of his own. Hoffman told the secretary of war that, although he had authorized the hospital, "I was very greatly surprised at this discovery [of the cost]." Hoffman assured Stanton that the hospital was "against my judgment and without my approbation." Having covered himself with his superior, Hoffman apparently thought the matter settled.[40]

It was far from settled. Not only did Danforth publish articles about the "alarming mortality," but every week the surgeons at the Barracks submitted reports to the Northern Department's medical director, Charles S. Tripler, who agreed with J. B., and in almost exactly the same language. He reported to Joseph Barnes, the acting surgeon general, that there were an "alarming number of deaths" at Rock Island. The statistics induced Tripler to call for a special report. Having no surgeons to send himself, he asked the current chief surgeon at the Barracks, Charles Watson, to make the report.[41]

When he received the report, Tripler noted that it was "somewhat confused." Watson can be forgiven any confusion. He had been at the Barracks less than three weeks, and conditions, although not as infernal as they had been earlier, still left much to be desired. Despite Watson's incoherence, Tripler made some sense of the report, and he concluded that there was no good reason for 485 smallpox patients to be crammed into a space meant for fewer than 250, nor for the "great want of cleanliness" that Watson reported. As late as 4 March 1864, nearly three months after the first outbreak, as many as 25 new smallpox cases appeared every day, and this, too, perturbed Tripler. Moreover, even if a man survived the smallpox, he remained in the hospital because there was no new clothing to give him, and old clothing had to be burned. As Watson reported to both Johnson and Tripler, the mortality at Rock Island was "almost unheard of in modern hospitals."[42]

Johnson also responded to the report, explaining to Hoffman the need for the new hospitals. The facilities existing when Clark had first appeared on the Island, said Johnson, "were entirely insufficient, and many cases were never removed from the prison and the epidemic was spreading rapidly. . . . This hospital was only deemed a necessary provision." The colonel supported Reynolds and Watson, heartily endorsing their plans: "The plan was drawn with much care and seems to me to embrace all that is desirable in a point of economy, convenience, location & sanitary measures."[43]

Tripler referred all the reports to Hoffman, who at last relented. But being a political animal, he was not about to take sole responsibility for an $18,000 expenditure. He packed up the latest sheaf of letters and sent them to Stanton, with a recommendation that the hospital be completed and paid for from the prison fund. But the commissary general of prisoners was not happy about this turn of events, and he warned Johnson to observe "the closest economy in all things."[44]

It was a victory of sorts for Johnson, one he sorely needed. In February 1864, Watson reported treating 1,490 prisoners—nearly a quarter of the prison population. Permission to complete the hospital solved one of his greatest problems. But there were other demons to torment the colonel, and several thousand of them lived just across the slough in Rock Island City. While the officers bickered about the hospital, the citizens had gone blithely about their business.[45]

To the citizens, the Barracks meant money. As Danforth had pointed out, every Rebel confined on the Island was a potential customer. Of course, a man was a better customer if he was alive, so the citizens on both sides of the river did their best to keep the prisoners that way. As the hospital crisis deepened Johnson appealed to the community, begging for clothes. His stocks were exhausted, and when they could be replenished was a mystery, thanks to the weather. As reported in all the local papers, Johnson said, "[T]here is a pressing want of clothes for the sick, and he respectfully asks immediate contributions . . . of any kind of clothing old or new." The community, as well as sympathizers far from the River Bend, responded with a flood of comforts. Lafayette Rogan recorded in his diary, "Liberal donations of clothing continue to be made by the good ladies of Ky., Tenn., and by kind friends who do not reside far from this place." On 20 January 1864, a large delegation of citizens, led by the "notorious Copperhead" Judge Grant, descended on the Island in a body. According to Barnes, "Large amounts of provisions and other things were distributed by these people to the Rebels." Although not a doctor, Grant understood the medicine of the day and included as part of his contribution a barrel and a half of "good whiskey—an article very much needed by the sick."[46]

However, the "other things" did not include enough tobacco. A prisoner, a former printer, wrote to the *Davenport Gazette* and called on his brothers of the Fourth Estate to send him tobacco. The bonds of ink being stronger than politics, the typos of the paper sent over a generous supply. Only a few days later another printer, John Loughrey, wrote to Danforth. Loughrey, however, had his pride—he declined to beg, but instead asked Danforth to "tell the comps to send me in some [tobacco] and I will set a few thousand when I come out." The composing room crew sent the weed. A third prisoner, Arthur P. De Bardelabeu, decided his chances were better with the sympathizing ladies of the area. Bardelabeu had a fine sense of flattery. He told a Mrs. Taylor that he had heard she was a woman "who considers it a pleasure and a privilege to administer to the wants of the needy." Arthur also believed that beggars could indeed be choosers: "If you will send me some clothing, a light pr. Boots or shoes No. 9 and some tobacco you will confer a favor upon me and add one more Rebel to the list that will always think of you with gratitude." And, in case Mrs. Taylor wondered about clothing size, Bardelabeu included his vital statistics in a postscript: "I am six feet two inches in height and weigh one hundred eighty pounds."[47]

Despite the aid, the prisoners continued to die, but the citizens made money even from death. As the smallpox epidemic gathered virulence Johnson, scrambling for places to put patients, approached owners of buildings on the Island. He got one house from a man named Hartel for $75.00 a month, but for another, rented from Elizabeth Bromley, he had to pay $150.00. Charles Knox, a cabinetmaker, had come to Rock Island in 1841 from Massachusetts and "found a brisk demand for coffins." It was the custom at the time to make coffins only as needed, but Knox hit on the idea of keeping a stock on hand. His fellow citizens were aghast at such sacrilege, but Knox knew what he was doing—by the time the war started he had cornered the city's mortuary business. He provided the coffins for the dead prisoners, and his son helped bury them. The son, B. Frank Knox, worked nights baking bread for the prisoners he had not buried during the day. Knox subcontracted the interment side of the business. A gentleman listed as J. De Harpart did the actual work of hauling and burying the corpses. In March 1864, he received $2.00 a day from the prison fund, part of which presumably went to young Frank Knox. Sensing a rising market, however, De Harpart finagled a raise the very next month, to $2.50 per day. The adage had at last proved true: war was finally good business.[48]

Everything was for sale, including the city's fire engine, called in those days a rescue engine. In late December one of the barracks' roofs had caught fire from the heat of a stove pipe. Although quickly extinguished, it awakened Johnson to yet another omission: there was no way to fight a fire save with buckets. Johnson entered into negotiations with the city to buy its engine. He was careful to ask for permission from Hoffman, who approved the purchase—and it was lucky for Johnson that he did, because Johnson did not wait for authorization: he made the request and immediately sent an officer to the city to close the deal. The officer, Captain Collins of the Quartermaster Department, showed up at a city council meeting prepared to pay $2,050 for the engine, hose cart, and 500 feet of hose. But when he arrived, the aldermen reneged; it had suddenly occurred to them that if they sold the engine to the

Barracks, the city would be left unprotected. Collins, however, was himself a very shrewd operator. He merely explained to the city fathers that the winter was bitter; that over on the Island stood 84 wooden barracks in which red-hot coal fires roared day and night; and that if those wooden buildings caught a spark and the prison burned to the ground, there would be no further business for the good burghers of the town. Faced with such an appeal to the better angels of their natures, the aldermen immediately sold the engine. Mayor Davenport arranged to borrow another from Davenport until the city could replace its own. Unfortunately for the city treasury, Johnson quickly decided that a new water system Reynolds had in mind would suffice. There is no voucher for the engine in the post records, indicating that Johnson either returned the engine or never took possession of it.[49]

Despite this disappointment, the money flowed endlessly. In the month of March 1864, J. G. Devoe, a hardware store owner, received $756.18 for awls, hammers, mucilage, and various other items. A tobacconist got a dollar a pound for the weed that Danforth's employees gave away free. T. J. Buford received $173.03 for some ironwork. When the hospital contracts were let, other firms found themselves thousands of dollars richer for such things as windows and lumber.[50]

Everyone benefited from the Barracks, and no one more than Danforth. The prison was a godsend to him—he could fill his paper with the antics over on the Island. With friends in the prison office to feed him information and to keep the blackguard Barnes away, J. B. had the market cornered. On 11 January 1864 he began running a regular feature called "Jottings at the Barracks." "Jottings" served several purposes. Danforth could keep his readers informed about such things as the straw shortage; he could kibitz Johnson's administration, point out where the colonel went awry, and keep track of the numbers of prisoners pouring into the compound. And, much more to the point for political purposes, he could keep track of the prisoners who left the compound, especially those who left by way of coffins.

With the very first appearance of "Jottings," J. B. printed death lists he obtained from the provost marshal of prisoners. The name and regiment of every man who died, prisoner and guard alike, appeared in the *Argus,* in lists that grew longer and longer. Perhaps J. B. thought he was merely performing a public service. There were many people in the River Bend of southern origin, and in addition to their commercial interest the citizens also took a fraternal interest in the inmates. Even disguised as simple information, however, the lists were damning indictments of conditions in the yard. Every week the list was longer than the week before. J. B. had no need to waste further space on long diatribes about the horrors, nor did he. The lists spoke volumes for him.

With the Invalid Corps running amok in the city, the accounts of all the business being done on the Island, and the death lists, J. B. had material enough to fill his sheet every day. And he was about to get even more.

A few miles downriver from the Island stood the town of Muscatine, Iowa. To aid the war effort the citizens of Muscatine decided vegetables were the thing, and they spent the summer raising a huge crop of potatoes. It was a democratic enterprise: "side by side the lawyers, storekeepers, editors, doctors and ladies toiled, turning the products of the field over to the Sanitary Commission." This was far too tame for a 50-year-old Ohio-born farmer named George Kincaid. Although too old for combat, Kincaid felt the call and would not be denied. In August 1862, he proposed to Iowa Governor Samuel Kirkwood and Adjutant General Nathaniel Baker, a regiment of men over 45 years old to serve as garrison troops, which would release stronger men for the slaughter pens. Kirkwood and Baker snapped up the plan. Recruiting had become difficult as the war progressed, but the calls for troops were ceaseless. Although conscription was regarded with almost universal horror, Baker shrewdly noted its salubrious effect on volunteer enlistments and told Edwin Stanton, "I like a draft." He also liked Kincaid's idea.[51]

Kincaid's plan fit in with the theory that had produced the Invalid Corps, soon to be renamed the Veteran Reserve Corps (VRC), and Stanton authorized the regiment. Kincaid enlisted a smattering of young men, including one boy of 15, but in the main his men were old: nearly 600 were over 50, and 9 were over 70. They trained at Camp Strong near Muscatine, where they learned both rudimentary drill and cornhusking. At least some of them were immediately disenchanted with military life. Private John Wagner wrote that the entire camp was "covered in the greatest effusions of snot that human eyes have ever beheld." Stanton had authorized a regiment of "active and vigorous" senior citizens, but he got something else entirely. Company F of the regiment wrote a letter to Baker, outlining the shortcomings of their fellows:

> [Case] No. 1 is that of a boy in Co. F which has been represented to you as a drummer boy . . . the boy can never be learnt. . . . No. 2 is that of a man in the same Co., E. J. Mathis who was rejected . . . on account of rupture as well as being almost blind. . . . No. 3 is a Mr. Travis who was also rejected . . . on account of rupture. . . . No. 4, a man named Warner . . . is nothing more nor less than a walking bottle of morphine unfit for any thing but eating, at which he cannot be beat. . . . There is also a woman in the Co. that should be out as she does no washing.[52]

The regiment mustered in as the 37th Iowa 15 December 1862. Baker attended the proceedings and told Kirkwood that Kincaid was felt "large as life, happy as a clam, and proud as a peacock." The proud colonel led his withered troops to St. Louis, Missouri, where they guarded various warehouses, depots, and prisons. After a few months, the 37th was transferred across the river to the former Illinois State Penitentiary at Alton, which now housed Confederate prisoners. According to inspectors at Alton, the old men were a little lax about military discipline but nonetheless took good care of the prisoners and were careful about security: "Every precaution seems to have been taken to prevent escapes." Perhaps this praise went to their heads, for two months later, in December 1863, the old men allowed 23 prisoners to go over the walls and back to Dixie.[53]

The "Greybeards" and "Silver Greys," as they were quickly dubbed, were regarded by prisoners as "old gentlemen, kind and fatherly." Colonel Kincaid, however, was something else. In fact, he was a martinet and his men were a disappointment to him—they were old, sick, and possessed of the distressing habit of writing directly to Baker to air their myriad grievances. Kincaid attempted to instill discipline by such unorthodox measures as holding his men under hydrants until they were "perfectly suffocated and apparently dead." The regiment's chaplain stood by to make sure the punishment was sufficient, in one case calling out to Kincaid, "He can stand a little more." When not otherwise occupied, Kincaid strode through the prison yard, announcing to Confederate prisoners that their wives were "prostitutes of the very lowest class."[54]

After several months at Alton, the Greybeards, knowing they were in a democracy, took a vote on where they wanted to serve, and the winning candidate was Rock Island. Fortunately, Nathaniel Baker also wanted the Greybeards a little closer to home. He asked Edwin Stanton to send the old men to the River Bend. Stanton and an obliging department commander, Major General John M. Schofield, ordered the 37th to the Island. Both Barnes and Danforth got wind of the transfer. Barnes immediately laid claim to the regiment, saying that Kincaid was "a good commanding officer" and "universally beloved by his men." The troops themselves were possessed of "harmony and promptness to obey orders, and general good conduct." Danforth, of course, took the other tack, and he was closer to the truth when he concluded, "The regiment is a failure and a useless expense to the government." J. B. also had an opinion on Colonel Kincaid: "It would be a very grave mistake to place Col. Kincaid in charge of Rock Island Barracks. He is not a suitable man for a position of such importance and responsibility." This opinion would return to haunt the editor shortly.[55]

The train carrying the Greybeards pulled into the station on 19 January 1864, and the old men remained right where they were. Johnson flatly refused to accept them. Stubbornly adhering to the chain of command, he said Schofield had no authority over the Barracks, and he was neither obligated nor inclined to accept troops on Schofield's order. And although he did not say so, it was also true that Johnson had nowhere to put them. Some of the VRC men were still quartered in the compound, and work on the new buildings had nearly ground to a halt in the face of the weather. There was no room anywhere on the Island—the compound was bursting at the seams, with 24 barracks used to house guards and hospital patients, and 6,000 prisoners crowding the rest. The buildings outside the compound were either full or still under construction. There might have been a few tents left over from the construction days, but they would have been shamefully inadequate. Faced with this insoluble problem, Johnson did nothing. The old men remained on the cars for two days. It took an order from the War Department to force Johnson to action. As he told Reynolds, "As I am unable to furnish quarters . . . on the Island, I would request that you furnish them at Rock Island City." Reynolds housed the old men in the city in any nook or cranny he could find, including both public meeting halls and private homes. The rents he paid were doubtless exorbitant. The citizens knew a captive market when one rolled into town.[56]

The new guards immediately began demonstrating the truth of J. B.'s judgment. Within days Danforth complained: "The sidewalks . . . have been rendered a public nuisance . . . generally crowded with men, obstructing the passage of the public. . . . There is no necessity for this, or for a camp fire in the street." The 37th continued the tradition of the VRC and immediately began drinking heavily. One man was arrested for being drunk and hitting a policeman, another for trying to shoot a discharged veteran who merely wanted to embrace a fellow soldier. Also, some of the Greybeards were still virile: 59-year-old Crouch Thomas of Company B was very shortly sent home to die of syphilis. Others were merely ill. Of the 900 men who had mustered a year earlier, only 700 remained, and 140 of them were on the sick list.[57]

It would be the middle of February, and only after Baker complained directly to Stanton, before the 37th began transferring to the Island, and when they did six companies, along with all the regiment's laundresses, marched directly into the compound. It took two teams nearly two days to haul their equipment, which according to J. B. included household furniture, bedsteads, and rocking chairs. Once ensconced on the Island, the 37th made itself right at home and demonstrated to Johnson the same housekeeping techniques that had caused Danforth to complain. They stood at their doors and tossed garbage into the yard; they kept food under their beds, which was both against the rules and an invitation to vermin; those that bothered to bathe poured the dirty water into the mounds of garbage. Being farmers, the Greybeards also kept pigs. Johnson, still occupied with the smallpox epidemic, let everything go on until Surgeon Clark made a third visit at the end of March 1864, whereupon he began issuing orders concerning the proper disposal of offal and waste water, and forbidding the keeping of swine.[58]

These depredations went largely unnoticed by Danforth, who had other problems to deal with. Some citizens of the River Bend had little love for the editor, and one of them was about to demonstrate his dislike, bluntly and physically. Some months earlier the local soldiers' aid society had promised a financial report and then failed to produce it, at which Danforth took umbrage. He regularly led his paper with demands for an accounting, and about the time the Greybeards began cluttering up the city's sidewalks he sent "an insulting letter" to the society. This did not sit well with Major James Beardsley of the 13th Illinois. Ten years earlier Beardsley had been the city prosecutor and charged Danforth with larceny, accusing him of stealing from his own partner. The grand jury, because of a quirk in the law, could not return an indictment, but the incident made enemies of the entire Beardsley clan. James's brother Ezra said, "If there is a creature on earth I hate, it is J. B. Danforth. I want him buried very deep." Now, Danforth's letter gave James Beardsley the opportunity to strike. According to Barnes: "During the morning the Major met the Copperhead . . . and accosted him by remarking that he was now prepared to make the report for the Soldiers' Aid Society. . . .[T]he Major [knocked] him through one of the large windows in front of Harper & Steel's. . . . Danforth commenced blubbering, and begged like a school boy to be let up." Danforth burst through the door of a store and tried to flee to the back. The proprietor, a man named Harper, tried to intervene, but Beardsley "told Harper to stand aside . . . that he was making a report for the Soldiers' Aid Society, and he wished to make a satisfactory one." Adding insult to the injury, Barnes reported that during the fracas Danforth lost his wig.[59]

The Greybeards, whom Danforth had abused since their arrival, applauded this effort by immediately getting up an oyster dinner in honor of Beardsley. Colonel Kincaid and most of his officers attended, and Kincaid offered the toast "Copperheads—may they all be scalped as clean as the Major scalped the Editor of the *Argus*." Another toast praised "The best of all beards—Greybeards and Beardsley." Kincaid then offered that any officer of his regiment would repeat the beating any time Beardsley called for it.[60]

It was a clear victory for everyone Danforth had ever harangued. His politics were the real cause of the attack, with J. B.'s plaintive call for a financial report serving only as pretext. Assuming a role utterly unfamiliar to him, J. B. did a little bootlicking: "We have not, and do not think all the measures of the administration the best that could have been devised . . . but we have been in favor of pushing the war with all possible vigor, from the start, and still are, and expect to be to the end." His paper for 18 months had given the lie to this pusillanimous utterance, but it was as close to an apology as the fire-eater would ever get. Because it was impossible to do otherwise, he also confessed in his columns that he had been obliged to wear a wig for 15 years. J. B. then dolefully noted that it was very ungentlemanly of people to make sport of the fact.[61] Danforth also tried a more official retaliation. He wrote his congressman, C. M. Harris, demanding an investigation into why an officer of the United States Army should be allowed to go around assaulting editors. The representative in turn wrote to Stanton, who thrust it all back on Johnson, who took affidavits from everyone concerned and sent them off to Major General Samuel Heintzelman, the district commander. That was the end of the investigation. Danforth dared not press the issue further, because Johnson controlled his access to the Island and the information J. B. needed to fill his columns.[62]

Despite being denied official revenge, Danforth had the last laugh. The Republicans might beat him in the streets, but they could not beat him at the polls, and only a few weeks after the attack J. B. proudly announced that the Democrats had swept every office in the city elections. And, although J. B. might have to be careful about abusing Johnson, there were others who could do as they pleased. One of them was Major Kingsbury, who was doing his best to add another ration of misery to Colonel Johnson's life.[63]

The Barracks were a nuisance to Major Kingsbury. The compound was full of unrepentant Rebels and the area around it full of something just as bad—volunteers. Moreover, citizens constantly wandered around. Since the Arsenal and the Barracks belonged to completely different departments, Kingsbury had no control over the Barracks. None of this suited the major. On 15 February 1864 he wrote the Ordnance Department: "In consequence of the proximity of the prison barracks, a guard is required to protect the Arsenal grounds from the soldiers and citizens who are constantly straggling and driving on the Island, breaking down the fences and cutting up the soil in all directions." Having had ample opportunity to observe the antics of the VRC and the Greybeards, Kingsbury added that he hoped "temperate, industrious and well behaved men may be sent." It would prove a vain hope—he was assigned a detail of men from the Barracks garrison.[64]

A few days later Kingsbury turned his attentions more specifically to the Barracks. He would always couch his complaints in his favorite term: whatever he disliked was an "interference with the public service." But Kingsbury had a far more personal reason for his crusade: Johnson had dared to defy the major. In truth, Johnson bears some responsibility for the feud. Although not nearly so small a soul as Kingsbury, Johnson suffered an extreme rigidity. Rules were to be obeyed without equivocation, and one of the rules was that nobody could visit the prisoners except under very explicit circumstances. Shortly after the prisoners arrived, Kingsbury applied to Johnson to visit one of the Rebels, who had formerly been a friend of the major's. This presented Johnson with a dilemma. As he later said, "I have been exceedingly desirous of avoiding any unpleasant contact with him." On the other hand, nothing in the regulations would permit him to allow the visit, so he denied Kingsbury's request.[65]

Johnson deluded himself that his strict adherence to the regulations "should have elevated me as an officer in [Kingbury's] estimation." Compounding the error, Johnson had been warned about the major. As the colonel put it, his desire to get along with Kingsbury "was occasioned by the general prediction of influential gentlemen in Davenport and Rock Island cities that he was so peculiarly made up that it was impossible for anyone to get along smoothly with him." Johnson labored under the misimpression that he and Kingsbury were both officers and were therefore kindred spirits. So he chose to ignore the warning, saying, "I had made the acquaintance of and had been associated with a large number of regular officers, that they had invariably proved to be high toned gentlemen; that my intercourse with them had been of the most pleasant character, and that I had no fears but what I could get along smoothly with Maj. Kingsbury." The citizens who had warned him were absolutely right, and, after Johnson denied Kingsbury permission to see his friend, the major made it his business to harass Johnson at every opportunity. The idea that a volunteer commanding old men and half cripples could brook a professional officer burned Kingsbury's soul. Adding to the fire was the fact that, in strictly literal terms, Johnson's refusal had been correct, and there was nothing Kingsbury could do about it, officially. But small nuisances and transgressions that might have been overlooked had Johnson been more flexible now became cause for a personal war.[66]

On 26 February 1864 Kingsbury began his vendetta. He wrote first to Captain Reynolds: "The teams which are hauling to the prison barracks have ceased following the road thither, and are traveling at will over the lower end of the Island. Several weeks since the fences were broken down, and two new routes opened through the Arsenal grounds, and not satisfied with this a new series has just been commenced." A few weeks later Kingsbury followed up his complaint, this time to Johnson himself: "The nuisance was abated for a short time, but today the teamsters are again scattering themselves as formerly." The fences particularly concerned the major, who asked Johnson to "order the fences to be replaced which within the last three days have been torn down by your guards, and used as I am informed, for fuel."[67]

Having spent his life in the army, Kingsbury knew how to manipulate the bureaucracy. Only two days after his complaint to Johnson, he wrote the Ordnance Department: "The prison barracks and buildings pertaining to thereto have been erected without much regard to locality. The structures are for a temporary object, and might have been placed on grounds previously cleared, and without the destruction of a large number of forest trees, many of which have been cut down without reason or necessity, and to the permanent injury of the Island." The point of this was to get Johnson under his thumb, although Kingsbury couched it in other terms. He suggested that "instructions be given to the commanding officer of the Barracks, that in all future operations the officer in charge of the Arsenal be consulted, and that no trees be cut down, or other buildings or burying grounds located without his approval." The appropriate orders were issued to Johnson, but Kingsbury was not satisfied. Almost immediately he wrote again to the Ordnance Department, this time with a view to getting the colonel evicted. Johnson rented George Davenport's house, because the building intended for the Barracks' headquarters was being used as a hospital. Kingsbury told his superiors that Johnson should turn over the house because the Barracks had more than enough buildings. Further, the major worried that without control of the house "the fences, gardens, orchards, etc., now belonging to the place, will soon be destroyed or rendered valueless."[68]

On 13 March 1864, the War Department ordered Johnson out of the house. A lull of a few weeks followed, but Kingsbury could not leave the offending Johnson alone. On 2 May 1864, he wrote the colonel to complain that Johnson's bridge guards had stopped the Arsenal's master mason. Kingsbury demanded to know "by what authority the public service is thus interfered with." Kingsbury sent a full report of the matter to the Ordnance Department, humbly pointing out that he had always been "anxious to avoid a conflict of authority." Johnson, however, had had just about enough of the major. He returned the letter, endorsing it: "Respectfully returned to Maj. C. P. Kingsbury Ordnance Department with the remarks that the within communication is not respectful in its tone and improperly addressed. . . . When Maj. Kingsbury forwards a proper communication I will be most happy to give any information that may be necessary."[69]

This retort represented a change for Colonel Johnson. He had for the most part suffered criticism in silence. But the silence did not represent equanimity; rather, it capped a spiteful temper. Thus far Johnson had controlled his anger, especially with respect to people outside his control. But Kingsbury's barbs had uncapped his temper, and Johnson had lashed out. It seemed to end the matter, because Kingsbury made no reply. Things were looking up. At least for the moment.

CHAPTER THREE

"A Disagreeable Place to Be"

In former days, Sauk Indians, and later whites, had used the Island for excursions and idyllic summer days. Now, there was smallpox, wind, and snow. Prisoners unprepared for an Illinois winter had been rushed northward to an unfinished prison. The sick and the hale had been crammed into barracks together. They suffered weather more brutal than many of them had ever experienced. There were too many of them, and more kept coming. When Ulysses Grant had captured Fort Donelson in 1862, he had overwhelmed the prison system with captured Confederates. Now, with his victories at Chattanooga at the end of 1863, he had done the same thing to Rock Island. It is doubtful the prisoners gave Grant's generalship much thought as they crossed the wind-whipped yard to go to the sinks or get water from the wells.

What they did think about was going home. Hundreds of the prisoners had had their fill of the war. As Danforth reported, "From the hundreds of letters they are now writing to their friends, as well as from themselves personally, it is known that they feel that the Rebel cause is hopeless, and that they would, generally, like to take the oath of allegiance and be liberated." This had been true for a long time. In July 1862, Hoffman had noted a lack of Confederate passion in many of the prisoners and had asked the adjutant general: "There are many among them who live in southern states who wish to be released on parole so that they may not again be forced into the ranks. Others wish to remain at the North and enter our service. Can these be singled out, and released on taking the oath of allegiance?" This inquiry, along with others from various generals and governors, was prompted by anticipation of the exchange cartel, which went into effect in July 1862.[1]

In 1863, when the exchange system sputtered and ground to a halt, allegiance oath releases also became more rare, and in October 1863 Hoffman notified his commandants that there would be no more releases, although the prisoners could continue to make application. By the time the Barracks opened, few prisoners were being released on oath. In January 1864, Johnson released three men, and in February, eleven. The process was fraught with bureaucracy. B. J. Gaston of the 10th Alabama Cavalry explained the process to his family: they had to write a petition, persuade the military governor of his home state that he was worthy of release, and get the governor's endorsement. This would be sent to the War Department. If Stanton approved it, the release order would be sent on to the prison. Of course, release was more assured if the prisoner had friends in high places. John Graves and John McClary counted Illinois Governor Richard Yates among their friends. On behalf of both men Yates wrote Abraham Lincoln and asked for their release. Lincoln replied, "See these men take the oath of Dec. 8, 1863 & be discharged."[2]

Eleven releases were not going to solve Johnson's space problems. Fortunately, Edwin Stanton still needed men for the killing fields. The idea of enlisting Confederate prisoners had been bandied about for some time. In February 1862, Colonel James A. Mulligan, an Irish-born Chicagoan who commanded at Camp Douglas when the Donelson prisoners arrived, noted a number of Irish prisoners whose ties to blood were stronger than their bond to country. He began recruiting for his own regiment, and although the War Department forbade the scheme, Mulligan took more than 200 men with him when he left Chicago for Virginia. Mulligan failed to appreciate the problems entailed in enlisting former enemies. It complicated the exchange system, since the cartel was silent on the matter of prisoners going over to the enemy; moreover, there was a certain Victorian delicacy about asking men to kill their former comrades. Stanton himself waffled, at one time denying enlistments, then favoring them, then turning against them again.[3]

Secretary of the Navy Gideon Welles also wanted men and did not suffer Stanton's equivocation: on 16 January 1864, as the smallpox crisis rose to a crescendo, Acting Master John Harty arrived on the Island to enlist prisoners in the United States Navy. Only three days later Johnson reported to Hoffman that 600 men had offered to sign up and head for the high seas. Men who volunteered, but whom the surgeons rejected, signed the allegiance oath and were turned loose. The more resolute among the prisoners did not take the defections well. William Dillon recalled being informed that men could join the navy and said, "I am sorry to add that a very large number are going to join their navy and turn traitor to us." Dillon kept track of the enlistees from his company, noting that one was his friend "Lytle Statham, who saw his brother die treated no better than if he were a dog by the men he is now going to fight for."[4]

Harty began shipping men to Boston, and at the end of January he left with the last group himself. If the new recruits thought they left their troubles behind them on the Island, they were wrong: on arrival in Chicago nine men fell ill. The former Rebels and current sailors were a new breed, and Harty found that the bureaucrats at neither the Marine Hospital nor the Soldier's Home would accept his men. He finally left them in a private hospital, hoping the government would pay their keep, and moved on for Boston.[5]

Back on the Island, the prisoners who remained cast about for other ways to stay alive, and some of them found an unexpected friend: Colonel Johnson. The paperwork Hoffman required was enormous, and Johnson had barely enough guards to man the walls, let alone fill out the endless rolls and reports, so he almost immediately began recruiting clerks from among the prisoners. One of them was Rupert Baird. Baird worked first in the adjutant's office and then for the surgeons. He reported that he was not only paid a small amount but was allowed the freedom of the Island and the cities on both sides of the river. Although city paroles were common enough at some camps, Baird is the only Rock Island inmate who claimed such a broad parole; since neither of the area's Republican papers mentioned prisoners wandering around loose, it is likely Baird's memory was playing tricks on him.[6]

Lafayette Rogan, however, confirms that some prisoners were paroled to the limits of the Island. Rogan also accepted a clerk's job, which earned him not only the parole but quarters outside the compound, as well as other favors. One of his jobs was to make out muster rolls for the navy recruits. Rogan was a man with a finely honed sense of integrity—it was treacherous for his friends to enlist in the U.S. Navy, but it was permissible for him to work for the Yankees, because he could be more help to his fellow prisoners on the outside than he could be inside. But Rogan never recorded the help he rendered his comrades, if indeed he rendered any. And, safely ensconced in his warm office, comfortably fed and clothed, Rogan noted that prisoners who did not want to be exchanged had been turning in their names, hoping for release, and said, "I hope they will get disappointed and have to remain in prison." Rogan was trying to justify his actions to himself, but his actions were perfectly understandable if not laudable. He and the other clerks were trying to survive an Illinois winter in a prison overwhelmed by weather and disease.[7]

Like everything else about the Island, the clerks proved a problem for Johnson. As he had with Kingsbury, he helped create the problem himself. In December 1863, Hoffman had suggested that a chief clerk could be found among the guards but that, if not, Johnson could hire one for $50.00 per month, to be paid from the prison fund. Unfortunately, the only man Johnson could find to take the job was a citizen named Winkless, who demanded $60.00 for January 1864, and $75.00 the following month. This caused Hoffman to remind the colonel that such expenditures had to be approved, and he had approved no such amounts. Johnson was in a tight spot. His guards were illiterate, and Hoffman kept a tight rein on the purse strings, so Johnson had little choice but to use prisoners as clerks. He should have known better. Barnes, noting both this and the *Argus*'s tendency to compliment the colonel, mused: "This looks rather suspicious. Is the Col. A New Jersey Copperhead, that he comes in for so much praise from his *peculiar* friends?" Barnes and the other Republicans among the citizens noted what Johnson was up to and wrote their congressman, demanding an investigation of the colonel's political proclivities.[8]

Johnson himself must have got wind of this, because near the end of April 1864, Rogan, Baird, and the other clerks were turned back into the yard. Johnson tried to cover himself after the fact. He wrote to Hoffman, explaining his clerk troubles and asking permission to parole and employ prisoners. Unfortunately, he asked this permission nearly a month after he had stopped using clerks and three months after he had started using them. Moreover, the very idea that he thought he could get away with anything says nothing of the colonel's perspicacity. He had been on the Island five months; he surely knew that anything he did favoring the prisoners would be reported by Barnes and the abolitionists, and anything that favored the administration would call down the wrath of Danforth and the Copperheads.[9]

Becoming a clerk for Johnson or enlisting in the navy were not the only ways out of the compound. The prisoners were finding exits on their own. As noted earlier, Hoffman had assured Rush that the prisoners had never shown any great predilection to escape. J. B. Danforth shared Hoffman's attitude. He reported on 25 January 1864, "Since the occupation of the Barracks it is not known or believed that a single man has tried to escape—an evidence that the prisoners are pretty well satisfied with their treatment and are in no hurry to return south."[10]

Two days later Thomas Lily of the 18th Arkansas made liars of Danforth and Hoffman. The only record of Lily's exploit is a note in the prison register, which says that he escaped from the smallpox hospital. J. B. failed to report the escape—perhaps it occurred too soon after his confident pronouncement—but neither did Barnes at the *Union,* and apparently neither did Johnson. In February another Arkansan, Edward Scales of the 8th, made a getaway; how is not recorded. A third man escaped on 26 February, and Johnson at last notified the newspapers. Both Barnes and Danforth reported the escape, although Barnes was nearly a week late in doing so. The next man out was Thomas Courteney, who was outside the compound on a work detail, constructing a new building. Courteney merely went in one door and out another, the guards having remained outside the first door. Johnson reported that the guards were being court-martialed for their laxity and that one of them had been "uttering sentiments of disloyalty previous to the escape of this prisoner." The wily Courteney apparently had no plan further than his door trick and was quickly recaptured.[11]

After Courteney there was a lull, but Johnson still had his hands full with his own men trying to get away and with citizens trying to get in. Despite the bitter winter, the lures of the city were too great for the VRC and the Greybeards, and they continued to swarm the place whenever they could, which was incessantly. Johnson thought this might change as the winter slowly turned to spring. Until now, the river had been a great road of ice, and anyone could get from Island to mainland at any point. But on 19 February 1864 the spring thaw began, and it impressed Lafayette

Rogan, a Southerner who had never witnessed such an event: "The ice came floating down the river in sheets acres large. The unevenness of the river banks caused the ice to pile up on dry land in heaps as large as a good sized house. It was truly magnificent to behold—it displayed the power and grandeur of God's works. The R.R. bridge finally checked the ice." It would take a few weeks more, but spring was coming. Rogan followed the ice's progress, and on 17 March he noted the first steamboat of the season working its way up the rapids.[12]

The thaw made things easier on the surgeons, who, although they had checked the smallpox epidemic, still had their hands full. It also made life easier for the guards on the walls. And it definitely improved matters for Johnson, whose drunken men could no longer slip unnoticed off the Island across the ice. But he was taking no chances. As the weather warmed he took steps to corral his boisterous guards. On 11 March 1864 he issued an order restricting passes to three per company. Another order required company officers to keep accurate lists of exactly who had passes and when they were due back to camp. On 14 March 1864 he issued yet another order, an eight paragraph set of instructions, which established guards at all four bridges leading off the Island, provided for the immediate arrest of anyone who did not have proper authority to be away from camp. The guards were also to keep a sharp eye out for "persons of suspicious character attempting to leave the Island." Perhaps fearing an escalation from rocks to rifles in the saloon battles, he forbade the troops to take firearms off the Island. Johnson also ordered A. C. Dart, the post sutler, to sell no more than three beers a day to any enlisted man. After considering the matter, he prohibited Dart from selling any beer at all. Finally, in an attempt to keep the peace with Major Kingsbury, Johnson told the guards that any team coming from Rock Island City should be prevented from wrecking Kingsbury's fences or wandering over the Arsenal grounds.[13]

Johnson should have saved the ink—the transgressions continued unabated. As Danforth reported only four days after the beer order, a VRC man was arrested for drunkenness; a few days later a pair were arrested for being drunk and breaking windows; each had a loaded revolver. By the middle of May, Major F. A. H. Gaebel, commanding the VRC, wrote Johnson asking for 13 men to be drummed out of the service, one for "drunkenness and running guard frequently," another for "willful disobedience & worthlessness," and a third because it had been discovered that he was "a notorious bad character, served term in state prison." Spring was in the air.[14]

In May Johnson added another to his long list of prohibitions: "All persons . . . are warned against conveying soldiers or other persons in boats to or from the Island. No boats are allowed to land on the shore of the Island." Anticipating that his men would wade a few yards out to a boat to evade the order, Johnson added another paragraph: "All officers and enlisted men on duty at the Post are forbidden to leave the Island by boat or other water conveyance." Johnson promised both confiscation of every boat that violated the order and the arrest of the owners.[15]

As Major Gaebel reported to Johnson later: "The guard at the several bridges has within the past few weeks confiscated quite a large number of canteens filled with very bad whiskey. The patrols under Lieut. Hazard have destroyed six rafts on the slough made by soldiers to cross over to town." Gaebel suggested allowing sutler Dart to resume selling the troops one beer per man per day, in the apparent belief that this would slake the men's thirst.[16]

Far from quenching their thirst, however, a single beer only increased the men's lust for strong drink. Despite all the measures Johnson took, the troops continued to find ways to get over to the city. If the bridge guards were effective, and if no boats were available, they could simply wade the slough much of the time. Tricks of bottom and current could make this a chancy proposition, but the delights of the city overcame fear of such obstacles. Johnson also instituted regular patrols of the city three times a day, with orders to "visit the public rooms at all the hotels and places of amusement in the evening." As a last link in his chain, the colonel finally decided there would be no passes issued at all, except for men desiring to attend religious services. Unfortunately, Johnson forgot to instruct the patrols to check churches on their rounds, and before long ministers in Moline were calling in the guard to remove soldiers who, on the way to church and anxious for salvation, had taken repeated communion at various saloons.[17]

Preventing his soldiers from getting off the Island was only half the problem; the other half was preventing citizens from getting on. The citizens persisted in thinking the place belonged to them, and they evaded guards and patrols to wander through the woods, watch the daily dress parade, and sneak peeks at the prisoners. It generally was not difficult. There were all manner of people on the

Island who had legitimate business there: contractors, laborers, suppliers, factory operatives, delegations delivering food and clothing to the prison. The thrill seekers were not always easy to discern, nor were the soldiers particularly eager to arrest anyone. Ella and Viola Lyman, daughters of the Greybeards' major, were in the habit of having their friend Will drive them from Moline over to the Island. As Viola recorded, "The guard at the bridge was a green gosling of a boy and he asked Will for his pass. Will said that he had none. The fellow looked a minute, then lowered his bayonet and said, 'Well, guess you can go on.'"[18]

Among the visitors, legitimate or otherwise, were some who wanted to do more than simply get a glimpse of living, breathing Rebels—they wanted to help them get out. William Hoffman had equivocated about putting the prison on the Mississippi, for fear of sympathizers. He had been right to worry: the River Bend was full of them. As Johnson told Hoffman, "There are residing in the cities of Rock Island and Davenport many families of secession proclivities who are thoroughly disloyal to our government and are known as Copperheads." One of the most disloyal was Kate Perry, a young Kentuckian who had relatives in Rock Island and spent long periods in the River Bend. Her politics, however, lay much farther south, and her own brother was held at Camp Chase, Ohio. She had witnessed the arrival of the first prisoners in December and had written, "I was quivering with contending emotions—grief, which I was too proud to show, and a deep and tender pity for these my people from the far-away Southland, who had battled for the cause they believed to be true. Here they stood, hopeless, forlorn, and seemingly forsaken!" Overcome with emotion, Perry called out to the prisoners, waving her handkerchief and shouting, "I am from Kentucky, and a friend." Perry prevailed on her friends in the South to send her clothing and other supplies, and under the guise of delivering comforts to the prisoners she also smuggled in letters and arranged "daring schemes" of escape. She was, in fact, a one-woman fifth column, if she can be believed, spiriting prisoners out of the prison and back to Dixie and enduring constant searches. As one of the Buford women would record, "Kate Perry has done more for the prisoners than anyone else."[19]

Parts of her story are demonstrably untrue. For example, Perry recounts in lurid detail the story of George Kern of the 9th Kentucky Cavalry. According to Perry, Kern appeared on her doorstep one evening after having spent a day and a night sneaking through the forests on the Island, hungry and cold. Perry hid him, despite the "squads of soldiers with gleaming guns marching up the avenue." After conferring with her fellow conspirators, Perry concluded that the best way to get Kern out of town was to disguise him as a girl. She transformed him into a woman, complete with hoops, hand-basket, and bonnet, and sternly lectured him on how to act the part. Despite a narrow escape at the train station, where Kern had to "act the role of a half-witted unfortunate" in order to escape detection by a federal officer, the boy got back to Kentucky.[20]

In 1901 this made a fine story for Perry to tell wizened veterans. In 1864, however, the truth was more prosaic. Kern was indeed a prisoner, and he did indeed escape. But he spent no time starving in the woods. As one of the surgeons left the compound near dark, Kern impulsively told a friend, "I believe I can make my escape with that buggy, and if I do, you can have my clothes," and swung himself under the man's buggy. The bridge guard was not interested in crawling around under carriages checking for contraband, so Kern arrived safely in Rock Island City only minutes after the surgeon left the yard. There he sought out not Perry but the Buford women and received not hoop skirts but a man's suit and $50.00. Kern made good his escape and wrote back to a friend still on the Island, describing the details. Kern said nobody bothered him as he hung around the train station, because he looked too young to be a soldier.[21]

Despite her propensity to embellish the facts, Perry, in concert with her landlady, did run an underground mail service, smuggling letters and money into and out of the compound. Even some of the guards aided Perry, smuggling letters and newspapers for the prisoners. The guards, however, evinced less enthusiasm for the cause and demonstrated their understanding of the River Bend's philosophy—they charged twenty-five cents an item, going in or coming out. Perry also enlisted the wagon driver who delivered bread to the Island. Perry's continued efforts earned her the name "Faithful" among the prisoners. Johnson eventually banned Perry and one of her friends, Mrs. Boyle, from the Island. He also began searching guards who had access to the compound; those found with contraband were strung up by the thumbs or otherwise punished.[22]

Denied their private mail service, the prisoners used onion juice or egg white to write secret letters under their regular missives home, hoping to avoid the censors and get word out to their friends of contemplated uprisings or escapes. This plan, however, was foiled by shrewd Federal mail clerks who knew onion juice when they smelled it. They simply held the letters to a candle and waited for the secret writing to appear. Egg white left the paper rather stiffer than it should have been.[23]

Although Perry was perhaps more open about her sympathies, she was scarcely alone, as Hoffman had suspected and Johnson quickly learned. The large Southern-bred population in the River Bend naturally favored the prisoners, so much so that Danforth soon took to calling them "our prisoners." Barnes's *Union* did not claim the prisoners, and he frequently pointed out: "It is amusing to witness the strong love and affection existing between the Copperheads of Rock Island, and the Copperheads over on the Island, who are prisoners of war. . . . Some of our 'first families' have made themselves almost sick in their anxiety for the welfare of their former associates down in Dixie." The Buford women's anxiety for Rogan was particularly acute. Not satisfied with the coat they had given him, because it fit poorly, they insisted on procuring one that fit better. As Mrs. Charles Buford wrote her daughter: "I could spend thousands on the poor fellows."[24]

The sympathizers' anxiety was not altogether misplaced. That first winter had been brutal and the camp administration chaotic. The citizens' generosity had made life not just tolerable, but possible, for hundreds of men. The visits of delegations bearing gifts and the work of Perry and her friends also provided diversion from the long and tedious days of prison life.

*I*f there was a time of peace during Johnson's tenure on the Island, it was the spring of 1864. The smallpox epidemic had crested and ebbed, although some cases continued to appear, and the last man to die of the disease, Phillip Nichol of Lewis's Alabama Cavalry, would not succumb until 19 March 1865. The improving weather allowed work to resume on the new buildings, so the Greybeards could be removed from the compound. By spring they were preparing to leave the Island, and they would finally move into their new quarters only three weeks before their departure. Work on the hospital also picked up. Despite the efforts of Kate Perry and her cohorts, there were no successful escapes from March through May.

Johnson also got a new provost marshal of prisoners. Born in County Armagh in Ireland in 1861, Andrew Patrick Caraher enlisted as a captain in the 28th Massachusetts, part of the Irish Brigade. Caraher would be described as "one of the best" of that famous brigade's officers. Promoted to major, he suffered a head wound from a piece of shrapnel at Fredericksburg, which caused dizziness and dim vision. Eventually this led him to accept an assignment in the VRC. He served for a time at Scranton Barracks in Pennsylvania and the Soldier's Rest in Washington, and on 15 February 1864 he was ordered to Rock Island.[25]

During the spring, even the eagle-eyed Danforth relented somewhat. J. B. was always careful not to attack Johnson personally, because it would cut off his access to the Island and its information, but in late May he positively gushed over the colonel. He had, for the moment at least, a new target: the post chaplain. Samuel L. Gracey had been the pastor of the Methodist Episcopal Church in Delaware County, Pennsylvania, and had enlisted, along with the Barracks' original commander, Richard Rush, in the 6th Pennsylvania Lancers. He served as the regiment's chaplain until April 1864, when he was assigned duty as the chaplain on the Island. One of Gracey's first acts on arriving in the River Bend was to offer some remarks at the dedication and flag raising of a new 130-foot flagpole, which had been erected just west of the compound. Lafayette Rogan could have done without the pole altogether: "The Stars and Stripes for the first time was unfurled at these Head Qrs. I have not the slightest objection to its waving over a free North, but I have serious objections to its waving over a subjugated South." The flag raising was a ceremonious affair, attended by throngs of soldiers and citizens. According to Danforth, Johnson offered some eloquent and appropriate remarks. Then, wrote the editor, Gracey

> made a violent political abolition harangue, in which he, in a very Christian (?) manner, wished "the God-defying, hell-bound and hell-deserving Copperheads might be exterminated from the earth." Those are his words, and they were uttered more in the spirit of a fiend than of a Christian minister. . . . He said "All the Copperheads are bound to go to hell anyway." . . . [His] conduct . . . was in such marked contrast to the dignified, patriotic and appropriate course of Col. Johnson, as to be the theme of universal remark among all right-thinking soldiers and citizens.[26]

Gracey did not respond to Danforth's diatribe. He had better things to occupy his time than replying to a virulent sympathizer who was at all events headed for the nether regions. Divine services for the prisoners, however, did not seem to be very high on Gracey's agenda. Church services had been held almost since the opening of the prison. Local ministers sometimes came to the yard, and sometimes preachers among the prisoners held the services. Gracey's arrival relieved the locals, at least as far as the guards were concerned, but as late as August 1864 prisoners still served as ministers to their fellows, offering services nearly every day. It is unlikely that the reverend's thoughts on Rebels and sympathizers endeared him to his flock. On the other hand, Gracey did concern himself with the physical welfare of the prisoners. Shortly after he arrived on the Island, the prisoners tried to form a school; one obstacle to this was lack of a place to meet. Nor was there anything like a library. Gracey wrote Johnson asking for permission to erect a small building as a school and library. This began the usual round-robin of correspondence, at the end of which Gracey did not get his library. He did prevail on the surgeon, however, to fit up a hospital ward as a reading room. Gracey also concerned himself with the garrison or, rather, the garrison's money—he became the post's treasurer.[27]

During the late winter and spring of 1864, more than 7,000 men were confined inside the fence, their lives circumscribed by the walls of the compound. The prisoners spent a great deal of time speculating on the progress of the war. Lafayette Rogan and his fellow clerks were lucky in this respect. Being outside the compound, they had access to current papers, and Rogan followed the news avidly, rejoicing over such Confederate victories as Nathan Bedford Forrest's capture of Fort Pillow, in the Mississippi River above Memphis. His access to current and accurate reports came to a halt when Johnson turned the prisoner clerks back into the compound. True, there were smuggled newspapers, but the delivery service was spotty. The rumor mill ran full time. By the second week of May, as Ulysses Grant's Federal forces began the long job of forcing Robert E. Lee toward Richmond, Rogan despaired of knowing the truth: "Rumors & rumors of rumors Federal defeats and Confederate disasters. Don't know what to believe." The fact was that after two days of inconclusive fighting at the Wilderness, near Fredericksburg, Virginia, Lee had fallen back toward Spotsylvania, with Grant's army hot behind him. By the time this news reached the River Bend, however, it had become a Confederate victory, with thousands of Federal prisoners in Rebel hands, but Rogan admitted, "All is yet doubt and suspense with us." William Dillon also believed the rumors, saying, "Cheering reports continue to come to us from the front—glorious news of successes in Louisiana and Virginia . . . at every point the Confederates have beaten back the enemy with great slaughter—the renowned conqueror of Vicksburg has been badly beaten by the Confederate forces under Lee."[28]

Fed up with contradictory reports and wild rumors, Rogan decided there was only one accurate way to gauge the Confederacy's fortunes: the price of gold. If reports of Union disasters were true, he reasoned, then the price of gold on Northern markets must rise; if the price fell, then things must be going badly for the Rebels. Colonel Johnson was not inclined to post market reports for the benefit of his wards, so Rogan still had to depend on smuggled newspapers, when he could get them. For a number of weeks he regularly reported the price of gold. When Grant in Virginia and Sherman in Georgia failed to make headway, the price rose to $2.29 an ounce. A few weeks later Sherman suffered a disaster at Kennesaw Mountain in Georgia, and Rogan noted that gold closed at $2.36.[29]

If any topic interested the prisoners more than the war news, it was exchange. Although hundreds had enlisted in the navy in January, and more hundreds when Master Harty returned in May, and still more hundreds desired to take the oath of allegiance, many remained who believed in their cause. Dillon noted, "All the true soldiers of the South are wishing earnestly for an exchange in a short time." Rogan thought the same, saying as early as February 1864, "High hopes of an early exchange have filled my mind today." Although both men continued to mention exchange for months, they were to be disappointed. General exchanges under the cartel had ceased long before Dillon and Rogan arrived on the Island, and when Ulysses Grant was appointed commander in chief of the Federal armies in March 1864, he confirmed the policy and refused to resume exchange. No matter how bad the conditions in the prisons both North and South, their inmates were condemned to remain there. But Dillon, the eternal optimist, wrote as late as July 1864, "The men . . . think we are in here for the war but I do not think so yet."[30]

The weather, the guards, and disease were not the only enemies: boredom also oppressed the prisoners. Although there were police details, three roll calls a day, a morning inspection, and details to bury the dead or perform various maintenance duties, Dillon noted: "Time still drags heavily along with us in our prison. Our health is very good but it is very hard to be . . . cooped up as we are." Rogan agreed: "Days in prison are so like each other that they fail to give items to record." To give himself a little variety Rogan, who had grown up in Alabama, decided to learn how to ice skate. After a couple days of practice he reported, "I can stand up pretty well but can't go forward at much speed."[31]

During the winter, indoor pursuits were more popular. The prisoners read avidly, although it was sometimes difficult to get reading material. Dillon wrote to friends in Missouri for books and received a copy of Shakespeare. He happily noted that one of his friends in another barrack also received some books, "so I have plenty to read which somewhat relieves the monotony of my life." Debating societies also formed in many of the barracks; Dillon's met three evenings a week. Also, mock courts were almost constantly in session.[32]

The *Union* painted a pretty picture of the prisoners' lives:

> But they are continually conjuring their brains for ways to kill time. Their theaters, glee clubs and debating societies are always well patronized. . . . Books are treasured up and handed from one to another; many find solace in the works of the Greek and Latin poets, for here we have graduates of colleges, professors of academies, civil engineers, book-keepers and booksellers, rice and cotton planters, mixed up with the gold grabbers of Georgia, the persimmon eaters of Tennessee, the "corn breads" of Alabama, and "our white trash."

Indeed, according to the *Union,* nothing better could happen to a Rebel than to be a prisoner on the Island: "To be well fed, to receive medical attendance when sick, to receive money and letters from friends, to be clothed and kept from the inclemency of the weather, to be treated like human beings . . . is the good fortune of the Rebel prisoners in the hands of the United States."[33]

There was also dancing. Among the prisoners was a violin maker. As one prisoner wrote home, "There is some splendid violins made here with nothing but a pocket knife." There were also fiddlers in the yard, one of the most prominent being "an old-time, break-down fiddler" named Tutt. Tutt would play while his friends would "music, dance, and kill time." Not everyone appreciated the diversions, though. Rogan, trying to read, complained that "such a continual clatter of tongue-whistling, singing, speech-making, dancing, hollering . . . renders it impossible to read with any degree of pleasure."[34]

Checkers was played constantly; chess also had adherents. Cards proved popular, as has been the case for centuries among armies. The prisoners played "all the games of cards that ever Hoyle mentioned"; moreover, they played for money. Prison regulations required that prisoners turn in their money on arrival, but thanks to Kate Perry's underground, sympathizing guards, and well-heeled relatives, the prisoners seemed to suffer no lack of currency, and it was only natural that they gamble some of it on the turn of a card.[35]

Gambling attracted the attention of one of the Greybeard's officers, Captain Graham. Notwithstanding regulations, some of the officers occasionally joined in the prisoners' poker games. Graham, an inveterate gambler, joined a game one evening. In addition to being a gambler, Graham was a bad loser, and when he lost his last dollar on a bad hand, "he sprang to his feet, accusing the others of being 'cheats,' raked in the stakes, put them in his pocket, and stalked out." Of course, there was no one to whom the victims could complain, since they were neither supposed to have money nor gamble.[36]

As the endless leaden winter gave way to spring, the prisoners moved their recreations outside, baseball being the most popular activity. But once again a Greybeard officer spoiled the sport. Graham's inseparable companion was a Captain John Hogendobler, dubbed "Hogdriver" by the prisoners. Hogendobler was a bully. He knew the prisoners could not defend themselves and made the most of his opportunity. One day during a baseball game a wild ball struck the captain. He approached J. W. Minnich, who had thrown the ball, and commenced to beat him, shouting the while "every vile epithet that would come to his base mind." Minnich turned his head to catch a blow on his ear rather than his nose, which further enraged the Hogdriver: he drew his pistol, put it to Minnich's head, and loudly threatened to blow his brains out. This in turn enraged Minnich, who with admirable courage if not prudence, shouted back, "Shoot, you coward!" Hogendobler, nonplussed by the retort, recovered his senses and took Minnich to the guardhouse and had him fitted with a ball and chain.[37]

Other prisoners, imbued with the commercial atmosphere of the River Bend, avoided the playing fields for more remunerative pursuits. One businessman was Lafayette Rogan, who began by making little souvenirs to remind himself in after years of his captivity. However, it soon occurred to him, and to many others, that the trinkets—breast pins, studs, and other such items carved of wood or oyster shell—could be sold. Rogan meticulously kept books on his enterprise. He paid fifty cents for a file, the only tool he needed, and soon had $2.50 worth of stock, which would show a clear profit of $2.00. He paid himself no wage for his time, "Time being out of the question." Indeed, time was all he had. Colonel Johnson, inspecting the prison, noted the makeshift workshops scattered about, and according to A. J. Cantrell remarked, "He had heard of Yankee tricks, but he had never seen the equal" of the prisoners' little jewelry shops. Nor did he like what he saw: Cantrell reported that "afterwards he had it all stopped." Even if this is true, it would not have required an order to halt the trade. The guards constituted nearly the whole market, and it quickly became glutted, as Rogan noted in relation to his shirt studs: "Now have 5 sets ready for sale—The trade however appears to be dull now and I may not find sale for them." He never mentioned his budding business again, nor did he bother to record his profit and loss.[38]

One man went into another business, albeit temporarily. The halyard on the new flagpole that had engendered Gracey's abolitionist diatribe snarled the flag, which became stuck at the top of the mast. Johnson could find no one in the garrison hale enough to climb the pole, so he sought among the prisoners. William Bennefield volunteered—conditionally. Bennefield had been sentenced to wear a ball and chain for some offense, and he told the Federals he would retrieve their flag, but only if they removed the shackles. The deal was struck, and Bennefield climbed the 130-foot mast and unsnarled his enemies' flag.[39]

One thought occupied the prisoners' minds more than any other: home. They wrote for news of home, and they filled their own letters with their longing to return to their families. The prison regulations allowed the prisoners to "write letters to their friends, of not more than one (1) page, and of a strictly private nature, which letters must be left open for inspection." They could say little about their treatment, certainly nothing that would reflect badly on Colonel Johnson and his guards, nor could they discuss the war. But they could ask their families to send them various comforts, and their letters are full of requests. B. J. Gaston wasted no time when he arrived on the Island. After only a few days of wind and freezing temperatures, he concluded, "We have reached quite a cold clime indeed. I would like to have some more clothing sent me." Gaston constantly asked his parents for money, noting that Johnson allowed the prisoners to receive anything that would add to their comfort. When his parents sent him ten dollars, he wrote, "I have been doing very well from what you have sent me, though I were *flat* before I received this today." He hastened to assure his family that the money was not being squandered: "Tobacco and eatables are very high and are the chief of my expense."[40]

Once the food and money questions were settled, two topics dominated their letters. The first was their prison life, and this was disposed of in short order. Elijah Hall and Gaston told their families that they were being treated as well as they could expect. J. W. Everett admitted to his wife, "I have been treated well ever since I have been in prison, but it is a disagreeable place to be." In view of the winter and the epidemic he had just survived, this was a vast understatement. Moreover, good treatment meant little to men deprived of their families. Hall told his family: "I am very tired of this place but have no idea when I will get out of the prison. I have been here going on eleven months and I can say to you that it has been the worst part of my life." Gaston said, "Each hour seems to be a day and each day a month. . . . I hope the time will come when we will be permitted to meet again." He later calculated that his 13 months of captivity were actually a century.[41]

The men wanted to return, if not to the rattle of musketry, then to the crackle of their own hearths. Both Hall and Gaston asked their families to petition for their release. Everett averred that he did not intend to be exchanged, adding, "I think I have friends enough to get me out of prison." Perhaps, but they did not act quickly enough, and Everett died of meningitis on 13 July 1864. Some of the men's families were as fed up with the war as were the prisoners themselves. A cooperative guard took the liberty of copying for Danforth one letter a prisoner received. J. B. printed an extract, despite the fact that it flew in the face of his own views: "Come home. Take the oath the first chance you get. Try to get to take it to-morrow, there is no harm in it, it will only make a man of you. Damn Jeff Davis and all of his sort, him nor his money is not worth a damn nor never was nor never will be. Don't stay no longer if you can get off."[42]

But few of them got off, and the next best thing was news from home. Nearly every surviving document contains pleas for news of friends and family. Gaston told his father, "Pa, I want you all to write to me often and I care not how long your letters are, for I would like for you to give me the particulars of the actions and proceedings of the people of that portion of the country—write often without fail." Hall echoed the sentiment: "I want you to write to me as often as you can and don't wait for me as I can not write often." And, thinking to spare his brother his own torment, Hall added, "Tell Thomas to be a good boy and stay at home." They were often disappointed. Perhaps their families wrote, but the letters often went astray. On 21 July 1864 Gaston received a letter from his parents and chided them that it was the first he had received since April. Fortunately both the ones he received contained money. Hall complained, "I do not know what is the reason you don't write to me. I have not got but 2 letters from home." And sometimes the letters they received were not the ones they wanted. On receiving a letter from his old lieutenant, Lafayette Rogan said: "Wish I could get one from Ella. One word from home sweet home. How much I desire to see my dear Ella & our boy and be in my home & in my country again." Receipt of a letter from his wife nearly overwhelmed him: "My heart was made to rejoice over two letters from my dear Ella. I read and re-read her sweet letters. She is cheerful, my boy is well—God be praised for it."[43]

The very lucky ones received visits. The regulations provided for visits only by immediate family members, and only if the prisoner was seriously ill. It was Johnson's rigid adherence to this rule that made an enemy of Major Kingsbury. But even the unbending colonel had a heart, deeply buried beneath his grim visage though it might have been. A Davenport paper reported that a loyal Mississippi woman traveled to the River Bend to visit her son, who had contradictory political views and had enlisted in the Confederate army. Accompanied by Judge Grant of Davenport, the mother went to Johnson to see her son:

> While the parties were engaged in conversation, at headquarters, and unknown to them, Col. Johnson had sent for the boy, and before his mother was aware of it, the boy was ushered into her presence. . . .

The mother had not seen her boy for two years, during which time he had been endeavoring to destroy the government, while his mother had remained true to the old Union. It is not proper to speak of the affecting scene of that interview—every mother knows that the erring boy is still the object of mother's love.[44]

This touching story appeared on New Year's Eve 1863. The boy's mother apparently had excellent sources of information if she had determined in four weeks not only that her boy had been captured, but where he had been sent; her alacrity in going to her son is commendable. True or not, the story did serve to paint both the prisoners and Colonel Johnson as men and sons.

More likely is the story of a correspondent who signed himself "SFF." He wrote to the *Union* after visiting the Island to deliver money and letters. SFF said: "We applied at Col. Johnson's headquarters for a pass, but were told that it could not be granted—that they were not authorized to admit any person into the prison barracks. We then asked the Adjutant to bring the prisoners to his headquarters; this too was refused. The failure to see the prisoners was a cause of much regret to us. . . . [W]e could but regret the stringency of the order relative to intercourse with the prisoners."[45]

Being deprived of liberty and home, cooped up in a pen and subject to rules the violation of which could cost their lives, the men grew restive and quarrelsome. The quarrels could be deadly. On 23 February 1864, Johnson reported to Hoffman: "On Saturday evening . . . Joseph Mullins, prisoner of war confined in these barracks was stabbed and instantly killed and that upon investigation, the circumstances clearly point to John G. Burt, a fellow prisoner as the perpetrator of the deed. I have placed the said Burt in close confinement and await further instructions from your office." Johnson did not mention any provocation, but Barnes was quick to point out that the accused was really a victim. Burt had volunteered for the Union navy, whereupon "a course of persecution was instituted against him." Burt took as much as he could and then snapped, taking a knife to Mullins. Hoffman never replied to Johnson, and Burt languished in the guardhouse until November 1864, when Andrew Caraher, provost marshal of prisoners, released him back to the yard.[46]

Besides murder, the prisoners committed lesser infractions, both against each other and against the authority of the prison. The latter was a rather easy thing to do: the prison regulations prohibited loud noise or required silence in half a dozen of their 22 paragraphs; further, crowds were prohibited. When Rush promulgated the rules, however, he neglected to define loud noise or explain what a crowd was; actual interpretation was left to the individual guards. To the prisoners' chagrin, what would go unnoticed one time would land them in the guardhouse the next. And the guardhouse was no place to be.[47]

Erected at the same time as the Barracks, the guardhouse was even more shantylike than the barracks themselves. During construction Hoffman had uncharacteristically suggested that Reynolds spend a little more money and erect a blockhouse in addition to the regular guardhouse, thinking "it would be nice." Reynolds did not take this suggestion. What Johnson ended up with was less than secure: "The guard houses are simply barracks, 20 x 40 feet and 1/3 of each end is divided off by a board partition, one being used as a place of confinement for prisoners, the remaining partition for the use of the guard. This arrangement is as productive of much evil as it is insecure." Not only was it relatively easy for men to escape, but the murderer Burt was necessarily confined with men whose crimes were no more serious than talking to a guard. Also, because everyone shared a single cell, those awaiting trial could spend their time concocting alibis: there was no solitary confinement. In a masterful understatement, Johnson concluded, "This building is in no manner adequate to the needs of this post." The men on guard duty did not think much of the building, either. Lieutenant B. R. Wagner noted on the guard report, "The officers' guard room is a place not fit to keep a beast in—rendered so by the cold." The next day he noted again that the guardhouse was unfit. And the day after that, in a stroke of insight, Wagner discovered why the place was so cold: "Would respectfully recommend the completion of the roof of the guard house." Evidently this was the information Captain Reynolds needed, because no further notations appear.[48]

In spite of the deficiencies, the guardhouses were used for the entire history of the Barracks. The prisoners continued to be crammed together in the single room, where they could plot both escapes and alibis. The number of men confined on any particular day ranged from a low of 4 to a high of 26, which included both prisoners and guards. Warmer weather found more men incarcerated than colder weather. The guards were confined with the Rebels in a common guardhouse, and it had a bad effect on some: James Mayfield of the VRC left his barrack after taps one evening and was promptly arrested. Upon learning he was to go to the guardhouse, Mayfield "commenced to demean himself by making hideous noises and using indecent language." It availed him nothing: he was held for trial and fined $16.00. In a vain attempt to keep his own men out of the place, Johnson ordered that all guards arrested were to have charges preferred within 48 hours.[49]

Many offenses, however, earned the offender a lesser punishment than confinement, in part at least because the guardhouse was often full. Some crimes warranted a 32 pound ball on a chain, but shackling hobbled the prisoners only when the guards were around. Prisoner Ben Hord, who wore a ball and chain for more than a month for trying to escape, said, "I could pick the lock with a small nail and stout cord as fast as it could be locked, and which I did every night after getting into my bunk." Another punishment was Morgan's mule, a narrow board turned upright and suspended between two posts. The offenders sat on the board, their feet just above the ground. When J. W. Minnich refused to go on a work detail he was tied up by his wrists. The charitable German guard who carried out the sentence pulled Minnich's jacket sleeves over his wrists to prevent the rope from cutting his flesh. Suspended from a tree, his feet barely touching the ground, Minnich endured "four short hours of sixty long minutes each, under a gray, sunless sky, with a sharp March wind blowing across the frozen river and cutting through my scant clothing till my very marrow seemed frozen." When he was cut loose, Minnich found his arms stiffened above his head, and it took vigorous massage by several of his barrack mates to restore the circulation.[50]

Offenders were sometimes put on bread and water. In the early days, at least, this represented a real punishment. In 1861, army regulations stipulated that prisoners of war would receive "one ration each, without regard to rank." That is, prisoners were to receive the same rations as troops. In fact, contracts for rations were let for both guards and prisoners as a single contract. But by the middle of 1862 Hoffman had instituted his prison fund, which depended in large part for its revenues on reducing the rations issued to prisoners. And on 20 April 1864, as part of a new set of regulations governing his prisons, Hoffman officially cut the ration, although only slightly. Indeed, the official cut amounted to only two ounces of hardtack or cornmeal (depending on which was issued), two ounces of pork, or six ounces of beef.[51]

The practice raised some eyebrows here and there, but Hoffman and his commandants were always a step ahead of critics. In response to some newspaper articles in Columbus, Ohio, which accused the Camp Chase administration of various crimes, the commandant, Major Peter Zinn, instantly rounded up some letters written home by the prisoners. They made Chase sound like Xanadu: "We have nothing to do but eat and sleep," said John A. Carson of Virginia. "We have plenty to eat and to drink and a very good bed to sleep on. We have no reason to complain. We have very nice officers here; as nice as any need have." John Haywood, also of Virginia, apparently had much experience with incarceration. He allowed, "This is the best prison I ever saw. We live as well here as in our hotels in Dixie." When complaints were raised about Camp Douglas in Chicago, Hoffman had a survey of barracks sergeants conducted, which concluded unequivocally that the prisoners were well fed and well housed. Whether any of this was true mattered little; such evidence allowed Hoffman and his commandants to continue doing as they saw fit.[52]

In 1862 and 1863 the ration cuts were not severe, as a rule. At Champ Chase in December 1862, the issue had been reduced from the regulation ration by only four ounces of beef and four ounces of bread; however, the potato issue was more than the standard, and vegetables were issued at the rate of more than half a pound per man per day. At least, that's what the commissary of subsistence reported. It is nearly impossible to determine exactly what the prisoners received. Although on several occasions Hoffman sent various commandants a scale of rations that had been found workable, those lists have disappeared. Whenever the scale is mentioned in the *Official Records,* the compilers noted that the scale was not found; further, Hoffman's records in the National Archives do not contain the lists. The reason for this remains unclear. Moreover, his suggested ration was just that—a suggestion. Hoffman made it quite clear that the reduction was in the hands of the commandant, as when he wrote to Colonel B. L. E. Bonneville in St. Louis: "It is left for you to decide what the reduction should be." On the other hand, if the commandants failed to produce an adequate prison fund, Hoffman wasted no time in lashing them into compliance. When James Mulligan was at Camp Douglas he consistently ignored orders from Hoffman to institute the prison fund. When Mulligan was assigned to West Virginia, he left behind in Chicago a chaos of missing money and records that led to an order for his arrest.[53]

Colonel Johnson began cutting rations almost immediately, but not severely: in March 1864, for example, the fund showed a deficit of more than $6,000. The prisoners themselves, while not as enthusiastic as the men at Camp Chase, had no complaint about the quantity of their food. J. W. Minnich reported that the amounts cut were "not a serious privation." Prisoner Charles Wright agreed that "no reasonable complaint could be made in regard to the food furnished the prisoners." E. Polk Johnson wrote, "We had no complaint to make of the rations issued us either as to quantity or quality." Indeed, the prisoners had so much food during the early months that they wasted a good deal of it. David Sears, the son of the original dam-builder Sears, operated a flour mill on a tiny island just a few yards off the upper end of the big Island, from which he supplied flour to the Barracks. Interviewed years later, Sears remembered the prison garbage dump containing "good fresh beef, sound loaves of bread, and some of everything that was issued to them." The day would come when the prisoners would repent such waste.[54]

If by chance a man's appetite was so voracious that 4,000 calories of bread and beef failed to satisfy him, there was yet more food available. Lafayette Rogan's diary contains many mentions of delicacies brought to the Island by the prisoners' friends. And for those who had money there was the sutler. Sutlers had long been a fixture in the army, providing household items and foods the regular issue lacked. Every regiment and every post was entitled to a sutler, and since the original prison pens were training camps and rendezvous, by the time Hoffman took over the prison system, his camps already had sutlers. At Camp Douglas near the end of 1863, Hoffman found the sutler selling "nearly everything (except liquors), including cider, butter, eggs, milk, canned fruits, boots, &c., underclothing, and all the minor articles usually found in a sutler's stock." In the prewar army, sutlers had been taxed at the rate of ten cents per soldier per month. At Camp Chase in December 1862, the tax was only four cents per prisoner, which Hoffman's inspector found less than satisfactory. Within a month the tax was raised to ten cents.[55]

The first sutler on the Island was John Burgh who, nearly as soon as Captain Reynolds arrived, erected a store to supply the construction laborers. Burgh lost out on the big business, though, to Albert

Dart, proprietor of Henry Dart's Sons grocery. Dart was not officially appointed post sutler, but he acted in that capacity to the exclusion of all others. He also served as the prisoners' sutler, although when he accepted the post there was no prison business. Earlier in 1863, Federal prisoners being exchanged began bringing back tales of their treatment in the South. As Army Chief of Staff Henry Halleck reported to Edwin Stanton, Federal prisoners were "stripped of their blankets, clothing, and shoes, even in the winter season, and then confined in damp and loathsome prisons, and only half fed on damaged provisions, or actually starved to death. . . . Not a few, after a semblance of trial by some military tribunal, have been actually murdered by their inhuman keepers." Not one to shrink from hyperbole, Halleck compared Libby and Belle Isle prisons in Richmond to the Black Hole of Calcutta. He then suggested that the North practice retaliation, noting that it would be completely justified, even though "it is revolting to our sense of humanity to be forced to so cruel an alternative."[56]

While Halleck spun his tale to Stanton, William Hoffman was sending inspectors to camps where returned Federal prisoners were kept, to ascertain for himself the inhumanity of the Rebel jailers. The reports he received did nothing to calm the growing hysteria. Hoffman's surgeon, A. M. Clark, reported that the prisoners suffered scurvy, hospital gangrene, pneumonia, and some, "though laboring under no disease, were actually dying of starvation. One poor fellow informed me that . . . for five days [he] had been supplied with but one cracker and a half per day." All of this was unconscionable, especially because, as Halleck was careful to note: "Rebel prisoners held by the United States have been uniformly treated with consideration and kindness. They have been furnished with all necessary clothing and supplied with the same quality and amount of food as our own soldiers." The item about quality of food would doubtless have been news to the scurvy-ridden prisoners at Camp Douglas, but Halleck conveniently ignored this contradiction.[57]

Arrangements were made to send provisions through the lines to alleviate the suffering, but this only caused more consternation. For one reason or another, much of the relief failed to reach the intended recipients, and a surreptitious report wended its way north stating that the supplies sent for Federal prisoners in Richmond actually were going to Robert E. Lee's army. A recently released chaplain, noting that the prisoners used Confederate money to ease their condition and that Hoffman's office held a quantity of this currency, concocted a scheme whereby the Confederate money could be smuggled to the Richmond prisoners in sealed jars labeled as preserved fruit; it did not occur to the chaplain that those jars, too, might be sent to Lee.[58]

Hoffman declined the fruit jar conspiracy but did begin retaliation, as revolting as it may have been to Northern sensibilities. On 1 December 1863, two days before the first prisoners arrived on the Island, Hoffman outlawed the sutlers. The stores were closed and the prisoners forced to survive on only the issued ration. Albert Dart accepted the sutler's post in spite of this. He was, after all, a citizen of the River Bend and a shrewd businessman. The prisoners might be denied him, but there were 1,500 federal soldiers who could fill his coffers. In addition to the individual soldiers, there was the camp administration, which would enrich Dart by as much as $1,000 a month.[59]

The prohibition against selling to prisoners did not last. On 29 December 1863, E. A. Hitchcock, commissioner of exchange, told Hoffman that Stanton was satisfied that the treatment of the Richmond prisoners had improved and that "tobacco, pipes, paper, and a few other things" could be sold to the prisoners. Hoffman sat on this letter. Only after Major General Benjamin Butler began complaining in February 1864 did Hoffman recommend to Stanton that the sutlers be allowed to resume sales to prisoners. And it was not until 3 March that Hoffman finally sent an order to his commandants allowing the sutlers and specifying what they could sell. A week later, Hoffman also relented on the question of receiving boxes from friends, as long as they contained "nothing hurtful."[60]

Dart went to business. There was a sutler's building outside the walls, put up during construction, but Dart made no use of it. He merely drove his wagon into the compound, accompanied by his bulldog. From the back of his wagon he sold such household items as stamps, buttons, tape, pins, scissors, and pens and, more important, such foods as syrup, lard, smoked beef, cornmeal, salt fish, canned fish and meat, apples, and lemons. Upon concluding his business Dart turned his wagon around and, the dog scampering under the wheels, returned to the city to count his gains. For a few months he did not even have to pay the tax, the camp administration being occupied with such things as smallpox and fires. When the tax was levied, it was not a dime per prisoner, but a paltry 5 percent. For June

1864, this meant $134.87 for the prison fund, which in turn meant Dart sold approximately $2,700 worth of goods to the prisoners. In July he did about $5,500 worth of business. This was a far cry from the $10,000 a month Danforth had predicted the prisoners would add to the local economy, but neither was it anything to be scoffed at, especially in light of the fact that it was more or less a sideline for Dart, who ran a thriving grocery in the city. Albert Dart had no reason to complain in the spring of 1864.[61]

Danforth never relaxed his vigil on the Island. It was the prime manifestation of Republican policy in the River Bend. He kept his readers informed of everything that happened on the Island, especially the mischief of the guards. J. B. lauded Johnson's order establishing bridge guards and prohibiting armed men from leaving the Island, saying that it would "effectually prevent any trouble about town." But two weeks later he reported that two more VRC men had been arrested with loaded revolvers. And if the guards were not causing trouble for the citizens, they were causing it for themselves: one VRC man was arrested for beating a Greybeard.[62]

Although Danforth never directly attacked Johnson, and sometimes even complimented the colonel, every time J. B. noted the soldiers' sins, he by implication attacked Johnson. When some amnesty men were released, Danforth reported that they "were in a pitiable condition." He did not say the fault was Johnson's, but the colonel commanded, and anything that happened at the Barracks could be laid at his doorstep. Johnson did not answer the implications, which was wise. His administration was far from the only target of the *Argus*'s broadsides. Indeed, some of the released prisoners that J. B. pitied turned out to be unworthy of such concern, as the editor dutifully reported: "John Holton . . . a discharged Rebel prisoner, got on a 'tear' last night and about midnight Policeman David Reddig locked him up in jail."[63]

Still, the problems caused by the installations on the Island were worth their trouble because of the business they brought. At long last Kingsbury had bestirred himself to lay the cornerstone for the Arsenal and to call for bids for brick, stone, cement, and gutter work. Reynolds needed carpentry, roofing, and plastering for the new barracks and hospitals he was constructing. Both projects brought more money to the citizens of the River Bend. The irritations of drunken soldiers and destitute prisoners were worth it, as long as the money flowed.[64]

CHAPTER FOUR

"Such Reckless Conduct"

Although much remained to be done, by the summer of 1864 the war had turned irrevocably against the Confederacy. In Georgia, Major General William Tecumseh Sherman's Federal army worked its way toward Atlanta. In the east, the Army of the Potomac had at long last brought Robert E. Lee to bay and besieged his troops around Petersburg, Virginia. Thousands of prisoners rolled north in the cars; by June more than 56,000 Confederates were confined in Hoffman's camps, and a training rendezvous at Elmira, New York, was being transformed into yet another prison. Some of those trains rolled to Rock Island, and June 1864 found more than 8,600 Confederates in the yard.

The flood of prisoners inundated Hoffman's department with work, but the commissary general of prisoners never neglected the prison fund. Hoffman was bound by duty all his life, and part of that duty was fiduciary; he was obligated to save his government money whenever he could. It is unfortunate that this obligation fit so well with Hoffman's personality, because the financial concerns outgrew their proper place in Hoffman's mind. In fact, the fund had become an obsession. In January 1864 Hoffman had reported to Edwin Stanton that the fund held more than $135,000, but this was not enough. On 20 April 1864 he issued a new set of regulations governing the camps. There were 18 paragraphs in the circular and eleven of them dealt, in whole or in part, with the prison and hospital funds.[1]

Of particular concern was Rock Island. The Barracks showed a balance of only $100. Johnson's Island, which had only a third as many prisoners, had a fund 130 times as large. Part of the problem was that Johnson, at least in the beginning, spent far more than he took in. For January 1864, he recorded savings of only $1,325, which, combined with $6,068 from December 1863, gave him a balance of $7,393. Unfortunately, he spent more than $10,000 during the same period. Much of the expense was for clothing and medicines, which clearly contradicts the idea that the camp administration was oblivious to suffering. Johnson also found a source for the Farmer boilers that Reynolds had been unable to purchase, and he bought them. All these things were meant for the prisoners' comfort. Just as Pratt's actions had condemned several hundred men to die of smallpox, Johnson's actions assured that some would live. But not all the money was spent for the benefit of the prisoners: one of the surviving vouchers for March shows that Johnson spent $36.00 for balls and chains—also for the prisoners, albeit not for their comfort.[2]

In March Johnson saved $6,500 from the sale of excess rations. Some 35,000 rations of bread (that is, more than 24 tons) were sold back to the commissary, which accounted for $1,300 of the savings. Ten tons of beef accounted for the same amount. Coffee, candles, sugar—all were cut. But during the same month Johnson spent $7,100. Among other things, Johnson bought 17 pounds of tobacco, at a dollar a pound. He also spent several hundred dollars on furniture and supplies for the provost marshal's office, and $75 for a bell. All this was minor: the main reason for the debt was the hospital. In the single month of March Reynolds spent $3,500 for lumber and windows, twice what Hoffman thought the entire complex would cost. And it was only going to get worse.[3]

The costs had grown, as was common with government projects even in the 1860s. Hoffman had barely reconciled himself to the idea of $18,000 when the bills began coming in. The estimate grew to $30,000. Johnson reported this to Hoffman on 16 April, which drove Hoffman nearly to distraction. He demanded to know just what the money was being spent on and Johnson, in a vain attempt to avoid being lashed by Hoffman's red-inked pen, claimed that Reynolds would not provide the exact figures. Hoffman was the more angered by Johnson's admission that he had no money. The prison fund held nowhere near $30,000, nor would it for months.

Between them, Johnson and Reynolds concocted a sort of install-
ment plan: Reynolds would pay for the construction with quartermaster funds, and Johnson would repay him from the prison fund
over the course of several months. They came to this agreement before bothering to notify either Meigs or Hoffman. It was completely
against regulations to do business in this manner, but both
Reynolds and Johnson were more concerned about humanity than
accounting; they went ahead with construction. It would in any
event be cheaper to do it this way, because Reynolds already had
contractors under retainer, thus saving some cost.[4]

Not a bit mollified by Johnson's mention of cheaper cost, Hoffman refused to ask Meigs for the money. Instead, he wore out pen-
cils scratching figures on waste paper, trying to make the cost of the
hospital come to less than $30,000. Arithmetic failed him, however,
and his failure was magnified by the waste on the Island: during
the tempest Johnson submitted a voucher for 1,565 yards of plastering for the surgeon's quarters, at twenty-six cents a yard. This,
Hoffman lectured, was completely uncalled for, "an extravagant al-
lowance." In the end, the prison fund managed to pay for the hospital without the intervention of Meigs. The contractors had to
wait on their money, which understandably upset them, but there
was little they could do. The fund balance was a mere $48.31 at the
end of May 1864.[5]

Fending off Hoffman's indignant inquiries about the hospital was
not the only problem Johnson faced. On 6 May 1864, Hoffman sent
Johnson the rather cryptic message, "It is possible that from circumstances which may soon occur, more than ordinary vigilance will be
required from the troops in charge of the prisoners of war." The circumstances were apparently the result of Nathan Bedford Forrest's
recent actions hundreds of miles down the Mississippi, just above
Memphis, Tennessee. While raiding through Kentucky and Tennessee, Forrest reported that he wanted to "attend to" a small fort
named Pillow. What followed was an outrage.[6]

Of the 557 men in the garrison at Fort Pillow, 262 were black. After a day-long battle and an alleged ruse involving a flag of truce,
Forrest's troopers gained the fort, and the defenders either fled or
tried to surrender. A massacre followed, described by a congressional committee as "a scene of cruelty and murder without parallel
in civilized warfare, which needed but the tomahawk and scalping-
knife to exceed the worst atrocities ever committed by savages."

Nearly 300 men died, many of them after the surrender, and a disproportionate number of them black. Although there was evidence
that Forrest not only did not instigate the slaughter but tried to stop
it, he took the blame. The North was incensed, and no one more
than Edwin Stanton. He wrote President Lincoln, urging that for
every man massacred at Pillow a Confederate officer be held hostage
for the delivery of Forrest and one of his brigadiers, James
Chalmers, and that, failing delivery of these two, "such measures
will be taken in reference to the hostages, by way of retributary justice for the massacre of Fort Pillow, as are justified by the laws of
civilized warfare." In other words, they would be executed. The retaliation was not carried out, but Stanton's letter did cause Hoffman
to warn his commandants that extraordinary vigilance would
shortly be required.[7]

The warning had little effect on the Island. The prisoners knew of
Fort Pillow, but not about the proposed retaliation. Lafayette Rogan
noted the victory briefly in his diary, along with the hope that Forrest would send all the Federals packing, and then never mentioned
it again. William Dillon, the other Barracks diarist, did not mention
Fort Pillow at all. In reply to Hoffman's order about increased vigilance, Johnson said he could not comply—many of the VRC men
had been taken from him and sent to Washington, D.C., and the
Greybeards were more or less useless. He did, however, increase the
guard as much as he could; not only because of rumors of uprising,
but because of Indians.[8]

On a bluff just above Davenport was a post called Camp McClellan, and in 1864 Sioux captured during an uprising in Minnesota
were sent there. Somehow the rumor gained currency that the Copperheads were going to liberate the Indians and then assail the Island and free the prisoners. On the strength of these rumors, Johnson sent some of his remaining VRC men to Davenport and doubled
the guard on the walls. However, as Dillon noted, "everything passed
off quietly." Johnson probably reacted properly. The Island was not
as secure as islands usually are, a fact Richard Rush had pointed out
to Hoffman months earlier. Johnson's reaction now was good training for the troops; there would be further scares. This one, though,
was a complete washout, as was the next, only a week later. This rumor started on the Island itself, and Johnson called out the entire
garrison, instructing the troops to sleep on their arms and be ready
for a break. But as a Davenport paper reported, "the only 'break'

apparent during their night's exposure . . . was the break of day."[9]

The Iowans remained gripped by fear, and rumors continued to circulate. N. B. Baker and a pair of Iowa congressmen thought the situation so precarious that in July they wrote to Hoffman, requesting artillery for the Island. Their concern was perhaps given rise by Confederate General Jubal Early's approach to Washington, D.C., but Hoffman was not alarmed. When he forwarded the letter to Stanton, he wisely refused to endorse the idea, saying that cannon could be taken from the guards much more easily than small arms and suggesting that more revolvers be sent to the River Bend to allay the Iowans' fears.[10]

Rumored revolts aside, however, increased vigilance was not a bad idea. With warm weather the prisoners grew restless. There were no successful escapes between February and June, but this is true only because of some creative bookkeeping. A prisoner was recorded as escaped only if he remained free past the end of the month, at which point a statistical report of the prison was submitted to Hoffman. Any Rebel the guards managed to recapture by month's end did not show up in that report, saving Johnson much explanation.

There was a break on 7 May 1864, involving five men according to Dillon and seven according to Rogan. A week later another squad tried to tunnel under the fence; for reasons known only to themselves, however, instead of tunneling out on the south side, they went north. This was unfortunate, as the compound nearly abutted the river on that side, and there would have been nowhere for them to go. The guards probably prevented an embarrassment for the tunnelers by discovering their hole before they finished it. Several of the prisoners were awarded balls and chains for their lack of foresight. On 1 June Isaac Morris of the 9th Tennessee Cavalry made a clean getaway, never to see the Barracks again. Two days later M. Lynch of the 39th Mississippi followed suit. Given all the escapes, Johnson probably rejoiced when he heard that some of his guards were about to be replaced. There could be little worse than the doddering, pig-keeping Greybeards. With the arrival of the new regiment, perhaps the security would improve.[11]

The guards were part of the latest scheme to put more men in the field. As the war dragged on and the casualty lists mounted, the manpower drain became acute. Such organizations as the Veteran Reserve Corps and the Greybeards were not enough to pay the butcher's bill, and the government continued to cast about for new ways to get men in uniform. One way was to enlist men for 100 days—three months instead of three years. As the theory went, men could spare a few weeks from their fields and shops to guard prisons and depots; veteran regiments could go to the front, at least for a while. The theory far exceeded the practice.

On 26 April 1864, Illinois Adjutant General Fuller called for 20,000 men to make up ten regiments of what the papers quickly dubbed "hundred dazers." According to Fuller, "the exigencies of the public service require the greatest activity in the organization of these forces." A little less activity and a little more preparation might have been wiser, but Fuller and his governor, Richard Yates, were determined to maintain Illinois's record as the only state that had exceeded all calls for troops without having to resort to the draft. The barrel had already been scraped by previous calls. Illinois had nearly 200,000 men in the field. Although Fuller did not get his 20,000 men, he did get 11,000, which he organized into 13 regiments and 2 battalions; nationwide, the scheme yielded 83,000 recruits. The first regiment to muster was the 133rd Illinois, and it would spend its hundred days demonstrating just how poor troops could be; it would make that demonstration on the Island.[12]

The 133rd would replace the Greybeards. The old men had been ordered away to Memphis, and Johnson was glad to see them go. He wrote Hoffman that the Greybeards were "very inefficient in officers and men." He further noted, "The 37th Iowa Regt. is ordered away, a hundred days' Ills. Regt. is to take their place. This change will occur in a day or two, when it takes place this depot will be better garrisoned than at present." Johnson labored under a delusion, although his joy at getting rid of the Greybeards is understandable. Over in the city, Danforth was also happy to see them go, especially the officers. On learning of their departure, J. B. commented that the Greybeard officers were "the most unprincipled set of men ever in charge of a regiment. They are boldly charged by their men with altering pay rolls, with entering the names of their wives and children on the pay rolls, as servants, and drawing pay for them . . . and with an amount of petty crimes too numerous to mention."[13]

The Greybeards departed for Memphis, where they would guard trains. As they marched away from the Island, the 133rd Illinois rode toward it on the cars from Springfield. Unlike the freezing, half-starved prisoners who endured two or three days of hell to reach the Island, the men of the 133rd enjoyed their trip. So much so, in fact, that the first official act of Colonel Thaddeus Phillips was to write letters of apology to the towns they had passed through. Among others, he wrote to the provost marshal of the 6th district: "Yours dated June 8 64 came duly to hand. . . . I must ask leave to differ with you in some of the language you see fit to express. I think you do injustice to the 133d Regt. when you say that the Regt. behaved in an unsoldierly manner. It cannot be denied that some of my soldiers did wrong but to include the whole regiment is false. . . . The claims which are presented shall be paid in full." The wrongs ceased, Phillips told another aggrieved party, only because "the men that committed the depredations referred to have deserted; consequently, am unable to bring them to justice. I will do all in my power to ferret out all those were engaged in the affair." But Phillips had no time to ferret out anyone: he was far too busy riding herd on the men who remained.[14]

The 133rd was much younger than the Greybeards. There was at least one 16-year-old and several 17-year-olds; one captain, Alfred Orendorff, was only 18. Being young, inexperienced, and, as Wilbur Norton of Company D noted, "guiltless of any knowledge of military tactics," the men of the 133rd communed with themselves and concluded that a soldier's duty consisted of shooting. And shoot they did, almost from the first day they were on the walls. Of the eight men listed on the death register as having died of gunshot wounds, the 133rd killed two, a disproportionate number for the length of time the hundred dazers served. They also wounded at least half a dozen others. They were only following the example of the Greybeards, who just a day or two before the 133rd arrived shot two prisoners for standing near the wall and trying to talk through it to a visitor. One of the men, George Ross of the 1st Arkansas, later died of his wounds.[15]

Profiting by this lesson, the 133rd wasted no time. Four days after their arrival, Samuel Frank of the 5th Alabama Cavalry left his barrack to go to the latrine. Although it was after taps, going to the latrine was permitted, especially for men who were sick, as Frank was. Danforth reported: "As he opened the door the guard . . . ordered him to halt, which order he instantly obeyed. The guard then said: 'Go back G—d D——n you, or I'll shoot you,' and immediately fired on him." J. B., properly abhorred, hastened to add that this "unwarrantable and indiscreet act" could not be blamed on the officers, but only on the rawness of the guard who fired. Dillon also noted the murder, and according to him the "cowardly miscreant" was proud of his act, saying "with an oath to his corporal 'I got one that time.'" Frank's shooting opened a deadly hunting season. The very next day Lafayette Rogan recorded another man had been shot, and two more on the 22nd. Charles Wright confirms the latter two, Bannister Cantrell of the 18th Georgia and James Ricks of the 50th Georgia. They were working in a ditch and stopped to take a drink of water, which unaccountably disturbed the guard.[16]

This was all a warm-up. In an incident largely ignored, the trigger-happy boys of the 133rd nearly committed a massacre; that they failed is due not to any restraint on their part, but only to their poor marksmanship. On 27 June, Danforth, yearning as always to abuse the *Union,* reported: "On Friday [24 June] the *Union* published a story of the shooting of several prisoners by the guard and the killing of one. On inquiry at the proper office we were told that the story is untrue." Unfortunately for the *Argus,* in this instance the *Union* was correct. The circumstances remain unknown. The official correspondence of the Barracks shows nothing, nor does the regimental book of the 133rd. Still more surprising is that not a single account by prisoners mentions it, either. But the hospital register corroborates the *Union's* story: 17 men were admitted to the hospital on 25 June, all with gunshot wounds, all from Barrack 78. Perhaps they were trying to escape; perhaps they made too much noise; perhaps the guards panicked at a sudden sound. The cause remains unknown, because Colonel Johnson did not report the incident, and someone in his office flatly denied to Danforth that it ever happened.[17]

There were enough shootings already in the public domain, and the incidents were not restricted to prisoners: some near victims were quarrymen working for Major Kingsbury. After their shifts, the guards marched a few rods up the Island and cleared their weapons, which they were supposed to do by firing at a target provided for the purpose. But the men of the 133rd were not content to shoot at a stationary round of wood nailed to a tree. As Major Kingsbury complained only days after the 133rd arrived, "It has been reported to me that men engaged in quarrying stone for the United States on the other side of the river, have been driven from their work by the firing of your men, and that their lives and those of the neighboring inhabitants endangered thereby. Will you please give such orders as will prevent a recurrence of such reckless conduct?" Johnson, according to J. B., "expressed sincere regret at the occurrence and pledged prompt measures to prevent its repetition."[18]

When no other targets presented themselves, the soldiers in the 133rd shot each other. William Sutton accidentally shot off two of his own fingers. He was luckier than George Lowe. While going on guard one morning, one of the men being relieved engaged in a bit of horseplay, bringing up his musket and making as if to attack his relief. Unfortunately, the hammer of his weapon caught on the strap of his cartridge box, cocking the weapon, and when the man untangled it the musket discharged, killing Lowe. In light of these activities, it had been wise of Hoffman to deny Johnson artillery.[19]

The men had other bad habits as well. One of them was losing their equipment. The regimental files show a phenomenal number of pay stoppages for lost haversacks, gun tools, canteens, and other equipment. To replace at least some of this equipment the men turned to theft, raiding the hospital for whatever they needed. Colonel Phillips despaired of apprehending the offenders because, as he told Surgeon Watson, "of the difficulty which generally attends the ferreting-out of the parties perpetrating these depredations." Phillips also tried to ferret out the men stealing commissary stores and selling them to citizens, but he could conclude only that it must be enlisted men, not officers, and they were probably not aware it was illegal.[20]

Women were another hobby of the hundred dazers. Although Johnson had ordered all laundresses to live in Laundressville, a set of buildings erected especially for them, at least some of the 133rd's women moved into the men's quarters with them, prompting an order sending the women to their proper place. Shortly after being deprived of the women's company, Corporal George Brown was reduced to the ranks for "committing an offense calculated to bring infamy and disrepute upon the command." Corporal Francis Woodcock was also reduced, not for masturbating, but for persuading another man "through misrepresentation to engage in an unlawful act which would and did result in pollution, disease, and misery."[21]

All in all, it was a rough crew, far beyond any ability of Colonel Phillips to control, especially since he seemingly had such a difficult time ferreting out the culprits. The regiment's order book is singularly lacking records for courts-martial. A number of noncommissioned officers besides Brown and Woodcock were reduced to the ranks, but for general incompetence rather than specific crimes. The troops apparently believed that military life consisted of plundering, theft, sex, and shooting anything that moved, and they understandably enjoyed it—so much so they wanted to continue. But they were not about to contribute their valuable services simply out of a sense of duty. As Captain Summers of Company K wrote to Fuller on behalf of his men: "Will you be so kind as to inform me the amount of bounty that would be given to this command reenlisting for the term of one year. Also the number of days that would be allowed them to visit their homes on furlough." Despite the neverending need for men, Fuller wisely declined the offer.[22]

Two other regiments of hundred dazers served on the Island that summer. One came all the way from the Keystone State—the 197th Pennsylvania. The 197th left behind it very few records of its service in the River Bend, and they were quiet enough that neither Johnson nor Danforth added much. So bland was this regiment that it is routinely misidentified. The Pennsylvanians apparently admired and emulated the 133rd's shooting habits, but they otherwise were quite reserved, at least by comparison with the other regiments. A third unit actually showed some interest in military matters. The 48th Iowa, a battalion rather than a regiment, was organized in Davenport under Lieutenant Colonel Oliver Hazard Perry Scott and moved immediately to the Island. The regiment held drill daily, and one of the captains wrote Nathaniel Baker asking for a copy of *Casey's Military Tactics*, because there was not a copy to be had on the Island. Even though the officers were interested in doing their duty, the men were not soldiers and it showed. A number of men were reduced for incompetence, being absent without leave, and conduct unbecoming. The 48th also seemed to want more laundresses than had been authorized. To determine who belonged and who did not, the captains were ordered to send in lists of the authorized women. The privates also took up freelance clerking and began writing passes for themselves. When Johnson responded with an order requiring that "none other than printed passes will be used," the men went into business trading and selling passes to each other.[23]

The men risked court-martial because the city was a powerful attraction. Life on the Island was in some respects as bad for the guards as for the prisoners. True, the guards were not incarcerated, but they were subject to the same numbing routines as their wards. What little of their correspondence survives mirrors the prisoners':

the guards, too, wanted to go home and wanted to hear from home. As R. Buckley told his wife: "Again disappointed. No letter." The guards' day began with reveille at 5:30 in the morning, followed by police call and guard mount, two periods of company drill, and a daily dress parade. Both guards and prisoners suffered the caprices of such officers as Hogendobler and Kincaid. They suffered the same weather and much the same food, although there was more of it, and the guards did have better access to the sutler Dart and his delicacies.[24]

During the winter, the guards were as much or more exposed to the bitter cold as the prisoners, who could spend much of their day huddled around the stoves while the guards stamped a beat along the exposed parapet. Dress parade was held on the river ice during the winter, causing one man to remark, "If the ice should break, wouldn't the Invalids go under." In the summer, the guards could ease the heat by bathing in the slough. The men of the 133rd did so too much, in the eyes of the surgeon, who said, "The injurious effects of which are becoming very visible and numerous." To forestall this, the men were restricted to bathing between reveille and guard mount; unfortunately, this caused them to make their ablutions at the same time some officers' daughters took their morning walk. But even the thrill of embarrassing young ladies paled beside the attractions of the city, and from the day the first guards arrived until the last ones left, they never ceased divining ways to get to town.[25]

By the end of July 1864, the only guards Johnson had were the hundred dazers. Although the trouble they caused no doubt wore heavily on the colonel, he remained silent. His aggravations were not yet hot enough to bring him to a boil. And as if he needed more trouble, the authorities in Washington decided to cut the ration. The government had had about all it intended to take of Southern mistreatment of Union prisoners and had decided the time for real retaliation had come. At almost the same time Stanton had relaxed the prohibitions on the sutlers in March 1864, having decided that treatment of Union prisoners had improved, a fresh set of invalid exchanges was proving him dead wrong. Reports of mistreatment continued to filter north, and in the spring of 1864 direct and incontrovertible evidence in the form of returned prisoners also began to filter back to the Union, bringing with them tales of horror that paled the earlier reports. Everyone began taking a renewed interest in the prisoners' treatment. Stanton sent Hoffman to the parole camp at Annapolis, Maryland, to look into the condition of the returned men. What he found moved even the emotionless Hoffman: "Some of these poor fellows were wasted to mere skeletons, and had scarcely life enough remaining to appreciate that they were now in the hands of their friends. . . . With rare exception, every face was sad with care and hunger; there was no brightening of the countenance or lighting up of the eye, to indicate a thought of anything beyond a painful sense of prostration of mind and body. Many faces showed that there was scarcely a ray of intelligence left." Hoffman concluded, "Our soldiers, when in the hands of the Rebels, are starved to death." He urged that "retaliatory measures be at once instituted by subjecting the officers we now hold as prisoners of war to a similar treatment." He discounted the Confederate excuse that prisoners received the same rations as that provided the Confederate armies in the field. Were Lee's troops receiving the same rations as the prisoners at Belle Isle in Richmond, Hoffman reasoned, Lee's army would be incapable of combat.[26]

Stanton turned this report over to the Joint Committee on the Conduct of the War, which immediately went to Annapolis to take testimony. The committee reached the same conclusions about the inhumanity of the Confederate authorities, but it also introduced a new twist. Realizing that it was "impossible to describe in words the deplorable condition of these returned prisoners," the committee "caused photographs to be taken of a number of them." This was one of the earliest uses of photographs as evidence. After appending testimony of a number of the prisoners, the committee's report closed with the statement of one of the attending surgeons, who said, "If there has ever been anything so horrible, so fiendish, as this wholesale starvation, in the history of this satanic rebellion, I have failed to note it." The committee ordered this report printed as part of the same volume as the report of the outrages at Fort Pillow.[27]

Another agency that interested itself in the prisoners' plight was the United States Sanitary Commission, which provided medical supplies and other relief to the Union armies. Not content with congressional reports, at roughly the same time the members of the committee were taking testimony the Sanitary Commission formed its own delegation and visited some Northern prisons and both hospitals where returned Union prisoners were held. Their purpose was twofold: to document the atrocities suffered by Federal prisoners and to verify that Rebels held in the North enjoyed the most humane of conditions. Given the growing hysteria, it is not surprising that the Commission accomplished both purposes.

The Commission examined the Confederate prisoners held at Fort Delaware and concluded that "they appeared in general, contented and cheerful." The bread provided the prisoners was "better indeed than is met with at hotels." In the matter of shooting, the commissioners noted, "Shooting was never resorted to unless a rule was grossly and persistently violated," which would have been news to the men on the Island, who spent the summer dodging bullets from the 133rd Illinois's muskets.[28]

All the reports demanded a response from the administration. Fortunately, one of Hoffman's commandants suggested one only a day after the joint committee's report was published. On 10 May 1864, the commissary of prisoners at Camp Douglas, L. C. Skinner, had proposed a ration cut. Hoffman had already ordered a reduction less than a month before, but Skinner noted that the prisoners continued to waste food. Hoffman sent the suggestion to Stanton, and it made the rounds. Henry Halleck, now chief of staff of the army, suggested an even deeper reduction, to make the ration conform to "that issued by the Rebel government to their own troops." The surgeons concurred that this would not endanger health, except for hospital patients.[29]

On 1 June 1864, Hoffman issued a circular cutting the ration. Skinner had suggested only tampering with the bread and some of the vegetables. After Halleck's suggestion, the meat issue was also reduced. When the prisoners received pork it would be only 10 ounces; when beef, 14 ounces. In other items, the actual reduction closely followed Skinner's suggestions, including the entire elimination of the candle issue, because, as Skinner shrewdly noted, there was no reason for prisoners to have candles, "except to be used in tunneling or in studying up some other means of escape." Satisfied he had done his duty, Hoffman turned to other matters. He would shortly be dragged back to the question of rations, thanks in large part to the activities in the River Bend.[30]

During the construction of the prison, Danforth had wondered what madness had possessed Captain Reynolds that he put the Barracks on the north shore of the Island. They were thus much closer to Iowa than to Illinois, and Iowa was always a source of concern for the editor. As it turned out, there were far more compelling reasons for locating the compound almost anywhere else. A low ridge bisected the camp from east to west, dividing it into northern and southern sections. Another ridge rose south of the walls, thus preventing drainage from the southern part of the camp. This problem was most apparent in the southwest corner, where water gathered. Surgeon Clark had noted this during his winter visits, saying, "At the present season this marsh causes no greater evil than inconvenience in crossing it, but in warm weather it will become a hotbed of miasma." Indeed, said Clark, the entire compound was "utterly unprovided with any system of drainage." The lay of the land demanded that any sewers should lead to the main channel of the river, on the north. Unfortunately, Captain Reynolds had placed the waterworks below the compound, so any sewers draining into the river would foul the water supply. Moreover, the waterworks were insuffient: a single unreliable steam pump provided water for the entire post. For several days in February 1864, the entire camp depended for water on one artesian well. When Clark pointed out these problems, Reynolds agreed about the "absolute necessity for an increase of the water supply and for a system of drainage" and promised immediate attention.[31]

For the short term, Reynolds installed a system of portable privies, which had to be emptied daily. The problem with the privies was where they were emptied: directly into the river. As Barnes pointed out, 200 barrels were dumped into the water every day. Moreover, the offal from the pest hospital was also thrown into the river. J. B. noted this and warned his readers: "Now that the sewers from the Barracks and pest house empty into the river people will hesitate somewhat about using river water for drinking and cooking purposes." The barrel solution was a stopgap; Reynolds agreed with Clark and wrote to Montgomery Meigs: "Already the twelve large sinks have been filled and the privies removed three times. In the spring the camp will be muddy and filthy. In the summer the stench caused by excrements will be insufferable and will certainly engender disease."[32]

All these problems could be solved by a water system that had its start in a 1.5 million gallon reservoir on the high ground south of the compound. A large sewer and a couple of auxiliaries would be dug through the camp, with bath and wash houses at the upper end and privies lower down. A constant flush of water from the reservoir would keep the sewers clean and sweet smelling. Potable water would be led from the reservoir through pipes to hydrants. None of this would alleviate the problem the citizens faced. Indeed, the problem would be exacerbated, because the new and improved sewers would still drain into the river north of camp, whence the current would carry the sewage directly down to the city's levee. This defect got short shrift from Reynolds. It was his job to improve the Barracks, and he submitted his plan to Meigs, carefully noting the cost: about $15,000 in quartermaster funds and, if Hoffman approved, $5,000 from the prison fund. Mindful that neither Meigs nor Hoffman would be cheerful about exorbitant costs, Reynolds suggested a way to reduce the expense: "It is proposed that the prisoners and troops quarry the stone, dig the trenches for pipe and sewer, tend the masons and do all the manual labor required." The troops Reynolds referred to had already proved themselves incapable of building simple barracks; such things as plumbing and masonry would be completely beyond them. In suggesting the prisoners, however, Reynolds had germinated an idea that would find him and the Barracks a small footnote in history. As his correspondence would show, Reynolds did not merely want to work the prisoners: he wanted to make them public employees.[33]

The idea of working prisoners was not new. Montgomery Meigs had long advocated prison labor. In August 1861, Meigs told Ohio Governor David Tod and Secretary of War Simon Cameron that army regulations allowed prisoners one ration each, and that was all they would get from him: "If they need clothing they should be placed where they can earn it by their labor." Meigs had no time for prisoners nor compunctions about forcing them to labor. In July 1862, when repairs were needed at Camp Douglas, he told Hoffman: "For these repairs the prisoners themselves should do the work. . . . If not willing to keep themselves and their camp clean and wholesome and supplied with water I presume it is in the power of the guard to compel obedience to regulations." Meigs had the law on his side. Francis Lieber, a prominent jurist and professor at Columbia University, had set down the laws of war, which in 1863 the War Department had issued as General Order No. 100. One stipulation regarding prisoners was that "They may be required to work for the benefit of the captor's Government according to their rank and condition." To some extent labor was voluntary: in January 1863, when some barracks were moved at Camp Douglas, a number of prisoners volunteered for the job. On the other hand, a year later, when the guards at Douglas needed a ditch dug, they impressed prison labor.[34]

On Rock Island Johnson also made use of prisoners, to clear brush and pull stumps for the interminable construction. And there were Rogan and his fellow prisoner clerks staining their fingers with Federal ink. Again, this was at least in part voluntary, although J. W. Minnich made it quite clear that some work gangs were impressed. The guards would collect ten men from each barrack until the detail was full. Minnich refused to go one morning, telling the sergeant of the guard, "We are prisoners of war, and you have no right to take us outside of the prison to do government work without pay." Minnich was not forced to work. But many others worked willingly, on the Island and in other camps, because labor passed the time and relieved the killing boredom.[35]

Policing camps and doing the odd bit of landscaping was one thing, but Meigs saw in the prisoners a huge and free labor pool, and it was more than he could stand to see it go to waste. Sent to Chattanooga after Grant's victories in November 1863, he noted the thousands of captured Confederates awaiting transportation to Rock Island. He wrote to Henry Halleck: "There are many prisoners here. To send them North will be expensive. . . . Does the present state of the contest permit works at Chattanooga and Bridgeport, where they can be very useful in building bridges, repairing railroads which they have destroyed?"[36] Halleck immediately dashed Meigs's dream of prisoners working to help defeat their own army, saying, "It is not deemed expedient to employ prisoners of war on public works or as laborers." Nor was it politic. Forcing the prisoners to work in such a fashion would have raised howls of protest from the Confederate government. The cautious Halleck thought it the better part of valor to ship the Rebels north. Montgomery Meigs, however, was not a man to let go of an idea. When Halleck turned him down, Meigs wrote directly to Professor Lieber. He noted that the generals in Chattanooga had no objection to his scheme except the trouble of guarding the prisoners, which trouble was not eliminated by shipping them north, but only transferred. Meigs's appeal was masterful, and made with an eye to the future:

> While at Chattanooga, . . . I advised the employment of some 6,000 prisoners taken in battles of Chattanooga upon public work, such as repairing the railroads . . . expediency, efficiency, economy, and

humanity appeared to me to unite in favor of the employment of these men on the public work. It was decided, however, by higher authority to be "inexpedient." . . . But I am convinced that, should the war continue, the policy of working prisoners of war must be finally adopted, and that public opinion will become so well instructed on this subject as to compel an advance in the true direction. . . . We feed, clothe, and shelter 40,000 Rebels rotting in idleness. . . . Why not give them a new lease of life by employing them upon . . . national work intended to strengthen the bonds of that Union which they have striven to destroy.[37]

Lieber agreed completely: "As a general thing, I say, as every one else will say, that it is very expedient indeed to make prisoners work and not to waste the capital that is embodied in thousands of lusty hands." Lieber's only concern was how strong the prisoners were: "I do not know whether our 50,000 prisoners are very lusty hands. The mass of Southern common people are, physically, worth very little."[38]

His opinion having been confirmed by the man who quite literally wrote the rules of war, Meigs next wrote to H. Raymond, the editor of the *New York Times,* whom he told, "We alone of all nations keep and feed and clothe . . . criminals as prisoners of war." Meigs intimated that "the subject is worth treatment in the public prints." The only barrier to forcing prisoners to labor, Meigs thought, was the misapprehension on the part of the public that "as a Christian nation we are bound to support these southern gentlemen in idleness, well fed, till we kill them with gout or inanition." The point of the letter was clear: Raymond should start educating the public so that when Meigs did drive the Rebels to work there would be no public outcry. But Meigs, being wise in the ways of politics, also told Raymond to keep him out of it: "I do not wish to appear in the public prints."[39]

At the Barracks, quartermaster Reynolds had not waited for the public to be educated. In March 1864, he had had no time to wait— he needed a hospital immediately. He asked Meigs about the propriety of hiring prisoners. Receiving no reply, he followed Johnson's lead in such matters and acted first, worrying about permission later. Reynolds and Johnson allowed the hospital's contractor, a man named McClellan, to comb the prison for carpenters, masons, and plasterers and hire them at forty cents a day, credited to their sutler accounts. Johnson notified Hoffman, but Hoffman said nothing. He probably did not care: after all, the money was coming not from his prison fund but from McClellan. When it came time to build the sewers, Reynolds again wanted to use prisoners. They would be much cheaper than citizen mechanics and, moreover, they were available; thousands of men sat in idleness in the yard. In authorizing the project, Meigs told Reynolds to employ prisoners when he could. By the end of May the contractor was working nearly 50 blasters. As Reynolds said, the prisoners were "doing as faithful and efficient service as if citizens were employed at $1.50 to $1.75 per day." But there was a problem: "I understand that these men expect some compensation." They expected compensation, of course, because the hospital crew was being paid. But Meigs now forbade Reynolds to pay wages. Knowing better than to make further requests of Meigs, Reynolds told Johnson that to get the work done he would need as many as 130 men a day, plus common laborers. As Reynolds noted, "I understand from my superintendent that there will be no difficulty in getting enough competent mechanics to do the whole of this work, who are anxious to work every day for a small compensation with which to procure additional food, tobacco, etc. to enable them to endure constant and severe labor."[40]

Johnson was nothing loath, and he sent the idea on to Hoffman, who approved the plan. Only a couple of weeks before receiving Reynolds's proposal, Hoffman had noted that the prisoners at Point Lookout in Maryland were paid nine cents in tobacco, "in consequence of the difficulty of obtaining laborers at this post." The prisoners at Lookout unloaded ships and did various construction tasks. What Hoffman did not know was the real reason the prisoners were willing to work: according to prisoner A. M. Keiley, it was the chance to gather up "pieces of plank, old iron, nails, and the like, which command a high price . . . within the 'pen.'" Given these fringe benefits, it was only natural that "the detail list is always full, and places thereon command a premium."[41]

Not surprisingly, Hoffman thought Reynolds's wage of forty cents a day exorbitant, the more so since this money would not come from a contractor but from the prison fund. He recommended that mechanics be paid only ten cents a day and common laborers five, payable in either cash or tobacco. Stanton also approved the scheme, and on 13 June 1864 Hoffman codified the system in a circular to his commandants. The prisoners on the Island had become public employees, and Captain Reynolds had found himself a small place in history. It was his proposal that moved Hoffman to make the system a regular part of the prison system, and Reynolds had been the first to employ prisoners, albeit without permission at the time. Moreover, Rock Island would make the most use of the system. Besides the longshoremen at Lookout and a few laborers at Elmira in New York, only on the Island would paid prison labor on public works became a regular feature of life, extending to the end of the war.[42]

At the suggestion of Henry Halleck, the work gangs also received full rations, and this represented a real bonus. Although the available records show that the rations were issued as ordered, there was contradictory evidence in the graveyard, where Cicero Faine went after he died of scurvy on 7 June 1864. He was not the first scurvy case, merely the first to die. He would not be the last. The announcement of the 1 June ration reduction, along with the death of Samuel Frank and the shooting of George Ross, moved the prisoners to action, action that was materially aided both by Captain Reynolds's lack of foresight and by the smallpox epidemic.[43]

During the epidemic, some of the barracks had been used as pest houses; two of these remained empty, for fear of infection. One of the two barracks abutted the south fence, which was different from the other three fences forming the compound. On the other three sides Reynolds had dug deep ditches between the deadline and the fence, to prevent tunneling. But on the south bedrock rose to within two feet of the surface. Reynolds had thought this too shallow for burrowing Rebels and had dug no ditch. The prisoners thought this all very obliging. On the night of 14 June a number of men gathered in the empty barrack next to the fence, pushed a quick tunnel under, and made a break for it. Ten made it through the tunnel and outside the fence before the guards were alerted. Three were captured before they reached the river, a fourth in the slough (who was erroneously reported as drowned), and three more a few miles downstream. The last three got away, and, although Johnson sent patrols into the Illinois countryside, the trio remained free, at least for the moment. The recaptured ones were awarded leg irons for their efforts, which offended the sensibilities of one young guard in the 133rd, who told a friend, "I cannot describe my reflections as I stood by and saw the great iron bands riveted to their limbs."[44]

The escape of ten men at once was a record for the Barracks, and Johnson was understandably embarrassed, so much so that he delayed reporting the escapade to Hoffman. Hoffman heard about it anyway, through the agency of the patriotic citizens who kept sending River Bend newspapers to Washington. Only after Hoffman wrote to him did the colonel belatedly report the escape. Somewhat lamely, Johnson added that the south wall would soon have a ditch.[45]

The lack of a ditch was the last shortcoming Reynolds would be allowed. His sins were too many to ignore. Back in April, Surgeon Clark had made another of his interminable reports and castigated the captain without mercy. Clark reported that there was no adequate supply of water for the camp, because Reynolds's pump and pipe kept breaking; the drainage was nonexistent (Reynolds had not yet begun the sewer project, although he promised that it would "be speedily executed"); and there still was insufficient straw for the hospital beds. At almost the same time, the inspector general sent his own inspector, John Marsh of the Veteran Reserve Corps, and in a single line Marsh exposed the cause of the captain's problems. Marsh said not only that Reynolds's books were in total disarray but that during the interview, "the captain was somewhat intoxicated." Immediately upon receipt of Marsh's report, Montgomery Meigs was told to relieve Reynolds. The War Department issued an order for the captain to report to Nashville, but it was 14 June, the day of the great escape, before the captain actually left the Island.[46]

Even though Reynolds was no longer a thorn in Johnson's side, the Democratic thorn over in the city continued to needle him throughout the summer. Danforth never let up. True, he did have other matters to impart to his readers. The summer was extremely wet, and J. B., along with his fellow editors, recorded every downpour, which were especially frequent in July. The draw span of the bridge burned, interrupting traffic for a month; a child was run over by a train; wolves were sighted above the town. Danforth chronicled a vicious plan of the VRC men to sack the *Argus* offices just before they left town, a plot thwarted when as many as 300 supporters showed up to prevent the outrage. J. B. was also elected a state committeeman for the Democrats.[47]

Despite his heavy schedule of political meetings and long hours spent thinking up new terms of opprobrium to use on the *Union*'s Barnes (after due deliberation, he decided on "cuttlefish"), J. B.

never neglected the Barracks. He was nothing if not persistent. Perhaps the frequency of the regular "Rock Island Barracks" column decreased, but little passed unnoticed. A VRC man, drunk, as Danforth noted, lay down on the tracks one day and was caught by a train, his body "horribly mangled" and one arm carried 20 miles down the road. The same day one of the hundred dazers tried to swim the slough, and he drowned. Another guard, trying to cross the railroad bridge after imbibing too much, fell between the ties into the slough. Not content with killing themselves, the men of the VRC also killed each other—a private named Willis sneaked up on a man named Farrell and broke his neck with a blow of a club. John Harty of the navy made a return appearance for more recruits, and J. B. proceeded to issue a screed about the draft credit going to Chicago rather than Rock Island. His diatribe came to nothing, because, as Illinois Adjutant General Fuller pointed out, prisoner recruits could choose the locality that got credit for them. The construction on the Island came in for approval, not just from Danforth, but from all the people. The hospital construction proceeded apace. New roads were laid down; every building got a fresh coat of whitewash. Indeed, enthused the editor, "[T]here is no prettier drive in the region than over the new roads on the Island."[48]

Of course, not everything on the Island was pretty. Danforth kept printing the death lists and in some cases singled out the dead for special mention. One was Edward Maxwell of the 28th Alabama, who was killed by a fellow prisoner in a fight over who got to use the cooking stove first. The clerks on the Island, more circumspect than Danforth, recorded only that Maxwell "died in barracks." Another man had a name too good not to use: Mountain Hill, of the 16th Georgia. According to the death register, Hill died of an abscessed hip; but J. B. could not resist the name and told his readers that Mountain Hill had died of emaciation.[49]

Despite all this, Danforth seemed supportive of Colonel Johnson. He excused the colonel for the short rations. When he reprinted the rules governing visitors, J. B. suggested, "The rule is an exceedingly harsh one, and ought to be so modified as to allow some discretion to the commandant of the post." Johnson, of course, responded to none of this. Every time the editor railed against the administration, it was an indirect indictment of Johnson. But unless he unburdened himself to his wife over the supper table, Johnson remained silent.[50]

*T*he completion of the new hospitals, including a larger one for the garrison, a pest hospital of six buildings, and a prison hospital with its own stockade, had taken months. Johnson had started guarding the new construction at the end of May, probably to prevent vandalism and thefts of material by the citizens who prowled about the Island. Two weeks later the first patients were admitted, among whom was Lafayette Rogan, who entered the hospital on 14 June with erysipelas and spent nine days enjoying what he described as "a pleasant place."[51]

Rogan must have had strange ideas about pleasantness. Men gripped by delirium would "rise from bed and run about the ward." The surgeons opened abscesses in the wards and let the pus run, in one case to the amount of a pint in a single day; diarrhea patients evacuated in their beds, sometimes a dozen times in 24 hours. The diseases and attendant discomfort were bad enough, but there was also the matter of research to consider. There were no teaching hospitals and research facilities in 1864. The surgeons used patients to test new treatments, sometimes bizarre ones. For example, one doctor near Washington suffered diarrhea, and the standard treatments, which included laudanum and ginger, failed him. So the doctor tried a new drug, and then excitedly wrote the surgeon general: "That pest of the army, diarrhea, or dysentery, can be relieved . . . by letting the person eat a gill or so of peanuts." Surgeon General Hammond took up the suggestion and ordered a test run at another hospital. Unfortunately, the self-treating doctor had a unique constitution, because the surgeon who ran the more extensive tests reported, "I have the honor to report that I have used peanuts in several cases of acute chronic diarrhea and dysentery and find them to be utterly worthless."[52]

About the same time as this strange experiment, a doctor on Rock Island was undertaking his own investigations into diarrhea. An assistant surgeon named H. F. Gilbert had somehow concluded that bromine would cure diarrhea and dysentery. Bromine is a corrosive used to make dyes and as an anti-knock element in gasoline. But in 1864, as Gilbert himself said, "Bromine is a new remedy, its status remaining unknown." Gilbert fitted up a ward and got 90 cases assigned to him, some of them men who had suffered diarrhea for more than a year. He administered bromine indiscriminately, giving three doses a day to everyone in the ward, regardless of symptoms, stage of the disease, complicating or underlying diseases, or response to other treatments. This simplified the record keeping a great deal. In the rare resistant case, Gilbert added creosote and lead to the pharmacopoeia. He further simplified his case notes by not keeping many, preferring to rely on his memory. When he submitted his report to Washington, he proudly claimed that, of his 90 patients, 10 remained under treatment, 79 had been cured, and only 1 had died. Gilbert crowed that he had discovered "an agent certain in its effects to cure all cases, I care not of how long standing."[53]

However, the doctors in Washington understood the experimental method somewhat better than Gilbert. They called for the hospital records and, comparing them to Gilbert's study, discovered that not only had a number of his cures been readmitted for the same complaints, some of them repeatedly, but that at least six of his patients had died; depending on how the data are interpreted, as many as 17 of the bromine patients gave up the ghost for the cause of research.[54]

Gilbert's were not the only patients administered bizarre concoctions, some of them experimental, some standard at the time. One treatment for pneumonia was "Dover's powder, camphor, quinine, turpentine emulsion, whiskey and milk." Not surprisingly, the patient "became very drowsy, falling into a semi-unconscious state . . . and dying next day." Alfred Driskell received medicines that included not only opium and silver but also "aromatic sulfuric acid." David Chapman's case demanded the strongest treatment of all: bromine, potassium, opium, ammonia, Dover's powder, wine, and whiskey. Chapman succumbed—if not to his disease, then to the treatment.[55]

The conditions in the hospital and the treatment accorded the patients, while seeming barbaric today, were not unduly harsh at the time. The causes of infection were understood poorly or not at all, and sterilization was unheard of. The more perceptive among the medical corps were beginning to notice the correlation between hygiene and the great killer, dysentery, but their pleas for sanitation were too often ignored. The soldiers who guarded the prisoners at Rock Island received much the same treatment as their wards. For example, turpentine and ammonia were both standard medical treatments at the time. This was no comfort to either the guards or the guarded. In fact, the best chance of staying alive for anyone, Rebel or Federal, "was the fortuitous one of his not contracting one of the great 'killer' diseases."[56]

It was nearly the end of July before the hospital construction was completed, and it was August before Danforth could report to his readers, "The corps of surgeons now occupy the new hospital headquarters." And by that time nearly 1,300 men, almost two-thirds of the men who would die at Rock Island, were already in their graves. But there was still work for the surgeons: during the summer months of June, July, and August 1864, more than 1,800 prisoners were admitted to the hospital. After the ration cut of 1 June the number of scurvy cases began increasing. There were men wounded by the guards' free-firing habits, and despite its being summer, hundreds of men went to the hospital with pneumonia. And as the *Union* reported, there were "considerable many cases of flux and diarrhea among the prisoners." The reduced rations doubtless produced much of the hospital's business, both directly, by causing scurvy, and indirectly, by lowering resistance. Dillon noted, "There is a great many men sick with scurvy now caused, of course, by our getting so much salt meat and no vegetables." The surgeons also did a little freelance pathology. A number of corpses were opened up so the surgeons could study the effects of various diseases. Autopsies of men who had died of pneumonia or other pleural diseases seemed to be the most popular. And no matter what disease killed a man, nearly every postmortem examination noted that the victim was emaciated.[57]

The sewer construction also gave work to the surgeons. A number of men were admitted for wounds incurred while working on the new water system. And on the afternoon of 11 July 1864, Adam Thompson of the 45th Tennessee, working on the sewers as a blaster, prepared a charge, lit the fuse, and turned to run. The charge exploded prematurely and a piece of wood struck Thompson's head, killing him instantly and earning him the dubious distinction of being the only prisoner to die in the public service. A few injuries and a death were no reason to stop the work, however, and it continued. The job was turning out to be larger than even Captain Reynolds had envisioned, and the need at least as great as Surgeon Clark had predicted. Andrew Caraher's weekly reports throughout the summer described a prison in pretty good shape. The buildings were whitewashed regularly, the yard policed constantly. Caraher's reports consistently pointed out only one defect: the sinks were not what they should be. Johnson's endorsements of the reports kept promising that the improvements would be completed any day; in September 1864, he was still making that promise. Hoffman seems not to have complained. The death of one prisoner more or less was meaningless, and except for the pittance paid the prisoners the costs were being borne by the Quartermaster Department. There were some other costs, however, that concerned Hoffman greatly.[58]

In early July Johnson received notice that the three fugitives from the great June escape had been collared. Neither his own patrols nor any provost guard had apprehended the trio, however. Some farmers near Mount Pleasant, Iowa, had rounded up the fugitives. The provost marshal in Burlington soon had the three in custody, and Johnson sent a Private McClure downriver to bring them back. McClure incurred $34.00 in expenses, and a Mr. Lynch of Iowa took the opportunity to bill the prison for the cost of hiring three guards between Mount Pleasant and Burlington. Johnson turned in all the bills to Hoffman for approval to pay them from the prison fund. This irritated Hoffman, who wrote back to Johnson that Lynch had gouged the prison by hiring three guards when one would do, and "unless the account is materially cut down I will not approve it." Further, the transportation to Burlington and back should have been paid by the quartermaster. Finally, McClure had apparently taken neither a weapon nor handcuffs with him on his trip and had purchased them in Burlington.[59]

McClure's expenses were not the only thing that worried Hoffman. Nothing seemed right on the Island. Johnson's report on the hospital costs, requested in April, did not arrive until July. Worse, the cost had ballooned to $30,000, and Hoffman could do nothing about it—the buildings were up and the contractors paid. Clerks' salaries continued to cause problems, and Hoffman sent Johnson an irritable letter demanding to know who had authorized the new quartermaster to pay them. As it turned out, it had been Hoffman himself who had authorized the money. But he had authorized enlisted men to work in the prison fund department, and Johnson had reported them as working in the Quartermaster Department, which confused Hoffman.[60]

It was small wonder that Hoffman forgot he had authorized two clerks. He was a man under pressure. Rock Island was only one of two dozen camps that held his prisoners. In addition, there were scores of jails and depots used to temporarily hold captured Rebels. Each and every prison required Hoffman's attention. Further, there was a huge correspondence dealing with exchanges, even though the cartel had broken down and exchanges were few and small. Despite all this, Hoffman thought the pecuniary disarray in the River Bend, as well as the question of Johnson's politics, demanded his personal attention. He told Stanton that, his office duties permitting, he would go to the River Bend himself and get to the bottom of things. It was a mercy to Johnson that Hoffman never made the trip. Further evidence that Hoffman had started to buckle under the pressure of his job was his decision on artillery for the Island. On 23 July 1864 Hoffman had told Stanton and Nathaniel Baker that the guards at the Barracks had no business with cannon. By 4 August he had changed his mind and wrote Meigs to request a barge "be purchased and fitted up for the accommodation of a guard of thirty-five men, armed with a 6-pounder field piece and a 24-pounder howitzer, to be anchored in the Mississippi River, off Rock Island, as additional security for the depot of prisoners of war."[61]

That settled, Hoffman again considered the sutler question. Governor Tod of Ohio had had his own inspection made of Camp Chase, and the inspector found the prisoners in a rather more luxurious condition than seemed proper. Not only did the sutler have a building built into the wall of the prison, with a counter in the yard itself, but "in addition to this convenience to prisoners their friends are permitted to contribute . . . liberal and frequent supplies of clothing, money, and food, which contributions are given them without hesitation and without stint. These comforts [are] an unpleasant contrast to the treatment received by our soldiers now languishing in Southern prisons."[62]

The report made the rounds in Washington. Hoffman was quick to note that he had never favored allowing sutlers in the camps but had been overruled. The War Department agreed with Governor Tod, and on 10 August 1864 Hoffman issued a circular addressing the matter. It was no longer allowed for prisoners to receive supplies of any kind from their families, unless the prisoner was sick. The sartorial splendor of his prisoners also concerned Hoffman: clothing could be provided only if the prisoner was destitute, and no prisoner could have more than one suit and a change of underclothing. Finally, the sutlers were nearly outlawed. Since March 1864, the sutlers had been selling an almost endless variety of things to the prisoners, including all manner of food, both staples and delicacies. Now, they could sell no food whatever to the prisoners. They could sell only tobacco, sewing supplies, hairbrushes, scissors, soap—and looking glasses. Apparently the prisoners had a great desire to admire themselves in mirrors.[63]

The ration cut of 1 June had its genesis in waste. Retaliation for the treatment the Confederacy accorded Federal prisoners was a secondary motive. But the regulation of 10 August had no purpose other than vengeance. In May, when Hoffman considered the ration cut, Andersonville was but a rumor; by August it was a reality that horrified the North. Without a backward glance Hoffman cut off the substantial foodstuffs both family and sutlers could provide the prisoners, forcing them to depend solely on the ration—the ration that two months earlier he had cut by a third. In the River Bend the effect of this order would manifest quickly.

Garrison troops. Guards from the 108th United States Colored Troops. (Courtesy of Illinois State Historical Library)

A view from outside the prison wall, showing the bell tower and what appears to be a work detail of prisoners. (Courtesy of Illinois State Historical Library)

Roll call in the prison compound. (Courtesy of Rock Island Arsenal Museum)

This sketch of the prison compound, dated September 1864, has several inaccuracies, including the number of roof vents and windows. The gate labeled "north" here was actually the west gate of the prison. (Courtesy of Rock Island Arsenal Museum)

(top) The prison administration buildings, west of the stockade. In the right background is the flagpole William Bennefield climbed for the reward of removing his ball and chain. (Courtesy of Illinois State Historical Library)

(bottom) North of the prison compound. On the right is the waterworks; on the left two soldiers stand in front of the photographer's studio. (Author's collection)

Inside the south wall of the prison, with stakes marking the "deadline." Reflective lanterns along the fence illuminated the area at night. (Courtesy of Illinois State Historical Library)

132

Sutler A. C. Dart (standing in wagon at right); the other men appear to be prison
staff. (Courtesy of Rock Island Arsenal Museum)

Prisoners making and displaying trinkets for sale or barter. (Courtesy of Rock Island
Arsenal Museum)

Prisoners riding Morgan's mule as punishment. (Courtesy of Rock Island Arsenal Museum)

These prisoners may be enlisting in the United States Army, but it is more likely that they are taking the allegiance oath in order to be released. (Courtesy of Illinois State Historical Library)

"The Glare of Wolfish Hunger"

Hoffman's unending correspondence about costs had its effect on Johnson. When not trying to corral escaped prisoners or keep his guards from killing everyone around them, Johnson sought ways to improve the prison fund's balance. The hospital had been a huge drain on the fund, and although that expense was paid, he now had to pay prisoners for labor they had previously done for free. During the summer the post council of administration hit upon the idea of a bakehouse, to make bread for both prisoners and garrison. It was not a bad idea; the prison fund had begun with such a bakehouse at Camp Morton in Indiana. Johnson snapped up the idea.

As far as the citizens were concerned, the bakery was just one more opportunity to make the government pay. A citizen named Otterman offered himself as superintendent—for $100 a month. Otterman hired eight journeymen at between $2.00 and $2.50 a day and was assigned three soldiers to act as clerks. The clerks apparently were not paid, but by November Otterman's bakers were earning, in the aggregate, more than $1,300 a month. On 20 June the bakery opened for business. For a few days Otterman baked for the garrison, but starting in July he also baked for the prisoners. When Danforth heard about the bakery he hurried to the Island for a tour of the place, which he described as "a large and convenient building, with three large ovens."[1]

J. B. was not the only one who heard about the bakery. Nine hundred miles away William Hoffman, his River Bend sources never

failing him, learned of Johnson's endeavors and fired off a telegram
to the colonel. Hoffman's concern was not so much that Johnson
had built the bakehouse but that he had failed to report the savings.
Hoffman followed his telegram with a letter, demanding that the
books be corrected. In reply, Johnson said the bakery had turned a
profit of $785.49 through the end of August and that he would
credit the fund properly.[2]

This was small change. After months of running a deficit, largely
because of the hospital construction, in July Johnson had saved
more than $22,000, and between June and August 1864 $43,000
had accumulated. The June ration cut had helped a great deal. September 1864 would see a new record for savings: that month Johnson saved more than $23,000 and spent only $53.00. The savings
are the more dramatic in view of the vastly increased cost of rations. Illinois contractors were no fools: in 1862 they had contracted to provide rations at 10.85 cents each; by June 1864, the
cost at Rock Island was 20.75 cents, and by September, 25.75 cents.
For the 30 days of September, the ration cost for each prisoner was
$7.72; of this, $2.86 (about 37%) ended up in the fund. The extremely low expense in September was unusual, the lowest of any
month the Barracks was in operation. Johnson had little time to
spend money during the fall of 1864; trouble brewed on every
front. Every new regiment of guards provided new depths of stupid-
ity, for one thing. For another, Johnson had to become a recruiter,
because Pennsylvania wanted his prisoners.[3]

In the fall of 1864 the war machine still devoured men. The
graveyards grew in Georgia, where Sherman had captured Atlanta,
and in Virginia, where Grant and Meade tightened their grip
around Richmond. A river of sick and wounded men flowed to the
hospitals. Moreover, enlistments were expiring. The thousands who
had answered the first calls in 1861 neared the end of their terms.
And even though furloughs and other inducements persuaded
thousands of men to reenlist, other thousands went home. With
the capture of Atlanta and the siege of Petersburg, the end perhaps
was in sight, but it remained on a distant horizon.

Recruiting was difficult; the draft unpopular; substitutes increas-
ingly scarce. None of this was lost on a Pennsylvania judge named
Newton Pettis and a lieutenant colonel named Henry Huidekoper.
Pennsylvania had already sent a quarter-million men to the slaughter pens, and meeting quotas was proving a nightmare. But Pettis

and Huidekoper saw a solution in the River Bend, some 800 miles from Harrisburg, Pennsylvania's capital. The prison yard on the Island held thousands of idle men. As Danforth had pointed out, many had lost whatever loyalties had induced them to serve in the Confederate army. Why not allow them to enlist in the Federal army? The prisoners would be free men again, the war machine would be fed fresh fodder, and Pennsylvania's draft quota would be that much closer to fulfillment.

The idea was not original with Pettis and Huidekoper. There had been Colonel Mulligan's freewheeling enlistment of prisoners at Camp Douglas. Major General Benjamin Butler had also been busily enlisting former Confederates, including, in a unique incident of the war, former black Confederates. At the outbreak of the war, free blacks in New Orleans organized a regiment of militia, which was called to duty when Union Admiral David Farragut approached the city. Despite their short career, these freemen, some of them slave-owners themselves, were bona fide Rebels. When New Orleans fell and Butler was placed in command, he feared an attack by the Confederates. His pleas for reinforcement falling on deaf ears, Butler promised Edwin Stanton that he would "call on Africa to intervene." Butler was as good as his word: he enlisted the former black Confederates and soon told Stanton that he neared completion of "a regiment, 1,000 strong, of Native Guards (colored), the darkest of whom will be about the complexion of Mr. Webster."[4]

The idea of enlisting former enemies took hold, and nowhere stronger than in Illinois. From Alton, from Camp Butler at Springfield, from Camp Douglas, inquiries about the possibility of enlisting former Confederates came to the War Department. Although Stanton denied these requests, in June 1863 he did an about-face and authorized enlistments, "when it can be reliably shown that the applicant was impressed into the Rebel service and that he now wishes in good faith to join our army." In August Hoffman sent a circular to every department commander, notifying them of the new policy. Almost as Hoffman was telling the generals about the new policy, Stanton, waffling, was revoking it. It remained for Butler to force the issue. He had come east in December 1862, and by late 1863 he was established at Fortress Monroe as the exchange agent. Butler wanted to enlist Confederates, and he was an influential politician. His request drew Lincoln into the discussion. On 2 January 1864 Lincoln wrote Butler that he could administer the oath to prisoners who would enlist in the Federal service. By the middle of March, Butler was asking Hoffman to send him every prisoner Hoffman could lay his hands on, because he already had nearly a regiment recruited and could get more "when I get more prisoners." Shortly after this, Provost Marshal General James Fry authorized the muster of the regiment for three years' service. This would become the 1st U.S. Volunteers. Butler immediately began recruiting another regiment of what were soon to be called "Galvanized Yankees."[5]

By the time Pettis and Huidekoper arrived in Washington, enlisting enemies was an old idea, but these two had a new twist: their intention was not to help end the war, but to grow rich. A young friend of Pettis's had been in the West, and when he returned to Pennsylvania he told the judge that hundreds of the prisoners at Rock Island wanted to enlist in the Federal army and would do so for $100 bounty per year of enlistment. Meanwhile, substitutes in Pettis's hometown of Oil City were being paid $1,000. The judge concluded that there was money to be made. Pettis enlisted Huidekoper, recently discharged after suffering disabling wounds at Gettysburg, and the pair betook themselves to the president.[6]

Although Lincoln may not have known about the pecuniary aspects of the plan, he had his own reasons for approving it. During the summer the Democrats had nominated George B. McClellan, former commander in chief of the army, as their presidential candidate, and despite the fall of Atlanta the election was proving a close run thing, nowhere more so than in Pennsylvania, McClellan's home state. Lincoln was a shrewd man, and allowing these men to enlist prisoners and giving Pennsylvania the draft credit might mean votes for him in November. In the meantime, draftees in Pennsylvania would pay substitution fees to Pettis and Huidekoper; indeed, Pettis was later quoted as saying that the draftees "were crazy to pay." The recruit would receive $100; the difference between that and the fees the draftees paid would remain with Pettis and Huidekoper. The plan would benefit everyone, and Lincoln wrote to Stanton on 1 September 1864:

> It is represented to me that there are at Rock Island Ills as Rebel prisoners of war many persons of Northern and foreign birth who are unwilling to be exchanged and sent South but who wish to take the oath of allegiance and enter the military service of the Union. Col. Huidekoper on behalf of the people of some parts of Pennsylvania

wishes to pay the bounties the government would have to pay to proper persons of this class, have them enter the service of the United States and be credited to the localities that furnished the bounty money. He will therefore proceed to Rock Island and ascertain the names of such persons.[7]

Pettis forthwith took the cars for the River Bend. Upon arriving, Pettis learned that Stanton had explicitly forbidden Johnson to enlist anybody. Ulysses Grant, now commander in chief of the armies, did not much like the idea, either. Another note from Lincoln to Stanton produced no results, and Lincoln eventually walked over to the War Department to deal with the matter personally. James Fry witnessed the interview between the president and the secretary of war. As Fry remembered it, Lincoln sat down on a couch, stretched his legs, and listened to Fry explain his and Stanton's opposition to the plan. Lincoln then ordered Stanton to execute the order and, according to Fry, Stanton

> replied with asperity: "Mr. President, I cannot do it. The order is an improper one, and I cannot execute it."
>
> Lincoln fixed his eye upon Stanton, and in a firm voice and with an accent that clearly showed determination, he said: "Mr. Secretary, it will have to be done."

Stanton buckled. According to one biographer, it was one of the few times Lincoln had to compel Stanton. But to take Stanton off the hook Lincoln also wrote to Grant, apologizing for going behind his general's back. Lincoln issued a new order, assuring the recruits that they would be sent west to fight Indians and not south to fight their former comrades, a stipulation Johnson believed indispensable.[8]

This solved the problem of unity in Washington, but Johnson remained reluctant to enlist prisoners. When Pettis arrived, Johnson in one breath told him that it was an excellent idea and should have been tried long ago, and in the next breath he said "there would be a difficulty." When Harty had returned to the Island in May to recruit more prisoners for the navy, those the surgeons had rejected were turned back into the yard, where they were "abused by the rabid and malicious secesh." Further volunteers would not be forthcoming, said Johnson, for fear they would be rejected by the surgeons and thrown on the mercies of their former comrades.[9]

The judge was not to be put off. He examined Lincoln's 1 September order and deduced that the president intended that volunteers who were rejected should not be returned to the yard but should be discharged. Having thus divined Lincoln's intention from an order that contained no such suggestion, Pettis explained matters to Johnson. Pettis also managed to have removed a requirement that the recruits be of Northern or foreign birth. The thing being settled, Johnson had the order read to the prisoners on 12 September 1864, and Pettis returned to Pennsylvania to count his money.[10]

These solutions solved one set of problems, but they also sowed the seeds of further difficulties. The first thing Johnson had to do was find a place to keep the "newly made Union men," as Danforth would immediately dub them. He housed them in the same area that had earlier served as a hospital, in the southwest corner of the yard. Eighteen barracks were fenced off, and anyone who enlisted would be transferred into what the prisoners called the "calf pen." Despite protocols for determining who was genuinely interested in joining the Union cause, some men enlisted under false pretenses. Dillon noted that a friend of his went to the calf pen, but only because it would be easier to escape. Dillon rooted for his friend: "I hope he will succeed as I think he is a good Rebel." Others might have gone over so they could help out their friends who remained behind in the "bull pen"—almost immediately food began flying over the wall to the unrepentant Rebels. Johnson established a new deadline and guard between the two pens to prevent such aid.[11]

Despite the blizzard of beef and bread that rained down on them, many of the prisoners were unhappy about this latest attempt to undermine their cause. Ben Hord said, "Never, since the Son of Man was tempted by the devil, was dishonor more cunningly devised or temptingly displayed." So strong was the reaction that the prisoners formed a secret society, called 7 C K, or Seven Confederate Knights, to counteract the attraction of bounty, freedom, and food. The Knights swore to "suffer death rather than swear allegiance to effect a release from prison." The order, according to an account left by Thomas Berry, had as its badge a seven-pointed star; each point of the star carried an initial letter, forming an acronym of the motto "Dulce et decorum est pro patria mori" (It is sweet and becoming to die for one's country). The seven points also corresponded to the seven grades of military officers. In his memoir, Berry modestly allowed that he was one of the originators of the order and its first commander and that 3,000 prisoners eventually joined. Because of his involvement, Berry was supposedly "an especial object of hatred to this cowardly monster, the commandant." Berry's account must be taken with much salt. Among other things, he thought the cowardly monster was someone named Carrier. Presumably he confused Johnson with the provost marshal of prisoners, Andrew Caraher. Berry did preserve the badge of the order, however, and he used it on the frontispiece of his memoir.[12]

The two prison diarists were not happy about the enlistments either. Rogan wrote, "This is the saddest day of all the days of my prison life. 15 men deserted us and take up arms against our cause. Oh, how depraved the present generation are become. Self, home, parents, dear wife, and children are abandoned for the sake of a few oz. of meat and bread—God forgive." Dillon recorded that "the number gone out [to the calf pen] up to this time will probably reach 1,800, a very large number of traitors." Dillon also accused Johnson of forcing prisoners into the ranks of the enemy: "the Yankee officers say that they will have another 800 or reduce our rations yet more. . . . There is no doubt but Lincoln holds on to us for the diabolical purpose of starving as many as possible into the ranks of his army."[13]

The defection of hundreds of their comrades was not the only affliction the prisoners suffered that fall. At almost the same moment the recruiting began, another indignity, one that struck at the very roots of the Confederate cause, was visited on the prisoners. The Emancipation Proclamation went into effect on 1 January 1863. Lincoln said that it was his government's intention to arm former slaves for service in the field. Edwin Stanton had already begun laying plans for black troops, and he hoped by the summer of 1863 to have 200,000 blacks under arms. But even Stanton lagged behind the field commanders: in yet another example of citizen soldiers making policy to suit themselves, several generals had been enlisting blacks for some time. While Benjamin Butler was signing up his Native Guards, an Illinois officer was blazing an even more visionary path in North Carolina: Brigadier General David Hunter was enlisting blacks and asking Stanton for 50,000 pairs of red pants, which he figured would be all the uniform his new soldiers would need. For good measure, Hunter declared all the slaves in his department free. Hunter not only thought blacks could serve, but that they must serve: when enlistments proved disappointing, Hunter swept the area and impressed blacks into his regiment. Lincoln annulled Hunter's enlistments and emancipation, but it was an idea whose time had come. In Kansas, acting on a new law that authorized the president to employ blacks to build trenches and perform similar duties, recruiting commissioner James Lane immediately began recruiting not black laborers, but black soldiers. He asked the War Department if there was any objection, but he did not wait for a reply.[14]

Lincoln's reservations were political. Sending former slaves in arms against their masters would enrage the South; some Northerners also took a dim view of the idea. On the other hand, the abolitionists would have no objections—indeed, Hunter and Lane were ardent abolitionists, and Governor John Andrew of Massachusetts yearned to get blacks into uniform. And, regardless of a Northerner's political persuasions, every black who enlisted was one more man toward a state's draft quota.

The blacks in Kansas and Carolina had not waited for the proclamation, nor had some of those in Illinois. Chicago's black community saw the war as a way to get the state's repressive Black Laws repealed, and black soldiers would be a powerful argument to that end. At the war's outbreak several companies organized and drilled, but the War Department would not allow Governor Yates to accept them. Not to be denied, some men, presumably rather light-skinned, enlisted in white Illinois regiments. One of these was Ford Douglas, a former slave and outspoken critic of slavery. Douglas enlisted in the 95th Illinois, where, according to his friend Mary Livermore: "his virtues, talents, and, above all, his fiery eloquence, gave him welcome. He was fraternized with as if he were a white man. Everybody respected him." Livermore may have gilded the lily a bit, but that Douglas was a member of the 95th is beyond doubt. After the Emancipation Proclamation, Chicago blacks could join organized regiments of what were called United States Colored Troops (USCT). In April 1863, recruiting rallies began in Chicago, but not for Illinois. Some 200 men signed up in Governor Andrew's pet regiment, the 54th Massachusetts, which would win fame at Battery Wagner in Charleston Harbor. Seeing these draft credits going to an eastern state, Yates renewed his cause and eventually recruited his own regiment of blacks, the 29th USCT.[15]

The black men who enlisted faced several problems unknown to their white counterparts. One was prejudice. Another was inequity. White soldiers received $13.00 a month plus a clothing allowance.

The blacks received $10.00, and the clothing allowance was deducted from this; nor would black recruits receive the Federal enlistment bounty. Far worse were the problems the blacks faced when they actually got to the front. Lincoln's effrontery had enraged the South, and Jefferson Davis promised to treat captured white officers of the colored troops as the leaders of servile insurrections. The black soldiers themselves would be returned to slavery, if ownership could be established, or sold into slavery, if free. In his report on the status of exchange, E. A. Hitchcock noted in November 1863, "In no single instance has the smallest evidence come to light tending to show that . . . any colored man employed as a soldier of the United States has been captured in the South and accounted for as a prisoner of war."[16]

Despite the inequities, some 180,000 black men took up arms. Nearly a thousand of these men were in the 108th USCT, recruited in Kentucky in the spring of 1864. They were commanded by Lieutenant Colonel John Bishop, who had enlisted as a sergeant in the 68th Illinois and been promoted to lieutenant. The 68th was only a three-month regiment and never saw combat, but based on his experience Bishop applied for the colonelcy of the 108th and was duly appointed.[17] Bishop's regiment was composed mostly of former slaves, although "some few were free men." Some of the men, including Nathan Shirley, were purchased from their owners, although the process was called "compensation" rather than purchase, and this process applied only to owners who could prove both ownership and loyalty to the Union. The owners also received the Federal bounty. The Cowherd family sent four men to the regiment. Woodford County, the ancestral home of the Bufords, also contributed some recruits. On their way through Illinois the regiment picked up a few free blacks, notably in Quincy; local historians would later claim these men were residents of Moline. Their patriotism must have been strong, because their lives were not easy. While still in Kentucky one man was shot and killed by an Indiana lieutenant for stealing apples from an orchard. Another private was killed by his own lieutenant for "insubordination." The private's precise offense was not deemed worthy of being noted. The regiment did garrison and guard duty for a few weeks, and in September 1864 it was ordered to Rock Island. The 108th replaced the 133rd Illinois, whose enlistment expired in September. The arrival of the black troops accomplished a rarity: it united everyone in the

River Bend in a single opinion. Nobody liked them. Danforth, honing his sarcasm, announced, "On Saturday morning, 980 'Free Americans of African Descent,' with their servants, arrived here from Louisville, carrying muskets and dressed in the uniform of the United States."[18]

The regiment arrived on 24 September 1864. Their trip from Louisville must have been difficult: three men went immediately to the guardhouse, and more than 60 reported sick. One man, 18-year-old farmer Isaac McMerkin, died the day after the regiment arrived. The paymasters docked his widow $17.50 for a musket and accoutrements the dying man had lost. The northern climate apparently did not agree with the Kentuckians: the sick list quickly grew to nearly 200, including one man, Clayborne Strauss, who would shortly be discharged for insanity. Strauss's exit was mercifully quick, compared to the ordeal another private endured.[19]

Ben Hord, a prisoner from Arkansas, many years later wrote an account of his time at Rock Island, especially his time in the guardhouse. Hord's account gilds many lilies. He spoke of a dungeon under the guardhouse, into which he was flung. In the dank and dark Hord found several other prisoners, including, according to a prisoner acting as Hord's host, "two Yankee deserters condemned to be shot and a crazy nigger that stands a good chance of going the same way."[20]

Of more than 20,000 people connected with the Barracks, Hord is the only one who ever mentioned the dungeon. The insane black man, however, existed. He was William Boyd of the 108th. Boyd, a 26-year-old farmer, had enlisted in Kentucky. There was nothing to distinguish him from the other thousand-odd former slaves he soldiered with. Shortly after coming to the Island, Boyd did distinguish himself, albeit in a less than exemplary fashion. By 7 November 1864, the day Hord came to the guardhouse, Boyd was already there. He had been originally confined on charges; by 9 November, the notation changed to "deranged." The nature of his derangement remains a mystery. Hord said that Boyd had "gone suddenly crazy while on post, and when the relief guard came around had fired into the squad, mortally wounding one of them." No records verify that this happened, but given the 108th's penchant for musket fire and the inept record keeping, it remains possible. Hord left the guardhouse after two days; Boyd stayed considerably longer. Eventually he regained his senses enough to be released and return to duty. By the middle of February, he was back, again listed as "deranged." Boyd led a peripatetic existence. The guardhouse evidently instilled some measure of calm in him, but every time he was released the air of freedom proved too much and back to the guardhouse he went.[21]

Finally Pearl Martin, the regimental surgeon, took a hand. Martin wrote the 108th's adjutant: "I have carefully examined the said William Boyd of Capt. Benton Tuttle's company and find him incapable of performing the duties of a soldier because of insanity. He has been insane since last August but not insane before enlistment to my knowledge." Tuttle, overlooking the implication that the army made men crazy, immediately applied to have Boyd committed to the Hospital for Insane Soldiers in Washington, where Boyd was forthwith sent. Behind him Boyd left a bill for two bayonets, a belt, and a scabbard, all of which he had lost "through neglect." Apparently insanity was no excuse for losing equipment.[22]

In a racist fashion, Hord confirmed Martin's suggestion that the army had made Boyd insane: "The case was by no means extraordinary . . . the negro was a weak-minded creature to start with . . . the violent and sudden change from slavery to a United States soldier, the change of climate, habits, etc., had evidently deranged his feeble mind." Regardless of the truth, Boyd went to the asylum, where he would remain for the rest of his enlistment.[23]

Two days after they arrived, the men of the 108th who felt up to it climbed the walls. The men in the bull pen greeted the arrival of the black regiment with universal horror. One prisoner told David Sears that the 108th contained three of his former slaves, and "it was more than he could stand to be guarded by his own niggers." Rogan dolefully reported, "8000 Southern men today are guarded by their slaves who have been armed by the tyrant." Rogan later noted, "Nigs all right," but by this he meant only that they had refrained from shooting anyone that day—he had been faithfully recording a litany of murders, woundings, and random shootings since the arrival of the 108th.[24]

The blacks liked shooting as much as the 133rd Illinois had, and whereas the latter's propensity could perhaps be ascribed to youthful exuberance, the new guards' tendency carried more sinister connotations. Minnich admitted that some few of the blacks "were good fellows, considerate, confining themselves to a strict discharge of their duty without any display of undue harshness." But Minnich could not remember a single one of these. Instead, the one guard he did distinctly remember "left the brutal impress of his brutal features stamped ineffaceably on my memory—a squat-built negro as black as any ever painted by nature's brush, low forehead, deep-set eyes, and the elongated jaw of a gorilla, a face denoting at once the low grade of mentality characteristic of the lowest type of the negro—a mere brute." According to Minnich, this man committed murder. During a coal shortage, a prisoner searching for fuel found a couple of tree limbs in the yard and picked them up. The guard noticed the man and "without warrant, authority, or cause, and in the most brutal manner possible, ordered the man to drop those limbs. . . . Clearly within his known rights, the man paid not the least attention, and the nigger repeated: 'Drop dem lim's, I say!' The man kept on, not heeding the order. When within a couple of paces of [his barrack], the nigger raised his rifle, took deliberate aim, and pulled the trigger. Shot through the spine, the poor fellow fell forward on his face in the snow motionless."[25]

The same guard shot another man a few days later, Minnich recorded, after which the prisoners took their grievances to Lieutenant Colonel Caraher. Surprisingly for a Federal, Caraher agreed with them, saying: "Well, men, you are right. I'll see that this man is taken out, and I promise you he will not come in here again." Unfortunately, Minnich's lurid account cannot be verified, since he named neither the man nor the date of the incident. But it is undeniable that the black troops climbed on the parapet and immediately began firing into the compound. During their first day on the walls they killed William Ford of Wood's Missouri battalion and wounded two other men. During the ensuing days they wounded two more and killed another. Even the 108th's own officers thought their men too prepared to shoot. Captain Matthew Kollock, officer of the day on 27 September, reported, "A shot fired at men that went out to work from 2d front without provocation as far as I can learn."[26]

Shot at and otherwise generally abused, the prisoners took umbrage and retaliated in about the only method available to them: they threw rocks. Rock throwing had actually begun during the summer when prisoners, for no apparent or recorded reason, began throwing stones at guards in the middle of the night. The pastime paled, and the barrage slackened until the 108th arrived, whereupon the prisoners again bombarded the parapet nightly for about two weeks.[27]

*D*uring the fall of 1864 the prisoners spent a great deal of their time seeking sustenance. Not only had the June ration cut reduced the food, but by issuing rations in bulk for ten-day periods, not to individuals but to each barrack, Johnson's commissary almost guaranteed that those prisoners with larger appetites would satisfy them at the expense of their weaker comrades. Far more important to the prisoners' health, however, was the August prohibition of the sutlers. With the sutler, a man could keep reasonably healthy on even the reduced ration. But without the sutler and with a constantly dwindling ration, hunger loomed large in the prisoners' vision.

The prisoners quite literally paid for their own keep. In October, Johnson added a staggering $24,600 to the prison fund. And the price was hunger—not a mere pang, but a constant craving, as E. Polk Johnson reported years later: "The rations continued to fall away in amount and deteriorate as to quality, and finally one meal a day, and a very small one at that, became the rule. The prisoners were hungry, not for a little while, but all the time." Polk Johnson was scarcely alone in his opinion: if there is one topic on which postwar accounts approach unanimity, it is that of hunger. Charles Wright wrote that from the June cut until the end of the war he and his fellows "were subjected to starvation and all its attendant horrors." "It was pitiful," noted Ben Hord. "Gaunt forms with the glare of wolfish hunger in their eyes, the very pictures of famine."[28]

H. G. Damon of the 2d Florida Infantry reported that his ration consisted of "1 loaf of bread so small it be easily squeezed into a pint cup, piece of beef, the length, width, and thickness of two fingers." Dillon also noted the rations, and his accounting, while less colorful than Damon's, is probably more accurate:

> 12 ounces of bread on an average per day—it was never more than 14 ounces and sometimes as low as 8 and 9 ounces, but as I said they will average 11 or 12 ounces—our meat remains the same: when cooked 4 or 5 ounces of fresh or 6 or 7 ounces of pickled beef three days in every ten—we will have 1 1/2 pts. hominy or rice for dinner— this is our whole amount of rations, less than half sufficient for us—I myself at the present am truly weak from hunger—my rations make me one small meal per day—I remain hungry all the time.

And the question of quantity aside, there was the question of quality. On this, too, the prisoners agreed: it was abysmal. Wright, still waxing eloquent, recalled: "The bread we received was made of corn meal, in loaves shaped like bricks, and about as hard. The salt beef had a most offensive odor. An orderly asked an officer of the prison to step into his barrack and smell the beef; he did so, but merely remarked he had often eaten worse. Depravity had reached its limit in his case, for he was doing violence to his stomach in even smelling that beef." Minnich agreed with Wright, noting that the beef was "sometimes, and often, green with age and odorous to a degree; and our ration of good white bread was changed to a square fourteen ounces of solid corn bread made of yellow corn with a taste of lye from too much soda or saleratus in it so strong that it made it unfit to eat." Of the bacon Minnich remarked that it was sometimes strong enough to "stand alone."[29]

It would have made little difference if all the food had been fresh; the ration itself was not designed to promote health. When the Sanitary Commission issued its report on the treatment of prisoners, the doctors went to great lengths to demonstrate the viability of the Federal ration. One of their points was that "it is necessary that the food of man should consist of a variety of substances, in order that the functions of the organism may be properly carried on; no fact in dietetics is better established than this." The doctors saw no incongruity between this statement and the ration itself, which they listed in the same report. The full ration was heavily weighted toward protein and starch, and the reduced ration even more so. Although the doctors said "fresh vegetables [are] furnished in large quantities," there is little evidence that this was consistently true anywhere in Hoffman's system. It was certainly not true at Rock Island in the fall of 1864.[30]

The short rations and the prohibition of the sutlers had seriously affected the functioning of the organisms in the yard. Of the eleven men who died of scurvy, five died in the two months of September and October 1864, despite the fact that scurvy patients were given potatoes. To avoid this fate men went into the calf pen, as Rogan noted, simply for bread and meat. A man dead of scurvy could serve neither the Confederacy nor the Union. Others volunteered for the work details, thus gaining a full ration and a wage. As John Kirby, a prisoner from Tennessee, said years after the war, "If not for detail service while in prison would have starved to death."[31]

They could, of course, give up their cause and go into the calf pen, where they would not only get enough to eat, but enough to throw back over the fence to their friends. Or they could go to work for the camp administration, constructing buildings, cutting roads, and clearing brush, thereby receiving not only a full ration but a wage as well. But for those who refused to work for the Yankee tyrant or join his army, not many alternatives remained. Some men took beef bones left from the rations and boiled them to a glutinous mass, crushing the unreduced bits of bone with their teeth. Others developed a taste for wild parsley that grew along the fence, begging the guards to pick the weed and hand it over the deadline.

Another dietary supplement was rats. It is a rare account from any prisoner that fails to mention this part of the bill of fare. Dillon reported, "Rats, owing to the way they have been hunted, are becoming scarce." Minnich explained the most efficient method of rat-catching: "All points of egress from under our barrack were carefully blocked, leaving only one exit beneath each window, and then men would station themselves at the window with a 'gig'; and if a rat stuck his head out, the gig would descend like a flash of lightning, and—well, sometimes overeagerness caused the hunter to miss, and then no rat stew for him." Some men caught rats not only for themselves but to supply the growing market for animal protein: "As our rations contracted the price of rats expanded until one could not be had for love or money." Most of the citizens could only suspect the hunger in the Barracks. The sutler Albert Dart, however, knew exactly how hungry the prisoners were, because he unwittingly contributed to the prisoners' diet.[32]

Although there was precious little he could sell to the prisoners in the bull pen, Dart still had the business of the recruits crowding the calf pen, and to reach their barracks he had to drive his wagon through the main yard. His bulldog was his constant companion until one day, while Dart's attention was occupied with peddling his wares to the newly made Union men, a squad of prisoners kidnapped the beast. Unable to find his dog, Dart returned to the city. The prisoners cooked Dart's pet that night and evidently enjoyed it a great deal, for when Dart returned the next day he found his dog's hide nailed to a tree, along with a note asking the authorities to "send in another dog."[33]

And other dogs were sent in, or captured. Dillon reported that at least three other canines became supper. But such delicacies as dog-meat were rare. Four dogs were not much for 6,000 prisoners. The rat supply fell off; Johnson put guards around the calf pen so the rain of food to the bull pen dried up; neither family nor friends could send in boxes; the sympathizing citizens of Rock Island City and Davenport were forbidden to send in delicacies. According to prisoners' accounts, the hunger grew as real and as threatening as the smallpox horror during the previous winter. But the smallpox epidemic had been an accident of mismanagement, and the hunger was at least in part an intentional infliction. In their accounts after the war, the prisoners reserved their most rancorous rhetoric for the subject of the rations.[34]

The ration cuts were, according to the prisoners, the intentional infliction of a "system of cold-blooded cruelty." Stanton and Johnson were no better than beasts. Indeed, according to J. W. Minnich, if Henry Wirz deserved to be hanged for his conduct at Andersonville in Georgia, then so did Johnson for his conduct at Rock Island. Another prisoner said Johnson and the other officers "committed this outrage on humanity for the sake of their commissions." In the absence of sufficient food and the abysmal quality of the available food, it was no wonder that "the dogs were missing."[35]

To a large degree, the prisoners had a point. Well-fed men do not hunt rats and dogs, and well-nourished men do not die of scurvy. But when they sat down to pen their accounts of the Barracks, the veterans let their remembered pangs cloud their judgment, and not one of them noticed a very curious anomaly in the records: the hungrier they got, the fewer of them died. Between June and November 1864, the time of the greatest hunger, the mortality dropped by 50 percent. By comparison, during the same period mortality at Camp Douglas quadrupled. That even fewer would have died had the rations not been reduced is probably true, but it is also moot. If Stanton's motive was to kill men by starvation, he failed. Adolphus Johnson, despite his reputation, kept the prisoners alive, if famished.[36]

The hunger, the humiliation of being guarded by former slaves, and perhaps the prospect of the coming winter spurred the prisoners to action. Escape from the Island had been a hobby; now it became an industry. During September and October 19 men made successful escapes, half the total for the entire history of the Barracks. One of these was Oscar Holland, who put on a Federal uniform and merely walked out the gates. Johnson surmised that Holland got his uniform from "some enlisted man of this garrison whose term of service is about to expire."[37]

For every successful escape there were a number of failures. Every man had his plan, it seemed, some haphazard, some intricate. Among the former was the flight of George Kern, the boy who swung under the surgeon's buggy and out the gates. Among the latter was the scheme of Ben Hord. Observing the prison routine, Hord noted that every morning details from each barrack carried the slop barrels through the gate to the river; each detail was accompanied by a guard. Inspiration flashed on the Rebel: "My idea was, disguised in a Yankee uniform, with a citizen's suit underneath, to take charge of a detail, march out with it, discard my uniform as soon as possible when safely outside, and in citizen's clothing the greatest danger would be past." Hord embarked upon elaborate preparations. A piece of pine board, inked and glazed with pencil, became a pistol; scraps cut from his boots became its holster. A coat stolen from a Yankee wagon driver became, laboriously and surreptitiously, Federal pants, "made without thimble or scissors, and much of the thread drawn from my old pants." When all was at last ready, Hord simply assumed authority over a slop detail that was conveniently awaiting an escort and marched his comrades out of the gate. All his careful preparations came to nothing, however, within a hundred yards of the gate, when a Federal captain noticed the newly made guard and challenged him. Hord went not to freedom but to the guardhouse.[38]

Disguise served a prisoner named Rowland no better than it had Hord. Rowland was still in the yard when the guards recognized him and exchanged his Federal uniform for a ball and chain. But disguise did work for two others: William Holt and William King disguised themselves as surgeons, bribed someone to provide them with surgeon's passes, and walked out the gate to freedom.[39]

Assembling uniforms and forging passes was both complicated and time consuming. Far easier and quicker for the prisoners, if more dangerous, was either to race from the deadline to the fence and burrow under like frenzied terriers or to drop into Reynolds's sewers and slither down to the river. Both schemes had their adherents. An unnamed prisoner tried the burrowing plan late in September and, when discovered, escaped death by pleading with the beat guard and relief corporal for leniency. The prisoner kept his life; the corporal lost his stripes. Three more men dug under on 3 October; five days later, yet another. Two days later an officer of the guard neglected to record a successful escape, perhaps out of embarrassment.

It was a rerun of the great June escape: ten men got out, and three eluded recapture. Colonel Johnson reported the escape to Hoffman. While he was at it he also took the opportunity to record his thoughts on the quality of the black troops:

> These men effected their escape by crossing the dead line and burrow-ing under the fence of the prison enclosure. The guard surrounding the prison since the advent of the colored troops at this depot, has been greatly increased (owing to their numerical strength) and with the addition of the prison being well lighted this escape can only be accounted for by the glaring negligence of the sentinels, which are composed of these troops; every pain is taken to instruct them in their duties by the officers who are at all times watchful and attentive. . . . I feel very insecure and fear they are likely to occur, so long as we must depend on this class of troops for guard duty.[40]

The black troops perhaps did not know much about their duties, but they did know how to make a dollar. James McClanahan of the 9th Tennessee bribed a private of the 108th to let him climb the fence. On the appointed night, according to Dillon, the guard shot him. Two of Minnich's friends failed to profit by McClanahan's ex-perience. They paid the bribe, built a makeshift ladder, and as they climbed the fence were greeted not by helping hands, but by flash-ing rifle muzzles.[41]

The most popular method for escape by far was the tunnel. When Reynolds had constructed the barracks he had raised the buildings two or three feet off the ground, which both provided ventilation and discouraged tunneling. But at the first breath of winter wind he had banked earth against all the barracks, thus enabling the tunnel-ers to work undetected. And they worked with a will: "Scarcely any barrack on either side was without a tunnel." Despite their popular-ity, tunnels were even less successful than other means of escape. One crew, industriously boring toward the river, found a ledge of rock barring the way. While they pondered alternatives, the guards discovered their work and put an end to their plans. Another tun-nel, this one on the south, was completed, and the escapees only waited for darkness before worming their way to freedom. But be-fore night fell a guard stepped on the thin crust of sod hiding the tunnel's egress and foiled the entire plan. Weather also exposed some of the tunnels, one being caved in by a heavy rain.[42]

By disguise, burrowing, climbing, and tunneling, the prisoners tried for freedom. Even when they failed they succeeded, for the attempts kept the guards busy, and those who got off the Island even for brief periods occupied provost guards and other troops in searching for them. That so many attempts failed was not entirely due to the prisoners' ineptitude or the haphazard nature of some of their plans; it was even less due to the diligence and perspicacity of the guards. It was due primarily to the fact that there were spies in the prison.

Some time during the early months of the prison's history, the provost marshal of prisoners called in a number of men, including a young soldier named Charlie Hemming. The provost told young Hemming and the others that if they would "report to him what was going on in the prison he would release them in a reasonable time." Hemming "was only a boy then, but when the proposition was made to him he declined so firmly and became so indignant that he was put in irons for three days and on bread and water. In prison and in irons he was true to his friends and his country." Hemming's loyalty was admirable. Or perhaps the price was too low. Freedom was worth a great deal, but in the early days the prisoners still cherished hope of exchange, and there were always the tunnels. Men like Charlie Hemming could hope for release without having to turn on their friends. Others, however, suffered fewer pangs of conscience at the idea of spying on their comrades. Then, too, Colonel Johnson raised the ante.[43]

On 29 January 1864, Hoffman had written to Johnson, "It is possible that by the employment of detectives among the prisoners you may be able to obtain information that may be useful to the Gov't or yourself in giving you notice of improper communications passing between the prisoners and ill disposed persons outside or in giving information of plans of escape and you are authorized if you can find a suitable man for the purpose among the prisoners, to pay him for such services according to their value out of the prison fund." Hoffman, never neglecting an opportunity to save a dollar, also said, "I do not think it advisable for you to pay by the month, but for each item of information according to its importance." The colonel took the hint: the prison fund accounts include vouchers to various prisoners for "services rendered exposing prisoners' plans for escape." The usual amount was $10.00. Rogan termed the spies "doves," and, although they undoubtedly prevented many escapes, they also sometimes amplified the plots they discovered, to increase their salaries. Rogan called one dove report of a general outbreak "moonshine."[44]

One of the most despised doves was James C. Cooper. Cooper received the usual $10.00 in November 1864, "for exposing prisoners' plans, etc." Unfortunately for Cooper, his fellow prisoners and former friends found out who he was, causing Johnson to recommend to Hoffman that Cooper be released because "his life is endangered by being confined with the prisoners." Another dove did not need Johnson's recommendation—he reported a tunnel, the diggers discovered his identity, and "the rapidity with which he went out of the prison could not have been taken with a stop watch. He must have had a vision of 'death on a pale horse and hell following after,' for not less than a thousand men were close upon his heels."[45]

The prisoners had no way of knowing it, but there were men outside the prison trying to help them escape. In March 1864, Confederate President Jefferson Davis "determined to send into Northern territory some Confederate officer who should especially undertake to effect the release of Confederate prisoners." The man sent was Captain T. Henry Hines, who had been captured with John Hunt Morgan and had escaped with him. Hines was to go to Canada, collect the escaped prisoners who had made their way there, contact sympathetic Northerners, and descend on the prison camps in the Midwest.[46]

Brave Hines might have been; an agent provocateur he was not. Nor were the thousands of disaffected Northerners he meant to recruit much good at keeping secrets. Many of these men belonged to an organization called the Order of American Knights (OAK), which later changed its name to the Sons of Liberty. There was also the Golden Circle, another subversive organization. Yet another organization, concentrated in Missouri, called itself the Corps de Belgique, because of the supposed involvement of a Belgian consul. The purpose of all these organizations was to form a Northwestern Confederacy, to overthrow the government, or both. In either event the result would be humiliation of the Federal government and an end to war.[47]

Federal authorities were on to the schemes almost from their beginnings. J. P. Sanderson, the provost marshal for the army's Department of Missouri, spent the spring of 1864 sending spies to ferret out the disloyals. He collected their reports and sent them to

William Rosecrans, the department commander. Sanderson's most active agent was Edward Hoffman (apparently no relation to William Hoffman), who spent months crisscrossing the Midwest and upper South, infiltrating the various cells of subversion and submitting long and detailed reports on the heinous plots he uncovered.[48]

The reports of Hoffman and the others read like a badly written spy novel. Despite the occasional close call, reported in breathless detail, the agents had absolutely no trouble penetrating the lairs of the disloyals, and they sent Sanderson complete reports of rituals, signs, creeds, and even membership lists. Indeed, secrecy seemed at a large discount among the conspirators. By September 1863, their existence was nearly public knowledge, and in Rock Island the *Union* warned its readers "to beware the Golden Circles."[49]

Given the loose security, Captain Hines should have had no trouble in contacting and organizing the armed hordes of Illinois. Unfortunately, the captain had far more trouble finding the conspirators than did Edward Hoffman. While Hoffman roved the country tracking down traitors, Hines met with Clement Vallandigham, a former Ohio congressman who had been sent south for traitorous activities and had then made his way to Windsor, Canada, across from Detroit. Vallandigham was reputedly the Grand Commander of the OAK, and he assured the captain that more than 80,000 Illinoisians, "invariably armed," awaited the call. Windsor hosted many clandestine meetings that summer, while Hines and others laid plans to liberate the prisoners and rise against the government. Hines was to lead the action at Camp Douglas, and Captain John Castleman would open the gates at Rock Island. Vallandigham was to return to Ohio and raise his voice against the government, which would be the signal for the uprising. One of the planners, a Mr. Thompson of Mississippi, enthused, "There are some choice spirits enlisted in this enterprise." The choice spirits, however, had weak flesh. As matters progressed the leaders began to realize the gravity of their plan. While Hines and Castleman urged instant action, the others kept postponing the date. Moreover, the two men had great difficulty in locating the armed legions of disaffected citizens that Vallandigham said awaited only the word, nor could the captains provide effective leadership even for the few whose hearts were in it. George St. Leger Grenfel, an English soldier who had thrown in his lot with the Confederacy, came to Chicago ready for rebellion but "could not find anybody, either Hines or

Marmaduke, who could tell him what to do. He afterward [said] that all they had to do was to go to South Illinois and drill Copperheads." Grenfel, disenchanted, instead took the opportunity to go hunting for two months.[50]

Faced with such problems, the plot's leaders repeatedly changed and postponed the plan, until finally the date was set for 29 August 1864, the day the Democratic convention was to open in Chicago. Instead of a simultaneous rising all across the Midwest, Hines would have to content himself with liberating Rock Island and cutting the telegraph wires in Chicago. Even this reduced plan came to naught. The convention opened, and all the prisoners remained right where they were, without a sign that anything was afoot, and the wires continued to hum. Hines and his cohorts, noting the utter lack of support from the citizens, "deemed it wise to leave Chicago." The aborted conspiracy did cause some consternation nonetheless. The district commander in Illinois, Brigadier General Halbert Paine, somehow learned of the plan and only a few days before the convention he ordered Johnson and the commandant at Camp Douglas to "report the number of prisoners in their custody; whether there is any probability of an attempt to rescue them . . . whether there are indications that acts of violence will be perpetrated . . . and, if so, at what time & upon what pretext."[51]

Hines was nothing if not persistent. The next date set was 8 November 1864, election day, and again the plan called for the liberation of only one camp, this time Douglas in Chicago. Freed of the stockade, the prisoners would "lay waste and destroy the city of Chicago, Ill." This scheme also went awry, thanks to the fortuitous intervention of a Federal spy, who came to Chicago in pursuit of a criminal and instead twigged to the plot of Hines and his friends. The unnamed spy alerted Colonel B. J. Sweet, then commanding at Douglas, and Sweet arranged a police sweep that caught up a hundred conspirators and cartloads of weaponry just hours before the planned liberation. The discovery put Chicago in a panic: "The city was horrified, and none knew certainly that the storm would not yet burst. Husbands and fathers shuddered at the thought of the city given up to the brutal control of that mob of eight thousand prisoners and their more brutal allies."[52]

Chicagoans were not the only ones shuddering. News of the aborted conspiracy found its way down the wires to the River Bend. Nathaniel Baker, fearing the prisoners on the Island were about to make a break, called out the militia in Davenport. When the papers chided him, Baker took it in good grace, saying that "he didn't want other Iowa cities such as Keokuk to have all the fun of military scares, and so treated the citizens to one of his own." Baker's source of information for the rumored plot was probably Johnson. The colonel warned his troops on 6 November 1864 that there may be a break and the following day the prisoners were all confined to quarters. The next day, Baker, snapping under the suspense, called out the militia. When the news of the Chicago plot reached the Island there was no further excitement, although the men did sleep on their arms on election night. Baker doubtless would have liked to have had the cannon-bearing barge Hoffman had earlier ordered for the Barracks. Unfortunately, the barge was stuck downriver in Keokuk, because of low water. And Johnson, not so given to alarm as Baker, did not even want it. He told Hoffman that it should remain at Keokuk or be returned to St. Louis.[53]

All of this passed unnoticed by the men in the yard. Neither of the prison diarists, Dillon and Rogan, noted anything amiss. Of the prisoners who later wrote of their experience in the River Bend, few mention a conspiracy to overpower the guards, and in those cases the timing does not match that of the adventures of Hines and Castleman. In any event, as Minnich noted, "Any such attempt must have resulted in a useless expenditure of blood and have proved abortive." Neither did Johnson mention any conspiracies or plots that fall. He had other things to occupy his mind, and he spent the weeks before the abortive Northwest Conspiracy trying to relieve the crowded conditions inside the compound. He would spend the weeks after it defending himself. In between, he had to take time out for yet another inspection. This time the inspector was not some spy for Hoffman or the Medical Department, but a real celebrity, by the name of Hooker.[54]

In the spring of 1863 Joseph Hooker had commanded the Army of the Potomac and prepared a brilliant plan to destroy Robert E. Lee's army and end the war. Unfortunately for Hooker, Lee paid no attention to the plan, soundly thrashed Hooker's men at a cross-roads called Chancellorsville, and then immediately invaded Pennsylvania. Lincoln and Stanton disliked both Hooker's results and his attitude and, when Hooker asked to be relieved, snapped up his offer. Hooker came west, and in November 1863 he directed the battle of Lookout Mountain in Chattanooga. When another general was promoted over him, Hooker again asked to be relieved and was assigned to command the military department of which Illinois was a part. One of his first actions was to visit the Island. He arrived toward the end of October 1864, while Johnson was busily enlisting prisoners. A crowd met him at the station. Hooker was a genuine hero for his battle in Chattanooga, memorialized as "The Battle Above the Clouds," despite the fact Ulysses Grant had said it was more a skirmish than a real battle. The citizens paid no attention to Grant: Hooker's stock was high, and all were "anxious to catch a glimpse of the man who drove the Rebels off Lookout Mountain [a number of whom now resided on the Island] and who planned the battle of Gettsyburg." Hooker had had nothing to do with Gettysburg, but that was overlooked in the frenzy.[55]

After spending the night at the Island City Hotel, Hooker went to the Barracks. He reviewed the troops and then entered the compound to review the prisoners. According to a witness, Hooker's "keen eye scanned each man as he raised his hat and said, 'Young men, I am very sorry for you. I hope our differences will be settled, so you can all return safely home again.'" According to one of the guards, even the prisoners "were anxious to get a look at the old hero, and they cheered him heartily when he addressed them." Whether the half-starved men in the yard cheered the man who had put many of them there remains in doubt. Neither Dillon nor Rogan even noted Hooker's visit, nor do any postwar accounts mention Fighting Joe Hooker's words of wisdom and the resultant cheering.[56]

Such interruptions as Hooker's visit could not long distract Johnson from the biggest problem he faced in the fall of 1864. Since June, the compound at the Barracks had never held fewer than 8,000 men, and as October opened nearly 8,200 prisoners crowded the yard. The prison had been designed for more than 10,000, but the design had not anticipated events. Two barracks, used as a pest hospital during the smallpox epidemic, remained unoccupied. The calf pen and administrative offices occupied another 18. On paper, none of this posed much of a problem: at 120 men to a barrack, the available buildings offered space for 9,600 men. But paper had little to do with reality.

The men who had volunteered for the Federal army numbered almost 1,800, but this represented only the number the surgeons passed and the mustering officer subsequently accepted. More than 4,000 actually volunteered for Uncle Sam. It is not surprising that the surgeons rejected more than half the volunteers; life on the Island was not calculated to keep a man fit for combat. Johnson's problem was that no matter how he arranged things he could not cram 4,000 men into the 18 barracks of the calf pen, nor could he leave the rejected volunteers in the bull pen, because Hoffman had stipulated that the men who applied to take the allegiance oath must be "treated with as much kindness as possible. Must be placed in barracks to themselves and to be allowed certain favors." The same stipulation applied to the volunteers, Johnson thought. Besides, even though the prisoners' postwar accounts claim that nobody blamed a starving man when he reported for Federal service, those accounts were written long after the fact, and not everyone in the bull pen could be counted on to treat a traitor with forbearance. Johnson had to do something with the 2,200 men the army refused to take.[57]

Johnson remembered Judge Pettis's interpretation of Lincoln's recruitment order and came to the solution of his problem: he would let them all go. He immediately proceeded to release every rejected volunteer. The gates opened and a flood tide of sick and disabled men hobbled out of the yard, over the bridge, and into Rock Island City. Until now, releases for all reasons had totaled only 467; in the single month of October 1864, Johnson released 2,294. That this was a mistake of the first magnitude would shortly become apparent, but at the time Johnson was blithely unaware of his transgression.[58]

As usual, however, patriotic citizens felt it incumbent upon themselves to report Johnson's actions to William Hoffman, who took a dim view of the colonel's new policy. On 27 October 1864 Hoffman telegraphed Johnson, demanding to know by what authority he had released these men. Johnson replied the same day with a detailed explanation of Lincoln's original order, which, said Johnson, had stipulated that recruits would be accepted only if they were of foreign or Northern birth. Pettis had intimated that volunteers who were "rejected by the examining surgeon would be promptly released," and Johnson had included this provision in his circular to the prisoners. When enlistments proved disappointing and Pettis prevailed on the president to remove the birth restrictions, Johnson made the assumptions that the "prompt release" clause was still in effect and that it applied to everybody. Colonel Johnson told Hoffman, "It was supposed by me that you were aware of all these facts."[59]

Hoffman could not do much about any of this, nor was his displeasure assuaged by Johnson's report, in reply to a further telegram, detailing the releases: 54 men on 24 October, 69 on the 25th, 63 on the 26th. And Johnson included a reminder in his report that these men had all been "released by order of the President." Hoffman could do nothing but stew about this end run around his authority. J. B. Danforth, on the other hand, was ecstatic. He welcomed the released men with open arms and poised pen. He was about to make things very difficult for Adolphus Johnson.[60]

CHAPTER SIX

"Had I the Power"

Ait the end of October 1864, the Barracks occupied J. B.'s mind a great deal, on two counts. One was a minor thing, dispatched in a paragraph on Halloween: a local man, C. Speidel, had done a lithograph of the Island, and J. B. thought it his duty to help increase sales. The artwork showed "Rock Island Prison Barr'ks and surroundings, which makes a very pretty and useful picture." The second matter was far more important, although at the beginning it seemed a single paragraph would handle this, too. When Johnson released nearly 2,300 men from the prison, he was doing more than relieving the crowding in the prison. He was providing Danforth with so many witnesses. As the tide of rejected and released recruits flowed into the city, Danforth spoke with them and reported, "Much complaint is made by them of the short fare in the prison."[1]

The editor had had access to prison officers off and on since before the Barracks opened. He had also had the opportunity to speak with prisoners released on oath. But the men released in October 1864 were a different breed: these were not Federal officers who perhaps had reason to gloss over prison conditions, nor were they men who were simply tired of the war and wanted to go home. The October men had volunteered for active service in the enemy's army—they were repentant Rebels who had come home and who would have no reason to lie about conditions in the compound. On Friday, 18 November, Johnson released another lot of rejected recruits. Danforth latched on to them immediately, and he spent the weekend preparing what would prove to be some of the finest editorial work of his long career. On 21 November, he spoke.

He began with a few paragraphs explaining the difference between a Rebel and a Union man; in the yard a man was either one or the other. He noted that the released men were no longer Rebels and that he had talked to some of the "newly made Union men." The ground thus prepared, Danforth attacked:

They all agree that the prisoners are kept on too short fare, in fact they are starved down to barely a living point; that they are allowed no vegetables, and only a small 8 ounce loaf of bread and piece of salt meat about as big as your two fingers for the whole 24 hours. Under this scanty and unsuitable fare they are pining away, becoming diseased, and fast filling the hospitals and grave yards. Under this treatment, that dreadful scourge, the scurvy, has made its appearance among them. . . . It is a shame that in this enlightened age of the world, white men, our own countrymen, should be confined in a pen, fed on such scanty and improper food, and reduced down almost to starvation point, until disease and death ensue. And more shameful still that, in a country like this, where vegetables are so plenty . . . that the scurvy should be produced for want of these vegetables. . . . There is no excuse for this deliberate torture of human beings, and the hand that does it or the heart that prompts it is hardened against the common instincts of humanity.

Not only does the government refuse to furnish these unfortunate people with proper food and clothing, but the friends of the prisoners are denied the opportunity to do so for them. There is scarcely a prisoner in the Barracks who has not some relative or friend within the Union lines, Union men, who would gladly send them proper food and clothes. . . . But even this is refused by those in charge of them. We do not know where the censure should fall for this inhumanity, nor do we care. Whoever is guilty of it is guilty of a great crime. Most likely it should fall upon the administration, and upon Mr. Lincoln as its head. . . . But whoever is guilty of this deliberate torture and death ought to be execrated by all mankind. . . . We are abundantly able to furnish all they really need, of food and clothes, to make them reasonably comfortable, and yet those in charge refuse to do so, or to allow others to do so. The case, then, becomes one of deliberate and willful torture ending, in many cases, with the death of the poor, helpless victims. Something should be done, at once, to stop the ravages of scurvy, and to render the condition of the prisoners so comfortable as to preclude the idea of deliberate and willful torture.[2]

This diatribe had an unexpected result: it moved Adolphus Johnson to speak. For a year Johnson had borne his troubles in nearly perfect silence. But the colonel had had enough. Although Danforth seemed to put the blame on Lincoln and Stanton, there remained that annoying implication: "who ever is guilty." If not the administration of the nation, then the administration of the camp certainly must be to blame, and Johnson had no intention of letting the matter rest there. It was time to answer the barrage of criticism.

When he sat down to reply to Danforth's attack, Johnson doubtless meant to write a reasoned refutation of the editor's fiery rhetoric. The colonel was not a man given to emotional displays. His correspondence up to November 1864 singularly lacks any emotional context, except for annoyance at the quality of his troops. He appears, in fact, cold and distant. He had suffered much at the hands of the citizens, the prisoners, Kingsbury, Hoffman, and Danforth; he had borne it largely in silence. At the outset, his reply was exactly what he intended—a calm, logical denial of nearly everything Danforth had written:

> In your issue of the 21st inst. I notice an article on the treatment of prisoners of war at this depot. Up to the present time I have passed unnoticed the numerous erroneous articles that have appeared in the papers . . . but in this case I will deviate from the established rule, and give your article . . . the notice it seems to merit. . . .
>
> Your assertions are founded on what you term a talk with several "newly made Union men," and it would be difficult to imagine it possible to put together a greater amount of error and misrepresentation in the same space.
>
> You . . . give large numbers the scurvy, and deliberately and willfully torture them to death, and call for fearful judgement on the guilty parties. Did you not blush when you published in your issue of the 22nd inst. the official report of the deaths of prisoners at this depot, *amounting to three (3) for the previous week*? That report was a scorching answer to your whole article.

Johnson then listed the official ration and continued:

The bread and meat issue is 2 ounces per day less than is issued to the troops. The prisoners have no labor to perform while the troops are worked hard. When prisoners are worked they do so voluntarily, and receive additional rations and also pay. Hundreds of dollars are expended every month to purchase tobacco to distribute among them. They have always been allowed to receive necessary clothing from their relatives, and scarcely a day passes without a large number of the most needy are brought out to receive clothing furnished by the government. . . . [T]he government furnishes more clothing to destitute prisoners in one day than friends do in two months.

The above issue of rations is made to the letter. Each company of prisoners receives ten days at a time, in bulk, they having the entire control of the distribution among themselves, and the few Union prisoners in each company are at the mercy of a Rebel majority.

Did it ever occur to you that while you can spend the necessary time to pen an article like that . . . that your files may be searched in vain for the smallest editorial paragraph in condemnation of the rebel authorities for the brutal treatment of our men in their hands?

You seem to be in doubt as to whom belongs the treatment of prisoners at this depot. I will enlighten you. The treatment of them here, and all issues to them, are made strictly in accordance with orders from the War Department.[3]

This would have been an excellent place for Johnson to put down his pen. He had stretched the truth a bit in places; for instance, "hundreds" spent monthly on tobacco does not match the available prison fund vouchers. Also, the idea of friends sending in clothes was sometimes true, sometimes not. But on the whole, he had explained the policies at the Barracks, ascribed responsibility for them, and defended his actions. But Johnson continued writing, and as he continued his anger poured onto the page:

I will embrace this opportunity to state that by a perusal of the columns of the *Argus* for the past year, I am enabled to form a correct opinion of your position, and I have no objection to give you, in plain terms, what would be my action in regard to the treatment of prisoners in my charge, if discretionary power rested with me: In the first place, instead of placing them in fine comfortable barracks, with three large stoves in each, and as much coal as they can burn, both day and night, I would place them in a pen with no shelter but the heavens, as our poor men were at Andersonville; instead of giving them the same quality and nearly the same quantity of provisions that the troops on duty receive, I would give them as near as possible the same quantity and quality of provisions that the fiendish rebels give our men; and instead of a constant issue of clothing to them I would let them wear their rags, as our poor men in the hands of the rebel authorities are obliged to do; or, in other words, had I the power, strict retaliation would be practiced by me.

Again, if discretionary power rested with me I would arrest and confine the known sympathizers with the rebellion, residing in Rock Island and Davenport, and quite a large number would be quickly added to our list of prisoners, and those communities would be relieved from a more dangerous element than open rebels in arms.

And here Johnson did stop, adding only a request that would prove completely gratuitous: "You will oblige me by publishing this communication entire." It would also prove that he had gone on about two paragraphs longer than he should have.[4]

Danforth could not get the colonel's letter into print fast enough, and he did indeed print the "communication entire." He had provoked Johnson into delivering up himself, the Barracks, and the entire Lincoln administration to the altar of Democratic politics. Johnson's own words confirmed everything J. B. had said for a year, and by the time he was finished the letter would also confirm precisely what Johnson had been trying to deny. Merely printing the letter would not do—J. B. included his own answers to Johnson's assertions, nearly two columns' worth. "We are gratified," he began, "that Colonel Johnson has officially contradicted the report of the newly made 'Union men' recently released." Danforth was gratified because the contradiction gave him the opportunity to turn Johnson's own words against him. Although Johnson outlined the rations, he did not address the issue of scurvy, which Danforth had raised in his original article. And, in J. B.'s world, silence meant assent: "By his silence on this point, we may regard it as fact that the scurvy exists." The colonel did not deny that relatives were prohibited from sending in vegetables, so "that part of our article may also be taken as confessed."[5]

As J. B. noted sadly, Johnson had changed: "We have also had recent occasion to speak, in high terms . . . of the humanity of Col. Johnson, in the treatment of prisoners, and we know of several cases where he . . . has taken a common-sense view of matters, and shown a feeling of humanity creditable alike to him as a soldier, and as a fellow-countryman of those under his care. But we do now 'blush' to say that his letter shows that he has sadly changed in that respect." Then Danforth issued an astoundingly accurate prophecy: "At his request we publish it [Johnson's letter] 'entire,' but we think he will live to see the day when he would thank us if we had expurgated from it . . . a wish on his part for revenge. . . . We think he will regret that he said, 'if discretionary power rested with him, he would place them in a pen with no shelter but the heavens, and let them wear their rags.'"6

After yet another attack on Lincoln, Danforth wrote: "We think we know our duty as a public journalist, and we propose to pursue it, without intimidation from anybody. The acts of Mr. Lincoln, and of all public officers, Col. Johnson included, are proper subjects for fair and impartial criticism, and in such a manner we propose to allude to them whenever . . . the public good requires it. . . . [W]e regret, on his account, that his letter had not been couched in less objectionable phrases." Having wrapped himself in the Constitution's cloak and Johnson in a shroud of pity, Danforth turned to other matters. There was nothing left to say. The politics of prisoners had been laid bare. Regardless of the truth, the reputation of Rock Island Barracks had been established.7

As the winter wore on, one of the most pressing problems at the Barracks concerned not the prisoners, but the recruits in the calf pen. The idea of the calf pen had been to separate the newly made Union men from the unrepentant Rebels and to offer the former an improvement over the bull pen. As so often happened on the Island, however, the reality differed from the concept. Although the men had volunteered for service and been accepted, no mustering officer appeared to swear them in or organize units. They remained cooped up, except for the occasional work detail, and suffered in an administrative limbo. At the same time that Danforth was composing his editorial bombardment, Johnson was writing to the provost marshal general, pointing out the plight of his recruits. The calf pen, Johnson wrote, "is close and tiresome and the men are becoming dispirited. . . . As they are no longer prisoners of war, clothing cannot be issued to them from the prisoners portion, and as they are not organized clothing cannot be issued by the Qr. Master. Consequently these cold days and nights find them shivering around the barrack stoves which are kept red hot in order that they do not freeze. These men are to be pitied."[8]

Johnson did not exaggerate the case. The recruits' clothing was so poor that the ragged, half-naked men in the bull pen actually tried to throw clothes over the fence to the men they considered traitors. One man, Robert Butler, was killed for his humanity. The guard, Eli Arnett of the 108th, stated during a hearing that he was "only carrying out the orders I received." The shirt Butler had thrown fell inside the deadline; when Butler stepped across to retrieve it, Arnett shot him.[9]

A few weeks later Johnson wrote another letter, echoing his earlier complaint, and noting, "I have done all in my power to better their condition, but as they were recruited under the direction of the Provost Marshal General, I have no discretionary power in the matter." In desperation, Johnson had already done the only thing he could. He had issued an order to his quartermaster in October: "Owing to the exigencies of the case [you] will sell to the enlisted men recruited from the prisoners of war at this post four hundred and forty-six (446) U.S. blankets at the Government price." The recruits doubtless wondered what sort of government they had signed up with, that would not distribute blankets unless they could pay for them.[10]

The confinement wore on the recruits, and a number of them found their way to the guardhouse. Several also found their way to the graveyard. F. M. Sympson died of a gunshot wound in November, another victim of the 108th's free-fire policy. Because he was not technically a prisoner, his death was not documented in the prison records; because he had not been mustered into a Federal unit, no strength return lists his death. The only record is the hospital register. Sympson was taken to the garrison hospital, rather than the prison wards, but this was cold comfort. It would have been even colder comfort for Sympson to know that, while he was not a prisoner, he had been a Rebel, and he, like several other Rebel recruits who died, was buried with the blacks in a separate section of the garrison cemetery.[11]

It was around Thanksgiving that Sympson was lowered into the ground beside men he might in former times have owned as chattels. The prisoners who buried him had little to hope for as

Christmas 1864 approached. Union General George Thomas at Nashville soundly thrashed Confederate John Hood's Army of Tennessee, ending the last Confederate offensive of the war. Having cut a 60-mile-wide swath of destruction through Georgia, William Sherman captured Savannah and presented it to Lincoln as a Christmas present. In Virginia, there was little action, but Ulysses Grant needed little action—he needed only to strangle the life out of Robert E. Lee's army, which he did with unrelenting pressure.

In the River Bend prisoners continued to die, but in far fewer numbers. In January 1865, only 108 men died, less than half the number who had died in January 1864. There was no smallpox to speak of, and although scurvy was present, it no longer killed so many. Nor was the weather quite as severe as the previous year. In fact, the river froze and thawed so frequently and unpredictably that an unusual number of teams crashed through the ice, causing Danforth to notify his readers, "On the ice between this city and Davenport *twelve dead horses* are to be seen—free of charge." Despite the milder weather, the men were just as cold, because there were periodic coal shortages. During the first winter Captain Reynolds had contracted for coal, and when the bad weather came early he had had the foresight to lay in extra stocks. Anticipating the second winter Reynolds's successor, Captain B. F. Reno, had in July started casting around for a coal contract. Nobody was willing to sell at less than seven dollars a ton because, as mine owner R. R. Cable put it, of "the great uncertainty of the cost of production and the risk of casualties to our mines and railroad bridges." This was fluff: the mine owners in the River Bend had long been known for their gouging skills, and Cable was merely applying the habit to the government. In Cable's defense, however, it should be noted that his labor costs were exorbitant. The war had driven miners' wages as high as nine dollars a day.[12]

Coupled with the coal shortage was a straw shortage. Bedding straw had been a problem since the day the Barracks opened. The problem, however, was not a lack of straw—some of the garrison companies drove their wagons out to the country and purchased straw for themselves. The problem lay with the quartermasters. Johnson told one of his captains that the quartermasters were not paying attention to their duties: "the wants of the command have been secondary and have not been properly attended to."[13]

Despite problems with coal, straw, and short rations, the decrease in the death rate bespoke conditions much improved over the first winter. But the men were still in prison and still far from home and friends. For William Dillon, it was the third Christmas of the war in captivity. In 1862 he had been in Camp Douglas; in both 1863 and 1864, he had been on the Island. As he morosely noted, "This is a gloomy picture of my campaigns." Rogan, too, had sad thoughts. On Christmas Eve he wrote, "Hopes have been entertained that I would be at home tomorrow." In Rogan's case, though, his sorrow was somewhat mitigated by Dart, who on Christmas Day provided Rogan and the other clerks, who were once again living outside the compound, with "mince pies and a goose . . . which we had well prepared and enjoyed much."[14]

Dart could afford to be generous to the men in the office, because Johnson had given him a lucrative Christmas present: for the four days before Christmas Dart was allowed to sell flour to the prisoners. Dart was no doubt glad of the business, since he had sold nothing to the men in the bull pen since August, and he took advantage of his monopoly. At the time, flour sold for $2.50 per quarter-barrel in the city. Dart laid in a mountain of flour, drove his wagon into the yard, and blithely announced that the prisoners could buy all they wanted at $4.00. According to J. W. Minnich, the stalwarts in the yard would have nothing to do with this scheme: "and great was his surprise when he found he could not dispose of a single sack among the hundreds of hungry men that crowded around his wagons. . . . I heard one man tell him: 'I have money and could buy all I want, so have others; but there are hundreds of others who cannot at that price, and I won't set the price.'" Dart, wrote Minnich, "communed with himself for a bit, then turned slowly toward the lower gate, and drove out, followed by hundreds of hungry eyes." If this story is true it must have occurred on 21 December, the first day Dart was allowed into the yard. A single temptation could be resisted, but continued temptation proved too much even for men loyal to their cause, and on the next day, according to Dillon, Dart sold flour as fast as he could fling sacks off his wagon, raking in between $2,000 and $3,000 for his trouble. Dillon's tale is confirmed by the prison fund accounts: for November, Dart's sutler tax was a paltry $46.38. For December, it soared to $261.84. At a 5 percent tax, this means the grocer sold more than $5,000 worth of goods to the prisoners.[15]

In addition to the largesse to Dart, Johnson gave himself a small, albeit spiteful, Christmas present. Danforth, ever the optimist, assumed that his attacks on Johnson in November had not hurt his relationship with the colonel. Early in December, as he had been doing for months, he requested the death lists. Johnson was quick to reply: "Respectfully returned to J. B. Danforth Jr., Ed. Rock Island Argus, with . . . the remark that this office has no authority to furnish the list of deaths occurring among prisoners of war at this post except to the Comy. Gen. of Pris. It is suggested he obtain the information requested from 'newly made union men.'" For the moment, Danforth let this pass.[16]

Conditions continued to improve. The waterworks at long last went into operation in January, providing water at a rate of 400 gallons a minute, more than enough for flushing the new sewers and for drinking. It had been a long wait, and all through the fall Andrew Caraher's reports to Johnson of prison conditions had included the notation "sinks—not good." By the third week of January, however, the water flowed. It was a welcome gift, but unknown to the prisoners, the authorities of the Union and the Confederacy were working on an even greater gift.[17]

On 10 August 1864, the same day Hoffman abolished the sutlers at his camps, Major General Daniel Sickles, a former corps commander who had lost a leg at Gettysburg, wrote to President Lincoln, suggesting that supplies be sent from the North to the Federal prisoners held in the South. As Sickles noted, "The condition of our officers and soldiers in the hands of the enemy is represented to reach the extreme limit of destitution and suffering." Sickles said the Confederates would be amenable to such supplies, inasmuch as the South was "without the means to supply clothing, medicines, and other needful supplies even to their own troops."[18]

Calling this "an old and very painful subject," Lincoln immediately turned it over to Stanton, who in turn bucked it to E. A. Hitchcock, the exchange commissioner. Hitchcock thought little of the idea, because when supplies had been sent earlier "the Rebel guards used the supplies before the faces of our imprisoned soldiers, and what they did not use, or much of it, was allowed to spoil in the boxes under the very eyes of our people." Still, Hitchcock was not without heart, and he allowed that, despite its pitfalls, "the experiment might be tried." Hitchcock's Confederate counterpart, Judge Robert Ould, agreed, although it took him five weeks to come to a conclusion. Ould finally said: "I see no very great objection to allowing the enemy to furnish plain clothing to the Federal prisoners in our hands. It is not like the case of furnishing luxuries." Some isolated and haphazard arrangements had already been made, but Ould soon suggested that the entire matter be systematized. He wrote to John Mulford, Hitchcock's assistant: "I propose that each government shall have the privilege of forwarding, for the use and comfort of its prisoners as are held by the other, necessary articles of food and clothing." Ould also sent a copy of his letter directly to Edwin Stanton, who referred the whole matter to Ulysses Grant.[19]

The only problem with this scheme was the dearth of supplies in the South. If the Confederacy could neither feed its own troops nor care for the Union prisoners in its hands, how could it possibly hope to send food and clothing to its soldiers held in Hoffman's camps? This obstacle was overcome by the simple expedient of sending not supplies but cotton to the North, where it could be sold and the proceeds invested in supplies for the suffering Confederate prisoners. Brigadier General William Beall, a prisoner, was paroled to take charge of the cotton, sell it, and then buy and deliver the supplies. Counterparts among the Federal prisoners were also appointed to take charge of the Federal supplies sent South.[20]

The usual bureaucratic web held up the cotton until well after the New Year, but the agents did not wait. Two colonels and a major were paroled from Johnson's Island, Ohio, and sent to the River Bend to supervise the distribution of clothing. They arrived in February. Hoffman, fearing plots, instructed Johnson that the three should be confined away from the prisoners, except when actually distributing supplies. Danforth approved of the idea, but he could not resist the opportunity to lash Johnson once again: "The action of the two governments does not show favorably to our side, in this respect [mortality]. For instance: At Rock Island Barracks prisoners of war are suffering from the scurvy, and, for aught we know (as the commandant refuses to allow a list of deaths to be published) dying in large numbers." This may have assuaged J. B.'s ego, but he let his umbrage cloud his logic: if Johnson's November letter had been true, and the government was supplying the prisoners, then why did this trio need to come and distribute supplies provided by the Confederates?[21]

The moment the supply agreement became public, the Barracks headquarters was deluged with requests from friends and relatives of prisoners, asking permission to send in boxes, the idea being that, if the governments had agreed to exchange supplies, what was the difference if friends also sent in clothing? Johnson, ever a stickler for the written rule, denied all such requests, even though he was so short of prison clothing the quartermaster had twice requested clothing for the prisoners in December. His requests fell on the same deaf ears that had failed to hear Johnson's request for blankets.[22]

Another change that winter occurred in the administration of the prison system. Apparently believing the duties of the commissary general of prisoners to be too arduous for one man, the War Department issued an order cutting the country in half at the Mississippi. Brigadier General H. W. Wessels took the eastern half, relegating Hoffman to the prisons west of the river. This represented a demotion for Hoffman—of the 62,000 prisoners listed on the rolls for November 1864, fewer than 2,000 remained under his control. It is possible that Hoffman requested the change because of his health. He would later report that prostate trouble had troubled him since the beginning of the war. Whatever the reason, Hoffman ceased to torment Johnson, at least for the moment.[23]

In some respects the prisoners' lot had also changed tremendously since the prison had opened. The smallpox had been defeated and largely kept at bay, new hospitals kept more of the patients alive, and the sanitation problems had at last been solved by the water and sewer system. Perhaps these things had taken longer to accomplish than they should have, but they had been done, and mostly under Johnson's aegis. The colonel was a strict man, utterly blind to anything outside the regulations, but he was not insensible to suffering. While the governments bickered and retaliated against each other, seemingly forgetful of the point of the argument, Johnson built a hospital and a waterworks. Some things, however, remained outside Johnson's control. For instance, he could not compel the Quartermaster Department to send him blankets for his recruits or clothing for his prisoners, so they remained cold. Some things remained the same from the day the prison opened until long after it closed.

One of those things was the guards. The garrison again included the 4th VRC, most of which had returned to the Island from adventures in the nation's capital. The men sought the same sort of diversions they had during their earlier tour. Private James Mayfield, ordered to be quiet one night, "said kiss my ass or words to that effect." Told a second time to shut up, Mayfield expanded on his earlier retort, saying, "Kiss my ass you son of a bitch." Mayfield's vocabulary exercises won him a court-martial.[24] Mayfield's sin was of a piece with the transgressions the guards had been committing for more than a year. But with black troops now forming part of the garrison the character of some infractions changed; the whites had a new set of victims. For instance, an enterprising VRC sergeant, Hady Moorehead, crossed the roadway to the quarters of the 108th, where he "did engage in sundry and divers games of chance with . . . enlisted men of Co. B, 108th USCT . . . winning money from them to the amount of $8.50." Moorehead lost his stripes. A companion, S. Brown, being a private already, was fined $5.00. The court also tried three men of the 108th for gambling and fined at least one of the blacks, Andy Bullit, twice what the white men paid. Bullit had been accidentally shot by one of his comrades during the fall. That and the discrimination in the matter of fines soured Bullit on the military, and a few weeks later he was brought before the court-martial again. This time the charge was insubordination. Found out of his bunk after taps and told by his sergeant to return to bed, Bullit replied, "I'll be damned if I go to bed for you or any other nigger."[25]

One of the captains of the 108th eschewed gambling for a more certain method of making money from the blacks: he wrote letters home for the illiterate men in his command and charged them for the service. This, said post adjutant A. F. Higgs, "is not warranted on moral or legal grounds." Moreover, Higgs said, "These ungentlemanly and unofficerlike practices must immediately cease." Perhaps to forestall such pecuniary adventures, either Johnson or Colonel Bishop thought to start a school. Two locals were hired, and an unoccupied barracks was turned into a schoolroom. Unfortunately, it appears few attended classes. As late as April 1865, Captain Charles Chase of Company C was keeping all the company records himself, because he could not find a sergeant who could do more than write his name, and several he tried could not even do that much.[26]

One reason for the school's failure was that the attractions of a poorly heated classroom and the admonitions of white teachers paled in comparison to the city lights. In this, and in many other ways, the 108th was no different from the other regiments that served on the Island. But there was one huge and obvious difference: these men were black, and most of them were former slaves. The citizens of the River Bend had very decided opinions on men of color. Indeed, after the black troops had been on the Island for a couple of months, J. B. had thought it expedient to refresh his readers' minds in the matter of Illinois's Black Laws: blacks were not allowed in the state without certificates of freedom, and they had to post a $500 bond that they would not become wards of the state. Any white found harboring an illegal black was liable to a $500 fine. The men of the 108th, however, showed little predilection to test the laws in Rock Island City. To the great delight of the citizens, the blacks preferred the Iowa side, despite the fact it was more difficult to reach. The reason was simple: Iowa belonged to a different military department, and Johnson's patrols had no authority there. Indeed, Johnson had never bothered to send his patrols to Davenport. Recognizing this, the men of the 108th, who managed to get themselves arrested whenever they appeared in Illinois, turned their attentions to Davenport, where they "carried their orgies to such a degree as to call out bitter complaints on the part of our citizens." The orgies took place at a few dance halls and saloons that catered strictly to them. These places soon became "an eyesore to all well disposed citizens, and a regular nuisance to those living in the vicinity."[27]

The outrages continued until finally the sheriff arrested a couple of the worst offenders. Their comrades worked themselves into a fury and went "to Davenport with arms in their hands and wool erect, for the purpose of rescuing their brethren." Led to the jail by a boy they shanghaied, they confronted the jailer's wife, who tried to reason with them while the mayor rode to the Island for help. Johnson, ignoring for once departmental boundaries, sent some VRC men to the city, where they met a few Iowa militiamen. Together these troops forced the men of the 108th into a precipitous retreat back to the Island, "where plenty of balls and chains awaited their delicate ankles."[28]

The Republican paper in Davenport castigated the blacks, saying that their pleasures were "in direct violation of all moral law." This was clearly racial; what the blacks had done differed very little or not at all from what the whites had been doing on the other side of the river for thirteen months. But on the Island, the colonel agreed with the newspaper's assessment. The jail liberation was merely the latest and most outrageous of a whole series of offenses, and to teach his unruly troops a lesson, eleven of the offenders were immediately cast into the guard house, and a flurry of correspondence

and orders followed. Captain John Cargill of the 108th recommended to Bishop that the "sale of all articles containing intoxicat-
ing liquors" be prohibited. For good measure, Cargill also suggested
that no pies, tarts, or molasses cakes be allowed either, apparently
lest a sugar frenzy take hold among the troops. Passes were forbidden altogether. The black troops retired to their quarters, where
they planned for a spring campaign.[29]

The hygiene habits of the troops—or, rather, the lack of them—
also caused Johnson consternation. The men of both the 108th and
the VRC were largely rural men, accustomed to relieving themselves
more or less where they were at the time nature called. They carried
this habit with them to the Island. Warnings had little effect, and finally Johnson issued an order on the subject: "The prevalent habit
of committing nuisances about the Island by the enlisted men of
this and other commands has rendered it necessary that stringent
measures be taken to correct it. Accordingly, tomorrow the guard on
the parapet will be instructed to fire upon any man seen committing a nuisance outside of the privies."[30]

No such shootings were recorded. On the other hand, the 108th
continued shooting prisoners at the slightest provocation. Although standing orders required that every shooting be investi-
gated, Johnson let many incidents pass without hearings. If he had
convened a commission for every incident, there would have been
no one to man the walls; besides, the officers usually supported the
troops. When Peter Cowherd, one of the four Cowherds in the regiment, shot a prisoner, his captain, Matthew Kollock, quickly wrote
to Johnson, explaining that Cowherd had discovered the prisoner
trying to dig under the fence, and, "According to instructions regu-
lating the actions of guards, said Private Peter Cowherd did there
and then shoot him to death." In this case, Johnson had reason to
doubt Kollock, and he did convene a hearing. As usual, it cleared
Cowherd. In only one case did a hearing find against a guard, and
in that case Johnson quickly overruled the findings. In one other
case a private named Grigsby was sent to the guardhouse for shooting a prisoner, but he was released the following day. In another incident six prisoners made a break for it. "They were detected in the
movement and fired upon by the guards. Two of them were shot
dead in their tracks, and the other four surrendered." In this case,
no official note whatever was made of the killings, other than in
the death register.[31]

The frenzy to get out that had taken hold of the prisoners with the arrival of the black troops continued through the winter. The statistical report for December 1864 is lost, but Johnson's correspondence for that month is little more than a list of the prisoners who managed to find their way to freedom. On 6 December, six men crawled through the sewers, pulled away a poorly fitted gate, and slid to freedom. One man escaped by slipping out of an ambulance on the way to the hospital. Three others left by climbing over the fence. For most of these escapes Johnson blamed his guards: "No excuse can be offered but the negligence of the guard."[32]

The colonel's ideas on carelessness would be vastly magnified shortly after all these escapes. As he reported to Wessels, John Langstaff of the 4th Kentucky Cavalry was "detailed on fatigue duty in the Q.M. dep't and by imposing on the guard, a colored soldier, made him believe he was foreman of the work they were then engaged upon, and desiring (as he represented) to go and see if another squad were performing their task, he slipped off. The guard will be duly made to suffer for his carelessness." Perhaps Langstaff had told his friends of his plan, because two weeks later another, quite similar episode played out. A man named Hendricks of the 3rd Alabama Cavalry, and another named Tucker, of the 7th Georgia, "with another prisoner had been working on the roof of a small building . . . and were returning to the prison under a guard from the 108th USCT when one of them told the guard that some of the tools had been left behind and proposed that the guard should go back with him to get them and the other two would wait until they returned. The guard did so and in the mean time the two that were left behind vamoosed. The guard is now in confinement." Langstaff, Hendricks, and Tucker all made it back to Dixie.[33]

Yet another escapee exhibited more avarice than sense, and his greed allowed Johnson to collar the man in Kentucky without ever leaving his office. A prisoner made good his escape, and afterward a box arrived for him from his brother in Kentucky. A few weeks passed, and a letter came from the brother, saying that he would like the box back, since his brother was no longer in the prison. As Johnson wrote to the provost marshal in the district, "How does he know his brother is not here only by seeing his brother and harboring him?" Johnson suggested the provost marshal grab the fugitive.[34]

Johnson perhaps took comfort in these minor successes. There was another comfort Johnson could take from foiled escape attempts: the failures increased the prison fund. As he told Wessels in January 1865, he found $93.00 on two prisoners trying to escape and immediately turned it over to the fund. Later, a search of the prisoners yielded $20.00 sewn into the lining of a man's pants; this, too, fed the fund. When a mother sent her son a box with $230 hidden inside, the guards found the money and it, too, went to the fund. Such minor finds, along with the savings in rations, helped Johnson save nearly $21,000 in December 1864.[35]

A still greater comfort was news from Washington about exchange. Since the July 1863 suspension of the exchange cartel, Federal authorities had tried several times to resume general exchanges, but their efforts came to nothing. When Ould tried to reestablish the system, the Federals balked. But in August 1864, the bipartisan intransigence softened a bit. In reply to yet another proposal to resume exchange, Ould wrote to John Mulford that he had for more than a year declined general exchanges because the Federals refused to abide by the cartel. But, wrote Ould, "In view, however, of the very large number of prisoners now held by each party, and the suffering consequent upon their continued confinement, I now consent to the above proposal, and agree to deliver to you the prisoners held in captivity by the Confederate authorities, provided you agree to deliver an equal number of Confederate officers and men."[36]

Mulford's superior, now Benjamin Butler rather than Hitchcock, responded to this offer with a very long letter, much of which concerned the old stumbling block—the black troops. Butler's response suggested an exchange of the sick and wounded. As always, lengthy correspondence and dickering followed, complicated by the negotiations for each side to supply its own prisoners, which were going on at the same time. Finally, Abraham Lincoln took a hand and instructed Edwin Stanton to tell Grant that, although he had full authority in the matter, "It is the desire of the President that no effort . . . be spared to effect the prompt release of all soldiers and loyal persons in captivity."[37]

The invalid exchange went forward. Next, all prisoners held in close confinement or in irons were ordered released and exchanged, culminating yet another months-long wrangle. This creeping expansion of exchange alerted the politicians in Congress, who immediately demanded all the correspondence relating to exchange, so that they could ponder whether these latest arrangements were warranted. While Hoffman scrambled to collect copies of 380 letters, orders, and memoranda, Grant, as persistent in this object as in his slow strangulation of Lee's army, continued to expand the exchanges. The two sides next struck an agreement about Confederates captured in Arkansas in 1863. Finally, on 11 February 1865, Ould and Grant came to agreement: the exchange would be general, as fast as prisoners could be transported to the exchange points. The issue of blacks was shrewdly covered by stipulating that those in captivity longest would be exchanged first. Since the blacks had been in the field a shorter time than the whites, and had generally been prisoners a shorter time, the race question was neatly sidestepped.[38]

Every one of these agreements affected Colonel Johnson and his wards, especially the one concerning the Arkansas prisoners. Many of those had found their way to the River Bend, and Johnson was charged with executing the order. The hopes of Rogan, Dillon, and the thousands of other prisoners were about to be realized at long last. As the old year ended and the new began, the prisoners began to journey home. On 15 January 1865 Dillon noted in his diary, "Our prison is full of the wildest rumors imaginable this past few days relative to an exchange." The next day he recorded that 250 prisoners were taken from the yard for exchange. These were the first of the Arkansas prisoners, and Dillon was disappointed: "it was only a special exchange." However, his time was coming. On 6 February 1865 Hoffman, who had again resumed control of all the prisons, telegraphed Johnson to prepare rolls for 3,000 men, arrange for transportation, and make sure the cars had water and lights.[39]

Despite three years' experience in guarding and transporting prisoners, the Federal system did no better in getting rid of them than it had in keeping them. The first group that Dillon mentioned left the Island on the evening of 17 January 1865, under the guard of Lieutenant A. E. Bennett and 40 privates from the VRC. Bennett and his charges rode the cars to Cairo, at the southern tip of Illinois, where they boarded a steamer for New Orleans. The trip was a nightmare. Hoffman's admonitions had been largely ignored, and the cars were insufficient in both number and equipment. Bennett, arriving in La Salle, Illinois, refused to move for 12 hours, demanding better transportation. But the railroad ignored him, and he finally moved on. While waiting for a boat at Cairo, two prisoners died. When they boarded the steamer, the only accommodation Bennett could find was on the upper, hurricane deck, exposed to the winds whipping across the river, and in desperation he pulled the tarpaulins off the life boats and stuck his men under them. Not surprisingly, two more prisoners died before Bennett's men stepped onto the dock at New Orleans, twelve horrible days after leaving the Barracks.[40]

Many of the prisoners went to the eastern exchange point, City Point, Virginia. One of the first groups went under command of Captain A. A. Lawrence of the VRC, and he had no easier time of it than had Bennett. None of his prisoners died, but two escaped, and the captain admitted he had no idea when or how. Moreover, two of the guards "left the cars at Elkhart, Ind. . . . and have not been heard from since." Lawrence took the opportunity to register a complaint about his men: "Some of the guard furnished me were utterly unfit for such duty, being actually incompetent to take care of theirselves on such a trip letting alone guarding of prisoners"[41]

News of exchange "elevated the spirits of the men very much," according to Dillon. Even men who wanted nothing more to do with the Confederacy had reason to celebrate. Johnson announced that anyone declining exchange could take the oath of allegiance and be released. On 18 February the prisoners were paraded and the rolls called, each man answering by saying "exchange" or "no exchange." Johnson told Hoffman that 1,330 men preferred not to be exchanged, and according to the colonel, a number of the men being exchanged had no intention of returning to the ranks but, immediately upon arrival in Dixie, "would desert and go home."[42]

When the exchange–no exchange roll was called that day, the prisoners suffered an excess of emotion. Whether it was joy at the thought of returning to their homes, or whether the stalwarts took umbrage at the men who preferred the oath, remains unknown. But there was some sort of celebration or altercation, which the guards quickly quelled through their usual method: gunfire. Twelve men were admitted to the hospital that day with gunshot wounds. As with the near massacre of the previous June, this incident was officially ignored by everyone. Johnson neither convened a hearing nor reported the incident to Hoffman. Even the newspapers remained silent. Only the hospital registers record the matter.[43]

The allegiance-oath men were released from the yard and sent across the bridge. Once out of the gates they were on their own, with only the clothes on their backs. Some had families that could send them clothing or money, but there were many who had nothing and no one to send them anything. Their plight moved Johnson to ask Hoffman whether he could provide bread to the released prisoners. Hoffman, however, was made of sterner stuff than Johnson and denied the issue. The men left the prison as they had come into it: without money, without food, without clothing.[44]

These men could not even enlist in the Federal army, although the army wanted them. Illinois Adjutant General Fuller's assistant, B. F. Smith, wrote to Johnson to ask whether he could enlist a further three companies to go fight Indians. Johnson replied that his prison had already sent 3,000 men to the army and navy, more than all other prisons combined, and that they "composed the best material." If Smith recruited any more men from the Island, said Johnson, "it is more than probable that the motive of nine tenths of them would be to get out of prison, with the intention of deserting." And so the men refusing exchange were turned loose to sink or swim.[45]

A few of them managed to swim, thanks to the sympathizers in the River Bend. One lucky man managed to get himself taken in by Lucy Buford, wife of Charles Buford. The prisoner was an amnesty man who had taken the oath, but Mrs. Buford forgave him because, as she wrote her daughter, the unnamed man was in poor shape: "Freezing and starvation has done its work & human nature could stand it no longer." She nursed the man to health and gave him money to see him home. Others were not so fortunate, as the readers of the *Union* learned. In February 1865, 40 people were admitted to the county poorhouse, 15 of whom were released prisoners. The Barracks, which had been a money fountain for 16 months, suddenly threatened to become a money drain. At the end of the fiscal year the supervisor reported that, of $4,886.07 spent at the poorhouse during the winter, $760.00 had been spent on released prisoners. Added to that figure would be the burial expenses for William Liggitt, who was released in November and ended up at the poor house, where he died in March 1865.[46]

Danforth did not make too big an issue of this new development. For one thing, the prisoners in question were released men, and no longer suffered the torments of the Island. For another, he had been busy. The satisfaction of having provoked Johnson during the November newspaper duel spurred the editor to new heights. He was determined to expose the prison as a charnel house, and, as he proudly told his readers, "We took especial pains that the authorities at Washington should see all we had said . . . as well as a copy of Col. Johnson's letter." Congressman C. M. Harris, the recipient of

Danforth's especial pains, demanded an explanation of the cruelty practiced on the Island. At the time, Wessels was in charge, and he told the congressman that nothing untoward was happening and that Johnson was doing a good job. Curiously, however, it was about this time that Dart was allowed back into the yard to sell vegetables. J. B. said Johnson had been ordered to allow the sutler to do business, and the editor claimed that his own exertions had caused the order; however, no copy of the order remains.[47]

As all this was going on, a lady purportedly from Chicago was writing to a friend in New York. The name of neither writer nor recipient survives. The recipient, however, was deeply moved by the description of suffering and sent the letter on to an editor who hastened it into print in the 7 January 1865 edition of the *New York News*. That worthy, being a Democrat, was only too happy to print the letter, which was worthy of J. B. himself: "The condition and suffering of the rebel prisoners at Rock Island is a source of agony to every heart not absolutely dead to the feelings of common humanity and the scantiest Christian mercy. . . . Many have taken 'the oath,' any oath, to save themselves from actual starvation." The writer recounted stories of eating rats and dogs and then worked herself into a truly righteous frenzy: "God in heaven! Shall these things continue? Will a merciful and just God bless and prosper [the Union cause] if such cruel inhumanity is practiced by our rulers?" Before ending with a paean to the heroism of the misguided prisoners, the writer also suggested a barbarity recorded by no one else: the clothing sent by friends and relatives for the relief of the prisoners was actually being taken across the river to Davenport and sold. Yet a third anonymous person, who signed himself "A sufferer," clipped the letter from the *News* and sent it to the War Department. It found its way to E. A. Hitchcock, who gave it very short shrift, calling it "a pure fabrication by some Northern Rebel." Nevertheless, he thought it wise to check into it. Called upon to explain things, Colonel Johnson told Wessels that the whole thing "bears on its face the finger marks of the editor of the Copperhead paper." Johnson assured his superiors that the "loyal press and the people of this section understand the matter." He was probably correct. Indeed, the letter showed such a fine command of language it is possible that J. B. wrote the missive himself and then engineered its various appearances.[48]

J. B. also wanted an investigation of the enlistment credits for the prisoners recruited for the army. He called on Congress to get to the bottom of the matter, and in a rare unanimity the Republican papers agreed with him. As the Davenport *Gazette* asked, "How, through whom, or by what authority, Pennsylvania and Ohio receives credit for the rebel prisoners who took the oath and enlisted in the U.S. service from Rock Island Barracks is to us, a mystery, and indicates a sharp practice on the part of someone." The whole River Bend was in an uproar. The town of Moline and the county board of supervisors passed resolutions demanding Congress to give Illinois the draft credits. The furor eventually moved Congress to action: led by Schuyler Colfax of Indiana, who himself may have wanted some draft credits, the House passed a resolution demanding Edwin Stanton to provide forthwith everything he knew about enlisting prisoners of war, including who got the draft credit and who paid the bounties. The congressmen were especially interested in Rock Island. Stanton's explanation satisfied the representatives, and the matter died quietly, except in the River Bend, where the plaintive but ineffective rumblings continued.[49]

Meanwhile, the objects of this investigation, the recruits, were at long last preparing to leave the River Bend. Brigadier General Alfred Sully, a career army man, had arrived to muster in the men from the calf pen and take them west. Unfortunately, as the general swore in the men, he allowed them to leave the Island and roam the area freely until departure. Not surprisingly, trouble followed. Five of them went to Davenport, took a room at the Burtis House, and "commenced a series of deviltry annoying to other inmates of the house." That is, they began ransacking the rooms. Arrested and hauled away to jail, they were released when Sully intervened with the judge and promised to make restitution. He immediately sent them out of town.[50]

In addition to those five, hundreds of other Galvanized Yankees left the River Bend, several hundred of them under the command of the former provost marshal of prisoners Andrew Caraher, who had been appointed colonel of the 2nd U.S. Volunteers, formed from the men at the Barracks. Other hundreds were going home for exchange as fast as the boats and cars could carry them; allegiance-oath men flooded the city and the poorhouse. Still, prisoners remained in the yard. The war was not over, and the Barracks was still in business.[51]

CHAPTER SEVEN

"All of the Prisoners Have Left This Island"

T he days of suffering were nearly, but not quite, over. What suffering remained was far reduced in scope. The death rate had risen slightly during the winter, but only slightly, and as spring approached it fell again. In February 1865 only 56 prisoners died on the Island, and, in March, only 34. Also in February, Hoffman had again authorized the sutlers to sell both clothing and vegetables to the prisoners. But Colonel Johnson, showing a basic if humorless mercy, had authorized such sales several weeks earlier, risking Hoffman's wrath. Dart charged outrageous prices, but the food was available—potatoes, apples, onions, turnips. Nor was the yard crowded any more. The Galvanized Yankees had all gone west, and more than 3,000 men had been sent for exchange. The yard, which had formerly been crowded with more than 8,000 men, now held only 5,000.[1]

Although with each passing day Johnson had fewer prisoners, he had just as many guards as ever, and they caused just as much trouble as ever. The men of the VRC carried on just as they had since arriving on the Island. Through the winter the 108th was confined to the Island, but that changed in March. As Lincoln's second inaugural approached, the post adjutant, Lieutenant A. F. Higgs, thought the regiment might enjoy getting over into the city, albeit in an official capacity. The inaugural day, 4 March, had been declared a national holiday, and Higgs requested the 108th to form part of a parade through Rock Island City. As adjutant, Higgs kept the records and doubtless knew the endless series of charges, courts-martial, and punishments accorded the black troops. Why he thought they could parade without incident remains a mystery. But on the appointed day the regiment marched through the city. They then added a new fillip to the record of their crimes.[2]

When the parade ended, the 108th continued marching down the street and "marched up to the Atlantic Brewery, stacked arms in front of the brewery, and made a general raid on the establishment. The proprietor, Mr. Schmid, was absent, but his lady protested against their acts, and so did his barkeeper." The soldiers helped themselves to beer and cigars and, still thirsty, went into the brew rooms and quaffed warm, half-brewed beer from the vats. According to the writer who reported these depredations to Danforth, "Mr. Schmidt is a 'loyal' Lincoln man—didn't he get about enough of the nigger?" After the January jail liberation, there had been balls, chains, and the guardhouse. This time, however, the perpetrators got away scot-free. There was no sudden increase in the number of prisoners held in the guardhouse, nor does the incident appear in the courts-martial noted in the post orders. In fact, the troops carried on as usual, and the regiment's commander, Colonel Bishop, reported just a few weeks later that men continued to smuggle whiskey into camp and that venereal diseases were on the rise in the regiment. But this appears to be just some regimental gossip that Bishop was passing on—he offered no solutions to the problems.[3]

Little ever changed with respect to the guards; their endurance in the face of regulation and retribution was remarkable. Despite having issued orders nearly a year before confining traffic to the roads, in May 1865 Johnson issued yet another circular, ordering his men to use the roads. Garbage continued to be a problem, and the colonel found himself repeating orders on that topic, too: "The indiscriminate dumping of refuse matter viz.—ashes, leaves, limbs, stumps, slops, offal, manure, sweepings, old rags, etc., along the river bank bordering this post is hereby strictly prohibited."[4]

As the guards sought places to dump their garbage, and as the prisoners continued to leave the Island to find their way south or to the poorhouse, the war was ending. Grant's coils constricted Lee's army, and the Confederate forces grew so thin that Lieutenant General Richard Ewell suggested to a Confederate congressman that the South should enlist its own Greybeards, men over 50, for the defense of Richmond. It was far too late: during the first week in April,

Grant's strangulation of Lee's army reached its climax. His lines broken, Lee abandoned Richmond and fled toward a crossroads named Appomattox Courthouse. As Danforth reported, "the glad news spread to all parts of the city. . . . The joy of the people was general and unrestrained . . . the cannon was fired, the church bells rung."[5]

Had they known of Edwin Stanton's plans for celebration, the citizens might have let the colonel borrow their cannon. B. F. Smith telegraphed Johnson, "By direction of the Sect'y of War you will cause to be fired a salute of one hundred (100) guns at meridian April 5th eighteen hundred sixty-five in honor of the capture of Richmond, Virginia." But the gun barge had never arrived, which allowed Johnson to reply, "Impossible. Have not a piece of artillery of any description." It was probably just as well: given the troops' penchant for gunfire, it is not hard to imagine the River Bend cities crumbling under the victory salute.[6]

A few days later the citizens celebrated Lee's surrender, while William Sherman chased down Joseph Johnston in North Carolina and Johnston, too, surrendered. Kirby Smith and Richard Taylor, commanding Confederate armies in the west, followed a few weeks later. The war was over. Johnson's men marched in another parade in the city, which provided J. B. with an opportunity to exercise himself on one of his favorite topics. Noting that the 108th formed part of the parade, he complained that they received preferential treatment all day and said, "You must give the white man a little bit of a chance, somewhere."[7]

During April 1865, 18 prisoners died on the Island. This was a far cry from a year earlier, when 139 prisoners went to their graves, but that was no comfort to 18 families. And 900 miles away another, single death shattered the nation and affected history more than all the deaths at all the camps: Abraham Lincoln was assassinated. From a pinnacle of exhilaration only a few days before, the North plunged into an abyss of despair. Even Danforth, the sworn enemy of Lincoln and everything Republican, put aside his rhetoric and played the story straight. However, J. B. could not quite bring himself to the same pitch of despair as most Americans. His columns dealing with the assassination and its aftermath ran under smaller heads than his coverage of the death of the great Stephen Douglas, almost exactly four years earlier.[8]

It is unfortunate that both the Barracks diarists, Rogan and Dillon, had already been exchanged, and their reactions to Lincoln's death remain unknown. J. W. Minnich did note the assassination years later, writing: "Then indeed were the dark days come. Worse than all else was the knowledge that we were crushed to the earth at last, all power of resistance gone, and uncertain of our own ultimate fate was our bitterest portion. Above all did we dread the effect of Lincoln's assassination." Events proved Minnich's fears groundless. Although the men of the 108th had every reason to loathe the prisoners, and Lincoln's death gave them excuse, they did not let loose indiscriminate musket fire into the compound; rather, no more so than they ever had.[9]

The demonstrations at Lincoln's death wrought a profound change on Danforth. He had castigated the black soldiers since the day they arrived in the River Bend. But their behavior during the procession in Rock Island worked on J. B.'s sympathies, and he reported, "Their sad looks, respectful and perfectly orderly behavior, scrupulously neat appearance, and real sorrow conquered our prejudices, and we could have walked in their procession as well as anywhere else, thinking only of the loss of our country and the uncertainty of the future."[10]

The releases continued through war's end and the assassination. Johnson, showing a bit more concern for his enemies than he is usually given credit for, had telegraphed Hoffman as early as February 1865, asking if he could pay for transportation for the destitute allegiance-oath men. To the first request Hoffman made no reply. To a second request made in May, Hoffman, in obedience to instructions from Grant but also conscious of the cost, told the colonel that only men who had applied to take the oath before the fall of Richmond could receive transportation. A few days later Johnson asked about feeding the former prisoners, saying: "Two-thirds of prisoners released . . . are destitute. Can hard bread be furnished them to their homes?" By this time, even Hoffman realized the war was over, and he allowed the colonel to issue rations to the prisoners, although he pondered the question for three days before allowing the issue. Later, Grant overruled him in the matter of transportation, too, and ordered all prisoners sent home by rail or boat at government expense.[11]

Two of the men released were Jesse Eley and Walter Porter, who had both been captured at Missionary Ridge and had been among the first prisoners to arrive on the Island. Like Rogan, they had served as clerks, and on their departure they received praise from the *Argus:* "They are both young men, accomplished gentlemen, and remarkably fine penmen and correct clerks. They were bred in the best and wealthiest circles in the south. . . . [T]hey will always be remembered . . . as gentlemen of the most agreeable manners and fitted to adorn any station in society." This paean suggests that perhaps Eley and Porter, in addition to being fine penmen, had also been fine conduits of information for J. B. Hundreds of others left with Eley and Porter, and the prison steadily emptied. But although the war was over, the Barracks was still a prison and Johnson its commandant. As the commandant, he was heir to problems that continued well past the surrenders. One of the problems, which had actually begun in 1863, came to a head as the war ended.[12]

After the departure of Captain Reynolds, Johnson suffered a series of quartermasters who all proved more or less deficient. The first and worst was Captain Mathew Marx, a Chicago lawyer. Marx had been a captain in the 82nd Illinois. At Gettysburg he suffered what he reported to be a severe and debilitating wound in his leg. The severity of the wound was later questioned by the Pension Bureau, and of the half-dozen witnesses rounded up not one could recall Marx's wound. Nevertheless, the wound and a recurring malarial fever got Marx out of active service. The regiment was glad to see him go: according to one man, Marx "was no good, he was a blower in camp and when the powder was burned he was not any good." In November 1863 Marx accepted an appointment in the VRC and was ordered to the Island.[13]

As Reynolds prepared to leave the Island, Johnson appointed Marx acting quartermaster and gave him charge of the post's council of administration, which administered the garrison's various funds. Trouble started immediately. According to Marx, Johnson had borrowed money to bring his family from New Jersey. When he asked for the return of the loan, Johnson not only refused to repay the money but said "I'll fix you, you d—d Copperhead." Noting some irregularities in the funds Marx supervised, Johnson relieved him in July and accused Marx of falsifying records in order to pocket $76.18 in quartermaster funds. By October 1864 Marx was under arrest and facing a court-martial for defrauding the government. The money cost Marx his career: on 31 March 1865 the court-martial found him guilty and cashiered him.[14]

This scarcely ended the matter, however. Marx had become enamored of the area, and he merely moved from the Island to the city, where he opened a law practice and planned revenge. In the spring of 1865 the revenge manifested itself: Marx brought charges against Johnson. To avoid accusations that he was merely lashing out at Johnson in revenge, Marx told the adjutant general's office that he had actually filed the charges in July 1864, before Marx's own troubles began. Johnson was not fooled. As he said in his response, "No such charges were ever forwarded by Capt. Marx, and in all probability never concocted until after he was placed on trial under charges preferred by me." But that made little difference to the bureaucrats, and Johnson was called to account. Marx charged that Johnson had not taxed the sutler, that he had failed to convene the post council of administration, that he had sold government hay for his own benefit, that he had paid for tons of ice from the prison fund and then let it go to waste, and that he had used a soldier as a personal servant.[15]

In his reply to the charges, Johnson was even more stinging than he had been in his letter to Danforth the previous fall. Johnson said that "only a disordered brain in a malicious heart could conceive" such charges. Speaking of the ice, he noted that Marx had had charge of it and, if any ice had been wasted, it had been the captain who had wasted it. Johnson wanted to prefer charges of maliciousness against Marx, but he consoled himself with the thought that the court-martial would undoubtedly cashier him, which indeed it did. An assistant adjutant general endorsed Johnson's letter, saying Marx's charges were "both frivolous and malicious." There the matter ended, officially. Unofficially, it was far from ended. The unblushing rascal, safe from further harassment by Johnson and making new friends in Rock Island City, wanted everyone to know the truth.[16]

One of Marx's new friends was J. B. Danforth. Marx was a German Jew, most of whom were at the time Republicans. Marx, however, was a Democrat, and J. B. welcomed him with open arms. When Marx produced a pamphlet entitled "A Word to the Public: Col. A. J. Johnson's Record Examined," Danforth was only too happy to provide space for it in his columns. J. B. opened his article by saying, "We have not room to spare for the publication of the pamphlet," and then proceeded to print much of it and summarize the rest. Marx alleged that much of Johnson's animosity had its genesis in two things: the loan Marx had made to Johnson, and Marx's politics. Marx recounted a conversation wherein Johnson said, "Captain, you know I have always been a friend of yours, but recently I have heard bad reports of you from prominent citizens . . . who say you are a Copperhead and will vote for McClellan." Marx replied that he would vote his conscience, to which Johnson retorted, "Unless you go slow and alter your gait, I will have you dismissed the service." When the 108th arrived, the colonel denounced Marx to them as a Copperhead, which was not calculated to endear the captain to the black troops. Marx's pamphlet ended by saying the affair amply demonstrated "the deep and malevolent wickedness of the man." To this J. B. added that Johnson was "a loafer and a blackguard."[17]

While Marx and Danforth were perhaps the sharpest thorns in Johnson's side, they far from the only ones. A more pressing, if also soggier, thorn was Captain Kollock of the 108th. The captain was a sensitive man, who thought Colonel Bishop and Johnson were persecuting him because he had erroneously reported that his men had never received their enlistment bounty. Bishop also questioned Kollock's administration of the company fund. To escape this persecution, the captain purchased a boat and spent his idle hours on the river, ignoring the orders that prohibited him from owning the craft. Unfortunately, Kollock was not much of a sailor. As Colonel Bishop noted: "Capt. Kollock owns and uses on the Mississippi river a sail boat—a frail unsafe thing. Four or five times, in fact nearly always when he has had control of the boat he has been upset in the river and in danger of his own life. . . . A few days ago . . . he took an enlisted man with him and was overturned in the water; he struck this man several blows with an oar." It was all too much for the captain. Distrusted and half-drowned, forced to give up the boat he should never have had, he tendered his resignation because he "desir[ed] to return to private life," presumably at some distance from large bodies of water. Kollock actually desired just to get away altogether. Less than a month after his departure it came to light that the abysmal sailor was a deserter from the U.S. Navy.[18]

Other boats also concerned Johnson. In the spring of 1864, Johnson issued his order forbidding boats on the Island. He had these orders published in all the newspapers, Republican and Democrat, English and German, and submitted the bills to the War Department, which refused to pay them. The colonel turned to Hoffman, explaining his position and noting that in at least one instance a boat tied up in the slough had materially aided a prisoner's escape. In light of this incident and the subsequent necessity for publishing the orders in all the newspapers so that nobody could claim ignorance, Johnson asked if he could pay the bills from the prison fund. Hoffman's reply does not appear in the records, but he probably allowed the bill. The fund could afford it. Despite his transgressions in the matter of the hospitals, Johnson had proved the most adept commandant in the army in terms of the prison fund. And even though the war was over, he did not relax his efforts. It had been nearly ten months since the fund had paid for the hospitals, and in that time the balance had grown enormously. Hoffman's quarterly report for the period ending 31 March 1865 showed Johnson's balance as more than $186,000. This was astounding in itself; it is the more amazing in light of the fact that through the same period the cost of rations increased and the number of prisoners decreased. It was a stellar accomplishment for the colonel. Although such serendipitous additions as money found sewn into prisoners' pants helped, almost all the money came from ration cuts. The records for the period from October 1864 until June 1865 show that the issue averaged about half the rations due.[19]

All through March 1865 prisoners were sent for exchange or released on oath. By the end of the month fewer than 3,000 remained in the yard. Despite their destitution, the exchange men left litter behind them, much of it in the form of clothing. The previous fall a local businessman named Job Ross had advertised in the *Argus,* offering five and a half cents per pound for rags. Remembering this, perhaps, and noting the threadbare, discarded clothing littering the yard, the colonel went into the recycling business. As he proudly reported to Hoffman in April, he had credited the fund with "two hundred and two dollars and fifty cents ($202.50) . . . the proceeds of old rags gathered up in the prison, cleansed, and sold at the market price." Another reason for the unprecedented savings is that expenditures also dropped. In February and March 1865, Johnson spent less than $400, of which $100 was for a fence for the Confederate graveyard. As the colonel pointed out to Hoffman, the graveyard had never been enclosed. The fund could certainly afford it. Johnson even did a second round of rag-picking, which garnered more than the cost of the fence.[20]

Johnson never relaxed an instant. He could scarcely afford to, because the guards had relaxed entirely too much. He still had prisoners left, and by Johnson's lights they were still prisoners; however, the men of the VRC and the 108th thought otherwise. John

Thornton of the VRC was one who thought the war was over; to him that meant the men he guarded were no longer his enemies. On the parapet one day, Thornton allowed some prisoners to cross the deadline. This in itself would have caused consternation, but then Thornton "did sit his gun down and leaning against the parapet enter into conversation with Confederate prisoners of war." Johnson did not approve of this sort of fraternization, and Thornton paid a $12.00 fine for his laxity. Three other men were hauled up on the same charge.[21]

Laxity was easy. The conflict was over, and for the first time in the history of the Barracks there were enough guards. The post returns show slightly more than 1,500 men in the garrison for both April and May 1865. In April, there were only 2,700 prisoners, and by the end of May the guards outnumbered their wards. The guards were healthier, too: in March 1865, the sick list of the 108th fell below 100 men for the first time since the regiment had come to the Island. Despite their number, the guards' lack of vigilance worried Johnson. Most of the guards thought as Thornton did. The war was over. Why not talk to prisoners? And why bother to maintain appearances? Ezra Race of the VRC appeared at dress parade one evening slouching and with his uniform unbuttoned. Told to straighten up and button his coat, he replied, "You are damned particular." This enraged the colonel, who only five days earlier had issued an order that coats were to be buttoned at all times. Race paid a $16.00 fine. There was some justification for Johnson's rigidity. The war might be over, but the prisoners were still prisoners until they signed the oath, were registered on another of Hoffman's interminable lists, and were led out the gate. And among the remaining prisoners were some diehards who refused to accept the inevitable and also refused the oath. During the month of June eight of these men managed to evade such alert guards as Thornton and escaped.[22]

Those prisoners were not the only diehards remaining on the Island. Major Kingsbury, commander of the Arsenal, remained in the River Bend. He had been quiet through the long winter, but spring energized the major, and the Barracks annoyed him as much as ever. Once again he attacked Johnson on the ground that the colonel was interfering with the public service, charging that one of Kingsbury's men had been arrested and "beaten like a dog" by Lt. Col. Caraher. Kingsbury demanded "to know officially by what authority he was arrested and for what offence, and why the facts were not reported to me." The major wrote to the Northern Department, outlining the whole episode. The day after this letter Kingsbury brought formal charges against Caraher. As he had in answer to Marx's charges, Johnson wrote an acceptable reply to Kingsbury's accusations. Nelson resisted arrest, according to Johnson, and Caraher was perfectly justified in beating him to compel obedience. Indeed, had Nelson been an officer, it would have been permissible for Caraher to shoot him. The colonel ended with an observation on his men serving under Kingsbury: "I have abundant evidence of the general demoralization of the squad."[23]

There the case of Private Nelson died. Kingsbury, however, was enraged. He next wrote to General Alexander Dyer, who had replaced George Ramsay as the chief of ordnance. From its opening line the letter dripped sarcasm bordering on insubordination: "My previous reports . . . having been considered of no importance, I had determined to make no further efforts in behalf of the permanent interests of the Ordnance Department." But the Barracks men were yet again cutting down trees, and the major could not let this pass. Kingsbury intimated, "I have no special interest in the subject, and if it is desirable that the Island should be thoroughly denuded, I have no objection." Kingsbury thought there was only one way to prevent the Island from becoming as barren as the moon: "a transfer of all the prisoners and also of their keepers."[24] General Dyer did not share his thoughts on denuding the island, but he shared instantly and sternly his thoughts on Kingsbury's attitude. On receiving Dyer's rebuke, Kingsbury filled several closely written pages backtracking and justifying himself. But even when he tried to be apologetic his sneer came through. He told Dyer: "It is of course impossible to comply with the instructions conveyed in the last paragraph of your letter, 'to report all instances wherein the interests of the Ordnance Department on Rock Island have been injured.' In my judgment the injury to those interests commenced with the erection of the prison barracks and will continue in an increasing ratio, until all the parties connected therewith are removed from the Island." Not surprisingly, this missive did not mollify Dyer, who fired back another demand for explanations, and Kingsbury again apologized. Kingsbury was merrily nailing shut the coffin of his career, but he scarcely had time to notice. Johnson continued to interfere with the public service.[25]

Johnson had issued orders that nobody was to leave the Island unless correctly attired, but he had failed to notify Kingsbury "what the costume is." And, Kingsbury said, Johnson had no authority to interfere with his men, even though they were actually VRC men belonging to Johnson. But the detachment's commander, Lieutenant Mellan, enthusiastically agreed with Johnson and had issued identical orders to his men. Also, the order about proper attire had its genesis not in Johnson's exactitude but in orders from the provost marshal general, and it applied to every soldier, regardless of such niceties as who commanded whom. If Kingsbury knew any of this, he did not care. The public service—that is, the major's business—was being interfered with, and off went another letter. This time Kingsbury bypassed Dyer and wrote directly to the War Department. Once again the adjutant general called on the colonel for an explanation, and Johnson once again made a satisfactory reply, at the end of which he wrote that Major Kingsbury "has endeavored to injure my reputation in which he has signally failed in this locality . . . and I trust his efforts will be equally unsuccessful at the War Department. . . . I regret exceedingly the necessity of making these remarks, but the character of Maj. Kingsbury's communication seems to call for it."[26]

While Johnson feuded with Marx and Kingsbury, the camps continued to empty. From Chase and Morton and Elmira and Douglas and Rock Island, prisoners signed the oaths and walked out the gates. Orders from the War Department sped the process. On 8 May 1865 Stanton decreed that all prisoners under the rank of colonel who had been captured before the fall of Richmond and who did not want to be exchanged could be released on taking the oath of allegiance. Hoffman sought to draw order from the chaos involved in releasing 50,000 prisoners and suggested to Grant that releases be restricted to 50 per day per camp, and those in proportional alphabetical order; that is, if 10 percent of the prisoners at a camp had names beginning with "A," then 5 of the 50 released each day would be men whose names began with "A." And, of course, complete and detailed lists were to be furnished to Hoffman's office. Hoffman's passion for an orderly release and accurate records smothered in the anarchy of 50,000 prisoners clamoring to get home. On the Island, Johnson released men every day, and it was always more than 50: 104 on 16 May; 70 the following day; 78 on 18 May. These were no longer exchanges but releases of a defeated enemy, and the limiting factor was not a decree from Hoffman but the availability of blank oaths for prisoners to sign and clerks to fill out. On 2 June 1865 a magnanimous Ulysses Grant issued General Order No. 104, ordering the Quartermaster Department to provide transportation by rail or boat for every released prisoner. Four days later Andrew Johnson, who had succeeded Lincoln as president, ordered the final release of all but a few prisoners. Hoffman's prison system was shutting down.[27]

In the east, Edwin Stanton busied himself tracking down the conspirators who had killed Lincoln and bringing them to justice. He also concerned himself with the capture of Henry Wirz, commandant of the notorious Andersonville camp, where some 13,000 Federal soldiers had died. Lincoln's assassin, John Wilkes Booth, was killed in a Virginia farmhouse, but seven other conspirators were captured, as was Wirz. After one-sided trials, Wirz and four of the conspirators were hanged. Also in the east, William Hoffman continued to worry about costs. Importuned by the commandant of Point Lookout to provide transportation home for nearly 1,900 sick, wounded, and maimed hospital prisoners, Hoffman approved the expense, but not on humanitarian grounds: he told the commandant that "transportation to their homes would soon be balanced by the expense of keeping them in hospital."[28]

In the west, Johnson continued picking rags and releasing prisoners. On 29 May 1865, 84 men left the yard, and Johnson reported that he had 1,100 prisoners left, every one of whom wanted to take the oath and go home. Also in the west, Danforth continued to keep an eye on the prison. During the spring, Danforth added another to the list of crimes perpetrated on the Island: body snatching. A Moline doctor had purportedly hired a room to some of the Island's surgeons, wherein they dissected dead Rebels. Not wanting to be left out, the doctor had asked if he could get some cadavers. Danforth himself had witnessed some dissections and had been told the prisoners' corpses had been purchased from some unnamed source. J. B. had dutifully reported this shocking practice to Johnson, but Johnson had done nothing. J. B. wondered in print if it was "'loyal' to steal or sell the bodies of deceased prisoners." Then there was the problem of Southern families coming to collect the remains of their loved ones, only to find empty coffins. There is some corroboration for the body snatching charge. The prison register shows a number of men who arrived on the Island and then disappeared from the face of the earth: "disposition unaccounted for" appears beside the names of at least 40 prisoners. Also, the morning reports show a number of prisoners who died but were not identified, or whose bodies were not accounted for.[29]

But there were happy notes, too. Danforth noted with satisfaction that as many as 15,000 Iowa and Illinois soldiers might be sent to the Island to be paid off and mustered out. This would, said J. B., "make business lively." A few of the returning soldiers who still had time on their enlistments were used to fill out the 4th VRC, which Danforth, forgetting his own earlier condemnations, called "a splendid regiment." Splendid or not, the VRC now constituted the only troops at the Barracks. With the number of prisoners rapidly dwindling, there was no need for two regiments of guards. By 7 June the daily guard, which had formerly numbered 100 men, was down to 40. For Colonel Johnson the choice of which regiment to release was an easy one: "I have the honor to report," he told Hoffman on 15 May, "that the services of the 108th USCT are no longer required at this station." Johnson bore the regiment no love; it had again and again embarrassed him, and he was no doubt glad when orders came for the 108th. He immediately notified Bishop that "orders have been received to remove your command to Vicksburg and that you will make the necessary preparation in order to be ready at a moment's notice." When the regiment embarked for the south, Danforth, more generous than Johnson and still under the spell of the 108th's dignity at Lincoln's obsequies, said, "The colored soldiers, as a general thing, have conducted themselves with great propriety."[30]

Some of the 15,000 troops Danforth mentioned were the Greybeards, who returned from Ohio to be mustered out. Danforth reported that the men were being cheated of their bounty. They had been promised $100, of which only $25 had been paid, and at muster out that $25 was deducted from their pay, leaving them no bounty at all. As J. B. said, "There is something wrong about the matter." He was also happy to report that Kincaid was not with his men, because "They have suffered great wrongs at his hands . . . and it would not be safe for some of the late shoulderstraps to come in contact with the indignant and sturdy old Graybeards." Indeed, it was not safe. When the regiment's second-in-command, Lieutenant Colonel George West, boarded a boat to go home, he found the boat crowded by his former soldiers. When the old men saw the officer, they "commenced hissing and groaning in the most agonistic style. Some pushed and jostled him about; a cry was set up to throw him in the river . . . but the captain of the boat interfered, and the persecuted ex-officio was taken away from his tormentors."[31]

A few of the Greybeards remained in town, to try to bring Kincaid and West to book. For some inexplicable reason they met under the bridge, where they passed a number of resolutions. Among other things they accused the officers of "gross swindle, fraud and intrigue" in the matter of the bounties, swore that they would "bring these men to justice," and declared "that they are unworthy of a place anywhere within the State of Iowa." The Greybeards also decided that, since Baker and Kirkwood had ignored their grievances the year before, they must be in cahoots with Kincaid. The privates further resolved that "the leading officers of our state, knowing and taking part with the officers of the 37th, we repudiate as unworthy of our confidence, as being accessory with them." Their resolutions came to nothing.[32]

The prisoners continued to leave: 101 men walked out the gates on 17 June; 163 on the 18th; 100 on the 19th. Many of these men got no farther than the city, where they crowded into a vacant building, awaiting transport home. There were now more dead prisoners on the Island than live ones, and the earth was still fresh on the grave of George R. Donaldson of Missouri. During Sterling Price's raid in the fall of 1864, Donaldson had been caught up and conscripted. Whether he was really a Rebel no one knows nor will ever know. Captured shortly after his enforced enlistment, Donaldson remained on the Island and still remains: on 14 June 1865, he succumbed to—no one knows that, either. The clerks kept records no better at the end than they had at the beginning. Donaldson was the last confederate to die on Rock Island.

On 21 June 1865, Johnson telegraphed Hoffman that he had that day released 160 men. The following day he released 182. Among these was William Bennefield, who a year earlier had climbed the flagpole to retrieve the tangled flag. This left only two prisoners, both sick, and both of whom were transferred to the garrison hospital. The three Confederate officers who had arrived in February to distribute clothing to the prisoners also left this week, sent on their way with praise from Danforth, who called Colonel Slemons, the leader, "a gentleman of cultivation and civility."[33]

The release of Bennefield and his friends had been delayed for a time because Johnson had no blank forms for the prisoners to sign. The captain of the incongruously named *Victory*, lying at the levee, was anxious to get downriver, and just as anxious to make money. The captain offered Johnson a deal: if the colonel would get the men released and on the boat before he was scheduled to cast off, he would cram on board every diabolical humanity he could carry, and carry them for $2.68 per man less than the chartered fare. This presented Johnson with a dilemma. He had requested more forms, but in the anarchy of war's end Hoffman's clerks had not yet sent them. However, Johnson's stay in the River Bend had taught him much about money. When the forms arrived two days after the *Victory* slipped into the current, he returned them to Hoffman with a smug note: "I have the honor to acknowledge the receipt this day of 2300 'Blank Oaths' and to return them herewith, owing to the time for their use having passed." Faced with a pecuniary conundrum, the colonel had not hesitated: he had the forms printed in Rock Island City, released his prisoners, and shoved more than 400 of them onto the *Victory*. The cost of the forms was $22.75; the fare saved was nearly $1,100. Hoffman's pupil had learned his lessons well.[34]

With all his prisoners gone save two sick ones, Johnson turned to the myriad administrative problems that remained. He retained a couple of companies of the VRC to guard the empty buildings until they could be turned over to the Ordnance Department. Instead of 100 men per relief, however, now there were only 12. The men would stand guard over the compound until 24 August 1865. Johnson also kept a few clerks, mostly hired citizens, to do the voluminous paperwork. There were rags to bundle up and sell. A week after the *Victory* carried her human cargo south, Johnson reported that he had garnered another $118 for the prison fund from a final rag-picking. An auction of property bought with the prison fund yielded another $754. Johnson also at last had time for a social life, and he invited the public to "a grand picnic" in the empty compound. Neither the colonel nor the citizens saw any impropriety in tables groaning with food in the yard where men had hunted rats and eaten dogs.[35]

While Johnson dismantled the prison, Danforth enthused over the Island. The war may have been over, but the Arsenal remained, and surely that would redound to the financial benefit of the citizens. J. B. got wind of a rumor that the Island would be used to store arms and ordnance. This, he said, was only right: where else should arms be kept than at an arsenal? He also speculated that the government would eventually require the entire Island for military purposes. But in case the Arsenal failed to throw a sufficient stream of revenue over the slough, J. B. began boosting the glories of Rock Island City. He told his readers that "there is no place where the hot season can be passed so pleasantly as in Rock Island." J. B. got a little carried away, however, in describing the wonders of the area. Forgetting the castigations he had heaped on the Barracks for a year and a half, Danforth noted as one of the area's attractions the "very large and superb military prison." Danforth also continued to report on the prisoners. Some of the released men had adopted the River Bend as their home, and J. B. believed it was his duty to report on them, especially when it made good copy. James Cooper made wonderful copy.[36]

Cooper had been one of the doves who reported escape attempts. He had been released in the summer of 1864 at Johnson's request, because his life was in danger. As Danforth told the story, Cooper was more than a dove: he was a businessman. Cooper told three Kentuckians that if they provided the money, he could bribe a particular guard to let them all escape. On the appointed night Cooper led his erstwhile comrades out the gate and straight into the arms of the soldiers. He pocketed the bribe money and then hied himself to headquarters, where he presumably collected his fee for exposing an escape attempt. Later, Cooper was sent to Davenport, where he rather ineptly pretended to be an escaped prisoner and begged a suspected sympathizer for money to get south. The sympathizer provided the money, and Cooper pocketed both that sum and yet another fee.[37]

After his release Cooper stayed in the area and "became the pet of a few malignants . . . and the scorn of all honorable men." He went to work in a woolen mill in Moline. Unfortunately for Cooper, one of his victims, named Herndon, was among the last prisoners released, and Herndon had no intention of going south without settling accounts. Rounding up another former prisoner named Foster, Herndon tracked down Cooper at the mill. As Danforth reported, Cooper proved a craven when Herndon demanded his money, begging Herndon, "*do* let me off—I have no money but I'll give you my clothes." Herndon declined the offer and proceeded to administer a beating: "Herndon gave him 33 tremendous blows with a heavy whip. . . . The blows were counted by Mr. Foster, who went along to see fair play"—fair play, apparently, consisting of counting the blows and reporting the whole thing to Danforth.[38]

Danforth also kept tabs on the colonel. Just before Johnson left the Island, J. B. reported: "Col. Johnson is still nominally in command of the Post, if anybody can tell what that is. . . . [If] Johnson is rendering the United States any equivalent for his pay, we can't see it." The colonel did not deign to notice this. But just as he was leaving the Island, Johnson wrote a pamphlet for the fall election campaign in New Jersey, and he made sure a few copies got over to the city. It was a mistake. The pamphlet and what followed served only to cement the reputation for himself and his prison that had come out of the earlier newspaper duel.[39]

Danforth, overjoyed at the thought that Johnson dared to cross pens with him again, latched onto the pamphlet at once. "It is," he said, "a jargon of horrible English, bad grammar, vulgar slang, and brutal attacks upon the living and the dead." Danforth told his readers, "Johnson is so excessively 'loyal' that he regards as a 'Copperhead' every officer and soldier who votes the Democratic ticket." Johnson was proud, said J. B., that he got four Democrats cashiered. One of these four was Mathew Marx; another was Captain John Gitterman, who had indeed been dismissed the service for drunkenness, although Johnson claimed to have caused the dismissal because of Gitterman's politics.[40]

Not content to let Johnson dig his own grave unaided, J. B. quoted Johnson's "had I the power" letter. Johnson needed no help, however: his character shone through every line. He revealed himself as vain, spiteful, petty, and full of hatred. Danforth pointed out that the pamphlet, meant to help defeat the political ambitions of a New Jersey general, a former commander of Johnson's, instead was "a shame and disgrace" to Johnson himself. Instead of letting the matter drop, Johnson wrote a letter to the *Union,* which Barnes duly published. It is a bizarre document. Rather than attacking Danforth on whatever issues hid beneath the exchange of insults, the colonel instead attacked Danforth on the matter of his wig, claiming that J. B.'s headpieces were made from the bodies of the dead. He also castigated the hair oil J. B. used on his beard. Once the hirsutal items were disposed of, Johnson accused Danforth of having attacked him personally and of being disloyal.[41]

This was only more ammunition for Danforth, who responded in kind. J. B. claimed that he had never attacked Johnson. This was sophistry. In the matter of wigs, however, J. B. nailed Johnson squarely: "He says that wigs are 'made from hair procured by mutilating the dead.' That Johnson is perfectly at home in the matter of 'mutilating the dead,' is proved . . . by the fact that, while he had charge of the rebel bull-pen . . . dead bodies of prisoners of war were sold and carried away, for dissection." And then J. B. gave away much of his position when he said that wearing a wig was not a disgrace but that "we had regarded [it] in the light of a misfortune, the same as with the little deformed child of Johnson's—a misfortune for which neither the child or its parents were censurable." Despite the fine turn of language, this was unworthy of J. B.; moreover, it was completely unnecessary. J. B. had had the upper hand since the colonel came to the Island, and he had refuted Johnson in language at once sharp, accurate, and entertaining. Despite this gratuitous insult, J. B. managed—barely—to hold the high ground. His reply to Johnson drifted off into a long discourse on beard dressings, plugs for recently published books by a friend of his, and an extremely twisted sentence about Johnson's attitude toward his political masters: "In his self-debasement he showed a willingness even to perform a labial titillation of the os coccygis of some African, if his masters required it—and the African would let him." He eventually managed to return to the subject, bringing up yet again Johnson's "had I the power" statement. J. B. demonstrated his acumen when he said, "It is really surprising that any man, having even a thimble full of brains, should . . . put himself in a position, in so many ways, for ridicule and contempt. He exposes himself in every line." And that line finally had some effect on Johnson. This bizarre exchange, one of the strangest and most jumbled duels to come out of this or any war, ended with J. B.'s reply. It had taken a long while, but Johnson perhaps at last realized he was both making a fool of himself and painting himself the monster everyone thought him to be. He made no reply.[42]

This tempest had started in May 1865, while the Barracks still held prisoners, and continued until the end of the year. While Johnson and Danforth tried to destroy each other with words, the war continued to wind down. Major Kress, who had replaced Kingsbury at the Arsenal, doubtless observed the duel, although his reactions to it are unrecorded. Kress also observed something else, something unnoticed by nearly every soul, citizen and soldier, in the River Bend: on 7 July 1865, J. W. Craddock and B. F. McCoy, the two prisoners who had in June been transferred to the garrison hospital, were discharged, and they walked across the bridge to freedom. One of Johnson's few remaining clerks sent the last roll to Hoffman, but it remained for Kress to pronounce benediction on the prison. He reported to the Ordnance Department: "All of the prisoners have left this Island." And while all the players were occupied with other things, the Barracks closed, 585 days after James Reeves had arrived.[43]

The captains and the kings departed, but the Island remained. Danforth was right: the government sent ordnance to the Island for storage after the war, much of it Confederate artillery. At one time the Arsenal boasted the largest collection of Confederate cannon in existence. In a sense, it still does: when the government erected stone workshops on the Island in the 1880s, many of the Rebel guns were melted down and recast as roof supports. J. B. was also right about the government requiring the whole Island, although it took until 1867 and cost $237,392, more than twice the original appropriation for the entire arsenal. Most of this went to the Sears family, which received more than $145,000. George Davenport and his sister, to whom Kingsbury had haughtily refused to pay $600 an acre, received more than $40,000 ($800 an acre). Even Rock Island City came in for a few dollars for its rights on the Island, and another $17,000 for the bridge. Kingsbury had been right when he called the Island the greatest natural site for an arsenal between the Alleghenies and the Rockies. The building he had so slowly and contentiously begun in 1863 was finally finished in 1867. From that beginning Rock Island Arsenal grew to become the largest military arsenal in the world; it has turned out ordnance for every conflict between the Civil War and Desert Storm. Although much reduced in scope, the Arsenal workshops still turn out ordnance. The Island remains.

Kingsbury left in 1865. The River Bend had stalled his career. In the greatly expanded postwar army Kingsbury had a right to expect, and given his opinion of himself doubtless did expect, to become a general. But he received only one more promotion, to lieutenant colonel. He spent the rest of his career in Watertown, Massachusetts, and in 1870 retired to Brooklyn, New York, where he died on Christmas Day 1879. Today thousands of people drive to work on the Arsenal past a stone building with a huge clock tower extending far above the roof. The Clock Tower is the original arsenal building, for which Kingsbury laid the cornerstone in April 1864.

Most of the men who served at the Barracks have not even a building by which they can be remembered. Charles Reynolds, George Kincaid, Mathew Marx—all have vanished from the Island without trace. Reynolds, despite his predilection for drink, remained in the service until 1887 and rose to be a lieutenant colonel, the same rank at which Kingsbury retired. Kincaid returned to his farm after leaving the Greybeards, no doubt embittered that his grand vision had come to so little. He died in 1876. Marx remained in Rock Island City for several years, serving a term as justice of the peace; but the pond was too small, and he began a peripatetic life that eventually found him in the Soldier's Home in Hampton, Virginia, in the 1890s. Andrew Patrick Caraher, the humane provost marshal of prisoners, remained in the army the rest of his life, although he rose only to the permanent rank of captain. His old wounds bothered him incessantly, to which was added the annoyance of Bright's disease. He refused retirement despite his disabilities and died in 1885.

The insane black soldier, William Boyd, recovered enough to be discharged from the asylum and the army. The surgeons, however, did not mention his mental trouble in their discharge statements. Instead, they swore Boyd suffered chronic gastritis and lumbago, both of which he contracted on the Island. This would have entitled Boyd to a pension, but his wife was denied his pension because they had been married in Kentucky while still slaves, and Kentucky did not recognize such marriages unless they were relicensed before a certain date. As the deadline approached, Boyd found himself trapped away from home by a race riot. By the time he reached his wife the deadline had passed, and she went unrecognized and unpensioned.

There have been other changes on the Island. The original railroad bridge was carried away by ice in 1868. Its replacement was located downriver. A single pier of the first bridge across the Mississippi still stands, just below the Davenport house, which also still stands. The government eventually built another rail and auto bridge across the lower tip of the island. The span from the Island to Iowa boasts the only drawbridge in the world that turns 360 degrees. The drawbridge is there because a lock and dam is there. After nearly 90 years' work on the rapids, the Corps of Engineers finally solved the problem by damming the river. The water level rose permanently above the dam, and the chains of rock that gave the Island its name submerged forever, as did part of the land the compound occupied. The span over the slough stands in the place where stood the original bridge, constructed by citizens lusting for the promised profits of the Barracks.

Some of the businesses that supplied the barracks also remain in the River Bend. Dimock & Gould, which made buckets for the Barracks, still operates. Funeral homes still carry the name of Knox. Some other names have left the area. The Bufords, ubiquitous in commerce, politics, and war, carried on for a while. T. J.'s son—T. J., Jr.—worked for the government until his death in 1950; he spent a number of years working on the Island. Napoleon, T. J., J. M., and their sons, nephews, and cousins—all the Bufords but one are buried in Rock Island's Chippiannock Cemetery. The exception is John, who in 1863 held the line at Gettysburg until the army came up. John's adoring troopers prevailed on his brothers and wife to allow him to be buried at West Point. After the war the family was largely given to daughters, and, although some distaff descendants fought in World War II, the name itself and the family have both left the River Bend. Not even their homes remain. In the 1960s a highway project swept away an entire neighborhood of antebellum and Victorian mansions near the river. One of the buildings destroyed was William Hoffman's home for the last 12 years of his life.

Hoffman had served his government well during the war. He had almost single-handedly constructed a prisoner of war apparatus that cared for a quarter of a million prisoners, and he had kept most of them alive. Hoffman's reputation is that of an inhuman fiend who intentionally denied care the Union was perfectly capable of providing. But Hoffman was not evil: he was narrow. He was unimaginative, humorless, hidebound, and very wise in the way of army politics. He had extremely strict ideas of duty, obligation, and his own career, and he followed those tenets blindly. From that came suffering.

But he did not blindly lash out at the prisoners simply because they were Rebels. Hoffman castigated quartermasters who failed to provide properly equipped cars to transport the prisoners. It was Hoffman who urged the installation of new sewers at Camp Douglas, only to be denied by Montgomery Meigs. When told of some shootings at Camp Chase and medical neglect of the victims, Hoffman berated the commandant: "Such treatment of prisoners, whatever may be the necessity of wounding them, is barbarous and without possible excuse." The record clearly shows that Hoffman, albeit grudgingly, often acted with human concern.[44]

What the record does not show is a single instance that is unequivocally the work of a monster out of control. Hoffman's whole life was devoted to control: control the prisoners and the camps; control the commandants; control the costs. The suffering that occurred at Hoffman's hand stemmed not from monstrosity but from rigidity, and from a character flaw formed in his childhood. Hoffman could not rest until Edwin Stanton had given him absolute power over the camps, the prisoners, and the guards. But in Hoffman's case power did not corrupt. It overwhelmed. To oversee every detail of transporting, housing, feeding, doctoring, and, in the end, releasing 250,000 men was a job too huge for any man. Hoffman's devotion to duty, however, compelled him to it, even if he failed.

And fail he did. Because he could not keep track of every detail, corruption and retaliation became part of the system. At Camp Douglas the contractors shorted both weight and quality of beef, and months passed before the cheating was discovered and rectified. At another camp the commandant used the prison fund to buy fish, which he sold to the sutler, who in turn sold it to the prisoners, who should have received it free to start with. Everybody profited, except Hoffman's wards. Commandants eager to please the commissary general of prisoners could cut rations as they chose, and despite the protestations of Federal apologists, men went hungry. In nearly every autopsy performed by surgeons at Rock Island, the first note about the body is "greatly emaciated."

But Hoffman did not starve the prisoners. Instead, the man of control merely gave up control in one specific area and let matters take their course. Time and again Hoffman told his commandants that the ration lists his office provided were only suggestions, that the commandants would find out for themselves what constituted a sufficient ration. If the prisoners happened to starve, the blame could not be laid at William Hoffman's door. In Hoffman's defense, it should be said that he intended good. The ration was indeed more than sedentary men needed. And Hoffman even stated shortly after he instituted the fund that it should be spent as fast as it accumulated. Legend has it that Hoffman never spent a penny. This is absurd. At Rock Island alone the fund disbursed more than $67,000 in 1864. And over the course of the war the commandants spent $1.2 million from their funds. That must be said in Hoffman's defense. But it is his only defense. As time went on, the balances worked their power on him. He brought the wrath of God on the head of any commandant who failed to account for every penny. As time went on, the expenditures drifted further and further from their original purpose: that articles purchased be "needful to the prisoners." By the time the Barracks opened Johnson could purchase shackles and pay spies without fear of censure. Born to penury and brought up in poverty, the commissary general of prisoners allowed his personal character to influence his professional decisions. William Hoffman was not evil. Rather, he was merely blind. But the point is moot: men died.

Hoffman has answered for his actions, although to a power higher than his government. Indeed, his government thought he had done well. Hoffman was brevetted brigadier general for his services as commissary general of prisoners. One of his services had been the prison funds: when Hoffman closed his books in October 1865, he returned to the government $1,845,125.99, the balances of the funds. Added to the expenditures, the total his commandants saved was more than $3,000,000.

After the war Hoffman continued in the army. He commanded at Fort Leavenworth in Kansas, where he argued with Illinois General Benjamin Grierson about Grierson's black troops. In 1870 Hoffman retired from the army, a major general with more than 40 years' continuous service. He spent the remaining 12 years of his life in Rock Island City. A widower during the war, Hoffman married a Rock Island woman and took up residence in a fine home near the Mississippi. From the cupola he could look up the river and see the Island. During the winter, when foliage did not block the view, he could even have seen the prison. Hoffman died in 1883 and was buried in Chippiannock Cemetery, directly behind one branch of the Buford clan.

The Ordnance Department took over the prison buildings and used some of them for storage for a while. But no one was interested in maintaining buildings constructed hastily and for a temporary purpose, and as the buildings decayed they were torn down. In 1907 the last remaining building, the garrison hospital, was razed. In later years a golf course was constructed on the Arsenal, and it covered much of the area formerly occupied by the compound; officers' quarters occupy the rest. There remain only a few historical markers and the Confederate cemetery to mark the Island as the home of 12,000 prisoners of war. The prison is gone. The Island remains.

Even many of the records are gone. Much of the original prison register is missing. Hoffman's office kept a copy, which is still complete, but parts are so faded as to be illegible. It is now impossible to determine exactly how many men were held at Rock Island. The official number is 12,192, but this is almost certainly wrong. The complete death register still exists, but parts of it, too, are nearly unreadable. Even if the register were pristine, it would be impossible to determine how many men died at Rock Island or who they were. The Commission for Marking Confederate Graves determined there are 1,960 graves at Rock Island, but this is little help. A few of those graves are empty, the bodies claimed by families. Some—including that of the first man to die, James Reeves—are mismarked. The cemetery was moved only a few weeks after it was started, and the headboards have been replaced at least once and probably twice. It is not difficult to imagine that in the replacement names and regiments got garbled. Indeed, that is exactly what happened: the commission's list has been used for decades as the more or less official list of Rock Island dead, but comparison with the death register and the headstones shows that the commission did its work sloppily. Moreover, some of the men who died are not even buried there, as Lieutenant Bennett pointed out when he noted that he buried a prisoner on an unnamed island on the lower reaches of the Mississippi. Men who died on the cars in Rock Island City were not always registered. Finally, the turmoil that accompanied the first months of the prison's existence and the frenzy to get rid of the prisoners during the last months contributed greatly to confusion: at least 40 names have the sinister notation "disposition unaccounted for." They died or escaped or were sold to local surgeons or were simply omitted from the rolls. No one knows. It can be safely said that somewhere around 2,000 men died on the Island, roughly 16 percent of the number held there.

Most of the men who lived in the Barracks survived. Lafayette Rogan returned to Mississippi. William Dillon went to Arkansas. Both lived long after the war. So did J. W. Minnich, who in 1905 recorded his experiences, somewhat enlarged by the intervening years, in a book called *Inside of Rock Island Prison*. Thomas Berry, who claimed to have founded the 7 C K, also lived to a ripe age in Oklahoma.

If an aged William Hoffman sat in his cupola and gazed at the Island, he probably gave little thought to prisoners, living or dead. He had done his duty, and pondering moral questions was not the sort of hobby Hoffman was given to. Besides, the prisoners were not the reason he retired to the River Bend. It is probable he came because he had a brother in Davenport, who extolled the virtues of the place. But it is possible that he came because the Island was the scene of his greatest glory.

When Adolphus Johnson left the Island he turned in more than $181,000 from his prison fund, nearly 10 percent of the total in all the funds. This is stupifying. Camp Douglas was larger than Rock Island and operated for a much longer period, but Douglas's savings were only $3,000 greater than Rock Island's. Elmira, in New York, was the same size as Rock Island, but Johnson's contribution dwarfed Elmira's. Chase, Morton, Johnson's Island—none matched Rock Island's savings. Although to a great extent Colonel Johnson suffered the same narrowness as Hoffman, Johnson could at least conceive of ideas on his own. It was Johnson's idea to print forms himself and save $1,000 on boat fares, and it was Johnson's idea to turn his men into rag-pickers for the benefit of the fund.

Johnson was unfortunate. He spent not quite two years in the River Bend, and he was cheerfully abused by nearly everyone he met. His own sternness helped engender that abuse, as when he stiffly refused Kingsbury a visit to a prisoner. Johnson served in the army until 1866. It is likely his old wound caused his resignation. He spent some time in Chicago but eventually returned to New Jersey, where he put his Barracks experience to use as warden of a county jail. He died in 1893 of paresis, which in those days was often a euphemism for syphilis.

The colonel left behind him a bitter legacy: the reputation of the Barracks. For nearly a year Johnson held his tongue every time Danforth castigated him. But when he picked up his pen to reply to J. B.'s November 1864 article, he assured both the Barracks' doom and his own. In anger, he wrote four words that branded Rock Island a charnel house: "had I the power." In those words was born the legend of Rock Island as a torture chamber. Moreover, that letter loosened Johnson's tongue. No sooner was the war over than he reopened the editorial duel with Danforth, revealing himself as spiteful, rancorous, barbarous, and cruel, reinforcing the charnel house legend. Johnson should have kept his thoughts to himself. Had he, he would today be a much more sympathetic character.

The legend Johnson created grew over the years as the veterans penned their memoirs. Understandably, they were bitter, and their bitterness crept into their accounts. As Ben Hord put it, "Every devilish device that could be conjured up in the brain of a savage to make us suffer was put in force." Minnich said, "The unspeakable treachery of the guards form about as black a chapter of crime as any ever recorded." Minnich even quoted Johnson's own letter to show what a hell Rock Island had been, and he compared Rock Island to Andersonville, saying that if Wirz was guilty, so was Johnson. And Johnson was not as smart as Hoffman, who had distanced himself from hunger by letting his commandants determine the ration. Johnson put on paper words that every man would turn against him: "had I the power." Johnson assuredly did have the power. He commanded. What was done was done by his order.[45]

Despite this, perhaps the legend would have died with the veterans were it not for a Georgia housewife, who in 1936 picked up her own pen and wrote a tale of the Old South that she called *Gone with the Wind*. Unfortunately for the Barracks and for Johnson, Margaret Mitchell decided to send the dashing Ashley Wilkes to Rock Island, and Mitchell's description beggared that of the most bitter veteran. A single blanket to every three men was the norm, according to Mitchell, and three-quarters of the men who went to Rock Island died there. This too is absurd.

There is a germ of truth in the legend, but the germ has outgrown its truth. Adolphus Johnson must bear responsibility for what happened at Rock Island, but Adolphus Johnson has a better defense than William Hoffman. He was, like Hoffman, humorless and rigid. But he was more sensible than Hoffman to the sufferings of his enemies. When the recruits in the calf pen were freezing, Johnson begged for relief; when it was not forthcoming, in desperation he told his quartermaster to sell the recruits blankets. In 1865 he let Dart back into the yard weeks before it was officially authorized. He asked Hoffman if he could give bread to the destitute men who had already been released. During the nightmarish first weeks of the camp, he impressed citizens to haul coal to keep his prisoners warm. Most important of all was what happened after the ration cut in June 1864. The prisoners were malnourished and hungry, but they were alive. In the five months after the ration cut the death rate increased at most of the camps: at Douglas it quadrupled, at Alton and Morton the mortality doubled, and at Elmira it increased tenfold. But at Rock Island mortality actually fell as the hunger increased: in June 1864 1.2 percent of the prisoners died; by November, after six months of the reduced ration and four months without the sutler, the mortality was 0.64 percent. There were not enough rats and dogs to account for this.

The ration cuts were at Johnson's discretion, and he swore that the issues were made to the letter of the law. The declining mortality corroborates him. On the other hand, men receiving 2,600 calories, roughly the amount of the reduced ration, do not eat rats and dogs and do not die "greatly emaciated." Issuing the rations in bulk caused part of the hunger. Strong men ate well, and the weak suffered, especially if the weak manifested any Union tendencies. The men who stole from their comrades must bear some of the responsibility, and it must be said that, although Johnson kept the prisoners hungry, he did not kill them.

All these things have been forgotten, and Johnson has been called the devil's archangel for his inhuman brutality. But in many respects Johnson did not control events; he was controlled by them. The horror of Rock Island was for the most part not a horror of cruelty but a horror of accident. Hoffman sent men to the Island before Reynolds had even completed construction, because he had no choice. Johnson left sick men in their barracks, because he had no choice.

Johnson has been blamed for the smallpox epidemic, but the accusation is unjust. Any blame for that chaos properly belongs to Captain Pratt, who knowingly sent smallpox north and said not a word about it. A quarter of the deaths on the Island are attributable to Pratt and Pratt alone. When the disease appeared on the Island Johnson did everything in his power to manage the crisis. He had no hospital, no serum, few doctors worthy of the name, paralyzing weather. And every day the cars rolled in. Johnson and Surgeon Temple moved mountains to stem the epidemic. But ignorance defeated them: no matter what they did with the cases on hand, every train brought fresh cases.

Although Johnson and Temple did turn the tide of the epidemic, A. M. Clark claimed the credit. The legend has it that smallpox was the scourge of the Barracks. This, too, is only partly true. Smallpox was the single greatest killer: 529 men succumbed to the disease. Diarrhea and dysentery killed 456, including Dr. Gilbert's bromine victims; pneumonia, bronchitis, and tuberculosis took another 439. Smallpox was but one killer among many. It killed nowhere near a majority of the 2,000 men who died. It is remembered because it caught the camp unaware.

There is also the matter of the guards, and here Johnson has little mitigation to excuse him. As a group they were not bullies, although they harbored bullies among them. As a group, they were not cruel, although there were cruel men among them. As a group, they were unfit. Except for the 4th VRC, not a regiment that served had a modicum of military discipline or the perspective that combat imparts. The Greybeards were old men, the 108th had mostly been slaves only weeks before arriving in the River Bend, and all the other regiments were hundred days' men, some of them only boys. Without adequate training and without the leavening experience of combat, these guards suffered vainglory, fear, and an abiding hatred of an enemy they had never met in battle. According to prisoner Charles Wright, the guards began firing in April 1863. Not coincidentally, that is also when most of the VRC left the Island for the eastern theater. The men of the Veteran Reserve Corps knew the difference between a prisoner reaching over the deadline to retrieve a ball and one trying to burrow under the fence. None of the other guards knew, and they were anxious to prove their worth as soldiers, so they shot at anything that moved.

Johnson did little to curb the trigger-happy men of his command. Despite orders, he failed to convene hearings for many of the shootings, and he failed even to notice the two riots that sent dozens of wounded men to the hospitals. In the single case where a hearing found against a guard who killed a prisoner, Johnson overruled the commission. A few more courts-martial might have drastically reduced the number of shooting incidents.

On the other hand, there were not enough courts on earth to keep his men away from whiskey. Despite orders and sanctions the men continued to drink as freely as if they were citizens. And the citizens, although they deplored the resulting vandalism, assaults, and general mayhem, also continued to sell them liquor. The soldiers got drunk, the barkeepers got wealthy, the papers reported the antics to the citizenry, and all the citizens could cluck their tongues. The only loser was Colonel Johnson. But the colonel lost in many respects. He was neither brilliant nor flexible, and, although he can be excused the smallpox epidemic and to some extent the drunken outrages of his men, he cannot so easily be forgiven their propensity to fire into the compound.

Johnson's command can be termed adequate by comparison with other camps. None, either north or south, were exemplary models of humanity. Although there were perhaps better camps to be in than Rock Island, there were also far worse. Rock Island ranked sixth in both the number of men who passed through the camp and the maximum number confined at any one time, but it was third in median population. Men sent to the Island were likely to remain there. For brief periods Rock Island's population was second only to that at the giant camp at Point Lookout. Mortality at the Barracks ranked fourth, exceeded by both Camp Douglas and Elmira as well as by the other island prison, Johnson's Island. Moreover, only at Rock Island can 25 percent of the deaths be blamed on circumstances completely outside the commandant's control. Were it not for Captain Pratt's actions, mortality at Rock Island would rank seventh instead of fourth among the major prisons. Rock Island was not Andersonville.

Rock Island's importance rests in part on these numbers; but much of Rock Island's importance also rests on its stability. Both the population and the command were stable throughout the prison's history. Other camps changed commandants; Rock Island did not. Johnson commanded for 583 of the 585 days the Barracks held prisoners. Prisoners came and went from other camps. For instance, Point Lookout fed thousands of men to Elmira, and most of the camps were temporarily emptied when the exchange cartel was signed in 1862. But what happened on the Island was not affected by changing commandants or shifting population. Moreover, Rock Island was the westernmost of the major prisons and more isolated from inquisitive generals and politicians than most of the other camps. Despite Danforth's best efforts to draw official attention to the Island, there was very little meddling with the camp administration by outsiders. What happened, to an extent greater than at any other prison, was what William Hoffman wanted to happen. True, Hoffman was sometimes thwarted, as in the matter of the hospital and in the October 1864 releases of the "newly made Union men." But these lapses arose through miscommunication, which itself serves as further illustration of the difficulty of administering the system. If there is a mirror of Hoffman's prison system, the mirror is Rock Island.

The prisoners at Rock Island are also mirrors, reflecting the prisoners at all the camps. There were rat-hunters at Elmira and trinket-makers at Morton; at Douglas the prisoners ate the commandant's poodle; Point Lookout inmates enlisted in the Federal army. There is a certain unanimity among prisoners' accounts, because they were in many senses all in the same place: prison. There was also unanimity in the guards and their actions. VRC and hundred days' men served at most camps, although only Rock Island could boast the old men of the Greybeards. Little of this is known or remembered. The reputation of Rock Island has never been that of a reflection. An angry Adolphus Johnson shattered the mirror on 21 November 1864 with four ill-considered words: "had I the power." Only the legend remains.

Although the legend was birthed by Johnson's own pen, it might well have been stillborn but for the midwifery of J. B. Danforth, Jr. It was J. B.'s constant needling that eventually provoked Johnson to respond. It was J. B. who kept it up, reminding his readers as late as 1867 that the prisoners had been starved, kept naked, and murdered. By then, with the colonel safely away, Danforth also suggested he was a philanderer, which gives credence to the syphilis theory of Johnson's death.

Excess in accusation was no vice, a policy Danforth maintained all his life, whether he was heaping abuse on the claw-sucking businessmen or skewering Johnson for starving the prisoners. His readers never had to wonder what he thought, because J. B. told them, repeatedly, forcefully, and with an unmatched command of language. To be an enemy of J. B. was to be sliced to very fine ribbons, and Danforth had many enemies, because of his outspokenness, his opinions, and his politics. But enemies never bothered J. B. Indeed, without them his paper would have been bland and mundane. He reveled in enmity and rejoiced at whipping anyone who dared to disagree with the *Argus*. Danforth was abusive, in some respects hypocritical, perhaps a thief, probably a craven, and certainly vain. But overshadowing all these flaws is a virtue that colored his life and work: he had passion. He would rather be wrong than silent. And whether wrong or right, he plowed ahead. What he put his hand to he did wholeheartedly. It is well his hardware store failed in 1852. Had it succeeded, the world would have lost an exquisite political editor.

Fortunately, the store did fail, and from that inevitably followed the feud with Johnson. In provoking Johnson, Danforth helped create the legend of Rock Island. Whether the legend is true or not mattered little: J. B. had papers to sell and a Republican administration to condemn. Besides, to J. B. Danforth, the legend was true in every detail. It is in the end this quality that is most attractive in Danforth: he believed every word he wrote.

And so did many others. In his November article J. B. noted that the meat ration consisted of a "piece of beef about the size of two fingers." Years later, several prisoners used that precise phrase in describing the ration. J. W. Minnich hoarded a copy of the *Argus* with Johnson's letter for more than 40 years. For good or ill, much of what people think they know of the Barracks stems directly from the articles that appeared in November 1864.

In 1869, perhaps bored by politics—Andrew Johnson was president and did not present nearly so rich a target as had Abraham Lincoln—Danforth sold out and went to New York for a time. But the River Bend had a hold on him. In 1872 he returned as part owner of the *Argus*. But the paper's politics had shifted too much to the right to suit Danforth, and he soon revived another, defunct newspaper, which he edited until August 1891. That month he wrote the last of his farewell columns and left the River Bend a final time, for San Jose, California.

On New Year's Day, 1896, Joseph Baker Danforth, Jr., died in California. His paper outlived him, and still lives. To this day the *Argus* publishes six days a week, only a few hundred feet from the location where J. B. dipped his pen in vitriol and seared those he called tricksters. Danforth is gone.

But the Island remains.

A Question of Hunger

item	ration 1	cal.	ration 2	cal.	ration 3	cal.	ration 4	cal.	ration 5	cal.
pork/bacon	12.00	1764	12.00	1764	12.00	1764	12.00	1764	10.00	1470
or beef	20.00	1800	20.00	1800	20.00	1800	20.00	1800	14.00	1260
soft bread/flour	22.00	2200	22.00	2200	22.00	2200	22.00	2200	16.00	1600
or hard bread	16.00	1920	*12.00	1440	16.00	1920	16.00	1920	14.00	1680
or corn meal	20.00	1520	20.00	1520	20.00	1520	20.00	1520	16.00	1215
beans/peas	2.40	211	2.40	211	2.40	211	2.40	211	2.00	176
rice/hominy	(and) 1.60	50	(or) 1.60	50	(or) 1.60	50	(and) 1.60	50	(or) 1.28	40
green coffee	1.60	0	1.60	0	1.60	0	1.60	0	1.10	0
or roasted coffee	1.25	0	1.25	0	1.25	0	1.25	0	**0.33	0
or tea	0.24	0	0.24	0	0.24	0	0.24	0	0.15	0
salt	0.50	0	0.50	0	0.50	0	0.50	0	0.50	0
sugar	2.40	261	2.40	261	2.40	261	2.40	261	**0.81	88
pepper	0.25	0	0.25	0	0.25	0	0.25	0	0.00	0
potatoes	4.80	81	0.00	0	6.80	115	6.60	111	2.40	40
molasses	0.33	30	0.00	0	0.00	0	0.35	32	0.32	29
vinegar	1.25	5	1.25	5	1.25	5	1.25	5	0.96	4
TOTAL calories		4637		4477		4592		4670		3197
Percent of ration 1		100%		97%		99%		101%		69%

(Table continued on following page.)

All calorie (cal.) counts are approximate; all calorie counts are calculated using beef, soft bread, beans, and rice, as opposed to alternatives; all measurements are in ounces; all rations taken from *OR*, Series II.

* 16 ounces allowed when on active campaign.

** Represents a daily average; actual issue was every other day.

Ration 1: Standard Federal issue according to Army Regulations, August 1861–June 1864.

Ration 2: Standard issue after the reduction of June 1864.

Ration 3: Contract for rations at Camp Douglas, 16 June 1862 (for troops and prisoners).

Ration 4: Contract for rations at Camp Chase, 9 June 1862 (for troops and prisoners).

Ration 5: Prisoner's rations after reduction of 1 June 1864.

N O T E S

ABBREVIATIONS USED

ISA — Illinois State Archives

ISHL — Illinois State Historical Library

LC — Library of Congress

NA — National Archives

OR — *The War of the Rebellion: A Compilation of the Official Records of the Union and Confederate Armies*

RIA — Rock Island Arsenal Museum

RICHS — Rock Island County Historical Society

SHSI — State Historical Society of Iowa

USAMHI — United States Army Military History Institute

USMA — United States Military Academy

VP — Virginia Polytechnic Institute and State University

1: "THAT IS THE WAY YOU DO HERE, IS IT?"

1. *Annual Reunion of the Graduates of the United States Military Academy, June 12, 1885,* 37; Henry R. Schoolcraft to J. C. Calhoun, 20 December 1822, Application Letters, USMA; William Hoffman to Calhoun, 21 December 1822 and 21 October 1824, Application Letters, USMA; E. Cutler to Calhoun, 3 December 1824, Application Letters, USMA; Leslie Hunter, *Warden*

for the Union: General William Hoffman (1807–1884) (Ph.D. diss., University of Arizona, 1971), 3–13; undated memoranda from John Hoffman to various Secretaries of War, 1845–1853, RG 92, Records of the Office of the Quartermaster General, Consolidated Correspondence, NA.

2. One of Hoffman's classmates at West Point was Robert E. Lee.

3. *Cadets Arranged in Order of Merit in Their Respective Classes, as Determined at the General Examination in June 1829,* USMA; George W. Cullum, *Biographical Register of the Officers and Graduates of the U.S. Military Academy at West Point, N.Y., from Its Establishment, in 1802, to 1890,* 2 vols. (Boston: Houghton, Mifflin, 1891), 1:433; Hoffman to George Cullum, 12 October 1859, USMA; *The War of the Rebellion: A Compilation of the Official Records of the Union and Confederate Armies,* 128 vols. (Washington, D.C.: Government Printing Office, 1880–1901) (hereafter cited as *OR*), ser. 2, 1:71.

4. Frank Weigley, *Quartermaster General of the Union Army: A Biography of M. C. Meigs* (New York: Columbia University Press, 1959), 23–24, 30, 33, 60–62, 66, 80; *OR*, ser. 2, 3:8.

5. *OR*, ser. 2, 3:8, 32, 48–49, 122–23.

6. Ibid., 10, 34, 49, 56, 123, 137.

7. Ibid., 169, 185, 211, 248, 269–71, 297.

8. Ibid., 156, 216–217.

9. Ibid., 390; General Orders No. 67, 17 June 1862, in *General Orders Affecting the Volunteer Force, 1861–1863* (Washington, D.C.: Government Printing Office, 1864).

10. *OR*, ser. 2, 3:360, 540–41, 617.

11. Ibid., 375, 541, 636.

12. Ibid., 317, 6:98, 5:247.

13. *Revised Regulations for the Army of the United States* (Washington, D.C.: Government Printing Office, 1861), 34–35; *OR*, ser. 2, 3:349, 361.

14. *OR*, ser. 2, 3:562, 586, 604, 647, 4:368, 682, 5:345.

15. General Orders No. 67, 17 June 1862, *General Orders; OR*, ser. 2, 3:621, 5:345–51, 367, 398, 4:240, 407–565, 700, 6:398.

16. *OR*, ser. 2, 5:225, 243, 713, 4:699, 3:590, 6:804.

17. Ibid., 3:647, 4:253, 263, 646, 5:383, 6:150; "Receipt Roll of Hired Men," RG 249, Entry 16, Papers of General Hoffman, NA.

18. William Hoffman to Edwin Stanton, 3 January 1864, and Brigadier General A. S. S. to Hoffman, 4 January 1864, Letters Received by the War Department from the Commissary General of Prisoners, RG 107, Entry 32, NA; *OR*, ser. 2, 7:784, 4:324.

19. George G. Lewis and John Mewha, *History of Prisoner of War Utilization by the United States Army, 1776–1945* (Washington, D.C.: Department of the Army, 1955), 29; *OR*, ser. 2, 8:986–87.

20. *OR*, ser. 2, 6:129, 395, 403; William B. Hesseltine, *Civil War Prisons: A Study in War Psychology* (Columbus: Ohio State University Press, 1930), 109 and chapter 5.

21. Meigs to Reynolds, 14 July 1863, RG 92, Entry 14, Miscellaneous Letters Sent, NA.

22. Francis Heitman, *Historical Register and Dictionary of the United States Army, from Its Organization, September 29, 1789, to March 2, 1903*, 2 vols. (Washington, D.C.: Government Printing Office, 1903), 1:825; *Chicago Tribune*, 3 August 1863; *OR*, ser. 1, 24(pt. 3):227; Meigs to Reynolds, 26 August 1863, RG 92, Miscellaneous Letters, NA.

23. *Rock Island Republican*, 17 March 1852.

24. *Rock Island Argus*, 1 August 1891, 5 March 1857.

25. *Republican*, 24 November 1852, 16 March, 29 June 1853, 1 June 1863.

26. Court Proceedings, 10th Judicial Circuit, 9 May 1853, Records of the Office of the Quartermaster General, RG 92, Consolidated Correspondence, NA; *Republican*, 4 May 1853; *Argus*, 25 August 1855

27. *Argus*, 15 December 1855.

28. *Republican*, 25 April 1855; McNeil to Jessup, 4 March 1854, RG 92, Consolidated Correspondence, NA.

29. *Argus*, 19 March, 2 April, 16 September 1857; *Past and Present of Rock Island County, Illinois* (Chicago: H. F. Kett & Co., 1877), 159; *Argus*, 25 January 1858.

30. "Slough" is regional parlance for a minor channel between the mainland and an island, as distinct from the main channel of the river; the term remains in use today.

31. Milo Milton Quaife, ed., *The Early Days of Rock Island and Davenport: The Narratives of J. W. Spencer and J. M. D. Burrows* (Chicago: Lakeside Press, 1942), 106–7.

32. *Argus*, 29 April 1861.

33. Ibid., 15 December 1855.

34. Ibid., 22 April, 8 May, 16, 23 June 1861. In one of the coincidences that abound in history, thirty years earlier Major Anderson, then a lieutenant, had escorted the warrior Black Hawk to captivity, in company with another young lieutenant named Jefferson Davis.

35. Danforth to Allen Fuller, 4 October 1862, Administrative Files, 51st Infantry, ISA.

36. T. E. Eddy, *Patriotism of Illinois: A Record of the Civil and Military History of the State in the War for the Union* (Chicago: Clark & Co., 1865), 56; *Argus*, 5 October 1864. Napoleon was the half brother of John Buford, of Gettysburg fame. Two other half brothers, James Madison Buford and Thomas Jefferson Buford (known as J. M. and T. J.), also lived in Rock Island. The family was prominent in politics and commerce from the 1840s through the end of the century.

37. Charles Buford to Louis [Buford], 24 September 1863, Charles Buford Papers, LC; *Argus*, 28 October 1863.

38. Arthur Charles Cole, *The Era of the Civil War, 1848–1870*

(Springfield: Illinois Centennial Commission, 1919), 302. Some Egyptians thought this very sound advice—a number of them slipped south and joined the Confederacy. This number included a company of Illinoisians who enlisted in the 15th Tennessee, making Lincoln's home state the only Federal state that sent an organized unit to the Confederate army (Ed Gleeson, *Illinois Rebels: A Civil War Unit History of G Company* [Carmel, Ind.: Guild Press of Indiana, 1996], xiii).

39. *Argus,* various dates in May 1863.

40. *Republican, Davenport Democrat, Davenport Gazette,* various dates in April and May 1854; *Republican,* 19 April 1854.

41. N. B. Buford to Secretary of War, 11 February 1851, RG 107, Entry 18, Letters Received, Main Series, NA; "National Armory: An Appeal to Congress by the Citizens of Rock Island and Moline, Illinois," 1861, ISHL; *Argus,* 27 July, 4 April 1861; *Rock Island Union,* 18 February 1863.

42. *Past and Present of Rock Island,* 108; *Argus,* various dates in April, 1 May, 8, 23 August 1863.

43. Michael Mullins, *The Fremont Rifles: A History of the 37th Illinois Veteran Volunteer Infantry* (Wilmington, N.C.: Broadfoot Publishing Company, 1990), 121–22; *Argus,* 27 May, 1 June 1863; *Union,* 23 December 1863; *Argus,* 12 January 1864

44. *Argus,* 28 July 1863.

45. *Union,* 5 August 1863; *Argus,* 29 July, 4 August 1863.

46. Meigs to Reynolds, 7 August 1863, RG 92, Miscellaneous Letters, NA; *Argus,* 31 July, 16 September 1863.

47. *Argus,* 14 August 1863.

48. Ibid., 1 August 1863; *OR,* ser. 2, 6:948.

49. *Union,* 5 August 1863. Part of the area of the compound is now under the Mississippi River, the result of a dam built by the Corps of Engineers.

50. Meigs to Reynolds, 12, 14 August 1863, Reynolds to Meigs, 19 August 1863, Meigs to Reynolds, with endorsements by Hoffman, 24 and 28 August 1863, Charles Thomas to Reynolds, 28 November 1863, all in RG 92, Miscellaneous Letters, NA.

51. *Argus,* 23 September, 15 October 1863.

52. Ibid., 12 June, 3 August 1863.

53. Ibid., 2 December 1863.

54. Cullum, *Biographical Register,* 24–25; *Annual Reunion, 1880,* 80–84.

55. Kingsbury to Cullum, 20 June 1867, USMA; *OR,* ser. 1, 2 (pt. 1):155; Kingsbury to Ramsay, 3 September 1863, RG 156, Ordnance Department, Letters Sent, NA.

56. *Argus,* 5 September 1863; Truesdale and Danforth to Kingsbury, 3 September 1863, RG 156, Letters Sent, NA.

57. Kingsbury to Ripley, 22 August 1863, RG 156, Letters Sent, NA; Meigs to Reynolds, 26 August 1863, RG 92, Miscellaneous Letters, NA; *Argus,* 30 September 1863.

58. Kingsbury to Ramsay, 8 October, 22 August 1863, RG 156, Letters Sent, NA.

59. Kingsbury to G. L. Davenport, 24 August 1863, RG 156, Letters Sent, NA; Kingsbury to Ramsay, 22 August 1863, Ramsay to Kingsbury, 21 May 1864, RG 156, Register of Letters Received, Rock Island Arsenal, Great Lakes Branch, NA, Chicago; George W. Burr, "History of the Rock Island Arsenal, 1862–1913," RG 156, NA.

60. Kingsbury to John Tracy, 12 January 1864, Kingsbury to Freight Agent, 23, 25 January 1864, RG 156, Letters Sent, NA.

61. Kingsbury to J. J. Lewis, various dates in October and November 1863, 28 January 1864, Kingsbury to Chief of Ordnance, 16 March 1865, RG 156, Letters Sent, NA.

62. *Argus,* 21 September, 6 October 1863.

63. Ibid., 19 August, 1, 5, 22 October, 22 November, 5 December 1863.

64. General Orders No. 105, 28 April 1863, *General Orders;* General Orders No. 130, 15 May 1863, *General Orders.*

65. *OR,* ser. 3, 5:549–52, 566; John Billings, *Hardtack and Coffee; or, The Unwritten Story of Army Life* (1887; rpt., Lincoln: University of Nebraska Press, 1993), 79; Endorsement, Johnson to Wood, RG 393, Part IV, Entry 1081, Register of Letters Received, NA.

66. Fletcher Galloway, Pension File, RG 94, NA.

67. Gaebel to Johnson, 20 May 1864, RG 94, Entry 113, Office of the Adjutant General, Regimental Descriptive, Order and Letter Book, 4th VRC, NA; General Orders No. 50, 10 March 1864, RG 393, Part IV, Entry 1083, General Orders, Rock Island Barracks, NA.

68. Guard Report, 30 December 1863, RG 393, Part IV, Entry 1088, Guard Report and List of Prisoners, NA (hereafter cited as RG 393, NA). It has been suggested that Civil War soldiers suffered what has come to be known as post-traumatic stress disorder. This has been examined by Eric Dean in *Shook over Hell: Post-Traumatic Stress, Vietnam, and the Civil War* (Cambridge, Mass.: Harvard University Press, 1997), but the malady does not seem to have affected either the prisoners or guards at Rock Island to any discernible extent; Adolphus J. Johnson, Service Record and Pension File, RG 94, Entry 114, Muster Rolls, 4th VRC, NA; *OR,* ser. 1, 2:487–88, and 31(pt. 1):816.

69. Thomas to Reynolds, 13, 18 November 1863, RG 92, Miscellaneous Letters, NA.

70. Samuel L. Gracey, *Annals of the Sixth Pennsylvania Cavalry* (Philadelphia: E. H. Butler and Co., 1868), iii, 135; *OR,* ser. 3, 5:544–45; Post Orders Nos. 1 and 2, 24 November 1863, RG 393, Part IV, Entry 1085, Post Orders and Circulars, Rock Island Barracks, NA.

71. Reynolds to Meigs, 14 October 1863, RG 92, Entry 19, Register of Letters Received, Quartermaster General, NA; *Argus,* 22 October 1863; Special Orders No. 9, 3 December 1863, RG 393, Part IV, Entry 1084, Special

Orders, Rock Island Barracks, NA; Meigs to Reynolds, with endorsement from Hoffman, 11 September 1863, RG 92, Miscellaneous Letters Sent, NA; *Argus,* 18 November 1863; Johnson to Hoffman, 28 June 1864, RG 393, Part IV, Entry 1081, Letters Sent, Rock Island Barracks, NA.

72. Rush to Hoffman, 24, 25, 26 November 1863, RG 249, Letters Received, NA.

73. Rush to Hoffman, 27, 28 November, 1863, RG 249, Letters Received, NA; Rush to Fry, 26 November 1863, RG 393, Letters Sent, NA.

74. Hoffman to Norton Townsend, 23 November 1863, RG 249, Letters Sent, NA; Hoffman to Rush, 25, 28 November, 1863, RG 249, Letters Sent, NA; *OR,* ser. 2, 8:992–93.

75. Hoffman to Rush, 25 November 1863, RG 249, Letters Sent, NA.

76. Donald Jackson, ed., *Black Hawk: An Autobiography* (Urbana: University of Illinois Press, 1955), 88; *Union,* 2 September 1863.

77. *Union,* 25 November 1863.

2: "They Are Dying Off Very Fast"

1. *Argus,* 3 December 1863.

2. *OR,* ser. 1, 31(pt. 2):36; ser. 2, 6:626.

3. Special Orders No. 4, n.d. [late November 1863], RG 393, NA; Charles Wright, "Rock Island Prison, 1864–5," Southern Historical Society, *Papers,* April 1876.

4. Rush to Hoffman, 24, 30 November 1863, RG 393, Entry 21, Telegrams Sent, NA.

5. *Argus,* 4, 7, 9 December 1863; *Union,* 11 December 1863; Alpheus Williams to My Dear Daughter, December 1863, in Alpheus S. Williams, *From the Cannon's Mouth: The Civil War Letters of General Alpheus S. Williams* (Lincoln: University of Nebraska Press, 1995), 278.

6. A. J. Cantrell, "Vivid Experiences in Prison," *Confederate Veteran* (May 1908): 216; W. C. Dodson, "Stories of Prison Life," *Confederate Veteran* (March 1900): 128; *OR,* ser. 2, 6:585–86.

7. *Argus,* 8, 14 December 1863.

8. F. A. Jennings to Friend John, 19 January 1864, Marsh Papers, IHSL; *Argus,* 8 December 1863.

9. *Argus,* 29 August, 1, 2 September, 28 November 1863; *Union,* 18 November 1863.

10. *Argus,* 19, 21, 31 December 1863; *Union,* 30, 31 December 1863; Lafayette Rogan Diary, 1 January 1864, ISHL (hereafter cited as Rogan); *Harper's Weekly,* 23 January 1864; *Argus* and *Union,* various dates in 2–18 January 1864.

11. Kate Perry-Mosher, "History of Rock Island, Illinois, 1863," paper read before the Henrietta Hunt Morgan Chapter, United Daughters of the Confederacy, n.d. [circa 1900], RIA; William Dillon Diary, 19, 31 December

1863 (hereafter cited as Dillon); Townsend to Hoffman, RG 107, Letters Received, NA; J. W. Minnich, "Comment on Rock Island Prison," *Confederate Veteran* (August 1908): 554; Rogan, 9 January 1864; *Argus,* 11 January 1864.

12. *Argus,* 1, 5, 14, 28 December 1863.

13. Death Register, RG 109, vol. 395, "Record of Prisoners Who Have Died at Rock Island Barracks, Illinois," NA; *Argus,* 14, 15, 22 December 1863; Rogan, 2 January 1864; Hospital Registers, RG 74, Entry 544, vols. 178–81, Office of the Adjutant General, "Register of the Sick and Wounded, Prison Hospitals, Rock Island, Illinois," NA; *Union,* 6, 13 January 1864

14. *Argus,* 14, 27 December 1863, 2 January 1864.

15. Ibid., 2, 18 January 1864.

16. *OR,* ser. 2, 6:848.

17. Robert M. Berkow, ed., *Merck Manual of Diagnosis and Therapy,* 13th ed. (Rahway, N.J.: Merck, Sharpe, and Dohme Research Laboratories, 1977), 30–31; Richard Gordon, *The Alarming History of Medicine* (New York: St. Martin's Press, 1994), 43–50; H. H. Cunningham, *Doctors in Gray: The Confederate Medical Service* (Baton Rouge: Louisiana State University Press, 1960), 200; *Argus,* 22 December 1863.

18. *OR,* ser. 2, 6:437–38, 865–66.

19. Pratt to Johnson, 31 December 1863, RG 107, Letters Received, NA.

20. Hoffman to Rush, 28 November 1863, RG 249, Letters Sent, NA; *OR,* ser. 2, 6:938; Temple to Clark, 7 February 1864, RG 107, Letters Received, NA.

21. Cunningham, *Doctors in Gray,* 199; *OR,* ser. 2, 7:23–25; Clark to Johnson, 6 February 1864, RG 107, Letters Received, NA.

22. Temple to Clark, 7 February 1864, RG 107, Letters Received, NA; Hospital Registers, RG 74, Entry 544, NA; Death Register, RG 109, vol. 395, NA.

23. Rush to Fry, 5 December 1863 (?), RG 393, Letters Sent, NA; Temple to Clark, 7 February 1864, RG 107, Letters Received, NA; Telegram, Johnson to Assistant Surgeon General R. C. Wood, 6 February 1864, RG 107, Letters Received, NA; *Argus,* 15, 21 January 1864.

24. *Argus,* 14, 23, 31 December 1863, 26 April 1864; Endorsement, Johnson to Woods, 17 April 1864, RG 393, Part IV, Entry 1081, Register of Letters Received, NA; F. A. Jennings to Friend John, 19 January 1864, Marsh Papers, IHSL.

25. Endorsement, Johnson to Wood, RG 393, Part IV, Entry 1081, Register of Letters Received, NA; Fletcher Galloway, Pension File; Special Orders No. 50, 10 March 1864, RG 393, NA. The Invalid Corps's name changed to Veteran Reserve Corps in April 1864. It was almost universally called the VRC, a practice followed here.

26. General Orders, various numbers and dates, RG 393, NA.

27. Johnson to Hoffman, 19 January 1864, RG 107, Letters Received, NA; *Argus,* 20 January 1864.

28. Death Register, RG 109, vol. 395, NA; John R. Brumgardt, ed., *Civil War Nurse: The Diary and Letters of Hannah Ropes* (Knoxville: University of Tennessee Press, 1980), 69–73.

29. Brumgardt, *Civil War Nurse*, 74–76, 106–8; *OR*, ser. 2, 6:758.

30. Clark to Johnson, 5, 6 February 1864, RG 107, Letters Received, NA.

31. Ibid.

32. Clark to Moxley, Clark to Hoffman, 10 February 1864, RG 107, Letters Received, NA.

33. *OR*, ser. 2, 6:1002.

34. Kincaid to Hoffman, 18 December 1863, RG 107, Letters Received, NA; *OR*, ser. 2, 8:990–94; Hoffman to Stanton, 19 September 1863, RG 107, Letters Received, NA.

35. Hoffman to Sangster, 31 March 1863, RG 249, Letters Sent, NA; *OR*, ser. 2, 6:462, 490, 503–4, 702.

36. Hoffman to Bucker, 3 June, 25 July 1863, RG 107, Letters Received, NA.

37. Hoffman to Sangster, 2 April 1863, RG 249, Letters Sent, NA; *OR*, ser. 2, 6:754.

38. *OR*, ser. 2, 5:720–21, 766–67, 6:754; Hoffman to Edwards, 25 July 1863, RG 249, Letters Sent, NA; Consolidated Statement of Prison and Parole Camp Funds During the Secession Rebellion, RG 249, Entry 16, Papers of General Hoffman, NA.

39. Johnson to Hoffman, 11 February 1864, RG 94, Entry 289, Adjutant General's Office, General Information Index, Rock Island, Illinois, NA; Clark to Johnson, 10 February 1864, RG 107, Letters Received, NA. How Hoffman reached this figure remains a mystery. No surviving correspondence mentions $1,800.

40. *OR*, ser. 2, 6:1037; Hoffman to Johnson, 10, 25 March 1864, RG 249, Letters Sent, NA; Hoffman to Stanton, 14 March 1864, RG 107, Letters Received, NA.

41. *OR*, ser. 2, 7:11.

42. Ibid., 12–15.

43. Johnson to Hoffman, 23 March 1864, RG 249, Letters Received, NA.

44. *OR*, ser. 2, 7:16.

45. Johnson to Hoffman, 23 March 1864, RG 393, Letters Sent, NA.

46. *Democrat*, 23 January 1864; Rogan, 13 February 1864; *Union*, 20 January 1864; *Argus*, 25 January 1864.

47. *Gazette*, 19 January 1864; *Argus*, 28 January 1864; Bardelabeu to Mrs. Col. James Taylor, 10 April 1864, private collection of Benton McAdams.

48. "Statement of Articles Purchased and Services Rendered and Prices Paid therefore in the Month of March 1864 Chargeable Against the Prison Fund at Rock Island Barracks, Illinois," February, March, and April 1864, RG 249, Letters Received, NA. (hereafter cited as Prison Fund Account); *War's*

Greatest Workshop: Rock Island Arsenal ([Rock Island, Ill.]: Arsenal Publishing Company, 1922), 213–15.

49. *Argus,* 28 December 1863; Hoffman to Johnson, 29 January 1864, RG 249, Letters Sent, NA; *Argus,* 8, 9 January 1864; Johnson to Hoffman, 2 February 1864, RG 393, Letters Sent, NA.

50. Prison Fund Account, March 1864.

51. S. H. M. Byers, *Iowa in War Times* (Des Moines, Iowa: W. D. Condit and Co., 1888), 463; Kirkwood to Kincaid, 20 August 1862, Correspondence, 37th Iowa, Iowa Adjutant General's Papers, ISHS; *OR,* ser. 3, 2:339.

52. *Roster and Record of Iowa Soldiers in the War of the Rebellion* (Des Moines, Iowa: Emory H. English, 1911), 5:745–832; John Wagner to Dinah, 9 November 1862, in Steve Meyer, *Iowa Valor: A Compilation of Civil War Combat Experiences* . . . (Garrison, Iowa: Meyer Publishing, 1994), 485; Company F to Baker, 7 December 1862, Correspondence, 37th Iowa, ISHS.

53. *OR,* ser. 2, 6:393, 8:993; Baker to Kirkwood, 15 December 1862, Iowa Adjutant General's Office.

54. Griffin Frost, *Camp and Prison Journal* (1867; rpt., Iowa City, Iowa: Press of the Camp Pope Bookshop, 1994), 31–32; Spencer Kotter et al. to Johnson, 25 January 1864, Correspondence, 37th Iowa, ISHS; *Democrat,* 31 May 1865.

55. Joseph Paschal to My Dear Children, 26 December 1863, Paschal Letters, private collection of Maggie Burmeister; Baker to Stanton, 9 February 1864, 37th Iowa, ISHS; *Union,* 13 January 1864; *Argus,* 20 January, 8 February 1864.

56. Johnson to Reynolds, 20 January 1864, RG 393, Letters Sent, NA; Baker to Stanton, 9 February 1864, Correspondence, 37th Iowa, ISHS; Johnson to Hoffman, 7 January 1864, RG 249, Entry 22, Telegrams Received, NA; Johnson to Hoffman, 19 January 1864, RG 249, Letters Received, NA; Johnson to Reynolds, 20 January 1864, RG 393, Letters Sent, NA; *Argus,* 29 January 1864.

57. *Argus,* 20 January, 29 February 1864; Returns for Alterations, 37th Iowa Infantry, ISHS; Monthly Returns, 37th Iowa Infantry, ISHS.

58. Baker to Stanton, 9 February 1864, Correspondence, 37th Iowa, ISHS; *Union,* 17 February 1864; *Argus,* 6 June 1864; *OR,* ser. 2, 7:24; Special Orders No. 80, 10 April 1864, and No. 88, 5 May 1864, RG 393, NA.

59. *Union,* 2, 17 February 1864; Court Proceedings, 10th Judicial Circuit, 9 May 1853, RG 92, Consolidated Correspondence, NA; Ezra Beardsley to Dear Emma, 27 March 1863.

60. *Union,* 17 February 1864.

61. *Argus,* 11 February 1864.

62. Johnson to Heintzelman, 1 May 1864, RG 393, Letters Sent, NA.

63. *Argus,* 3 March 1864.

64. Kingsbury to Ramsay, 15 February 1864, RG 156, Letters Sent, NA.

65. Johnson to Nichols, 23 May 1865, RG 393, Letters Sent, NA.

66. Ibid.

67. Kingsbury to Reynolds, 26 February 1864, Kingsbury to Johnson, 14 March 1864, RG 156, Letters Sent, NA.

68. Kingsbury to Ramsay, 16, 17 March 1864, RG 156, Letters Sent, NA.

69. Unnumbered order, 13 March 1864, RG 393, Entry 1086, Orders Received, NA; Kingsbury to Johnson, 2 May 1864, Kingsbury to Ramsay, 4 May 1864, RG 156, Letters Sent, NA; Endorsement, Johnson to Kingsbury, 5 May 1864, RG 393, Letters Received, NA.

3: "A DISAGREEABLE PLACE TO BE"

1. *Argus,* 14 December 1863; *OR,* ser. 2, 4:223; Lewis and Mewha, *History of Prisoner of War Utilization,* 29; *OR,* ser. 2, 8:986–87.

2. Gaston to Father, no date, RIA; Yates et al. to Lincoln, no dates, and memorandum, 16 January 1865, from Lincoln (unaddressed, but to either Stanton or Hoffman).

3. *OR,* ser. 2, 3:335, 4:566, 616.

4. *Argus,* 19 January 1864; Johnson to Hoffman, 19 January 1864, and Johnson to Hoffman, 17 March 1864, with endorsements by Hoffman and Stanton, RG 249, Letters Received, NA; Dillon, 13, 24 January 1864.

5. Rogan, 9 February 1864; *Argus,* 29 January 1864.

6. Rupert Baird, "In Camp and Prison," *Confederate Veteran* (February 1917): 95.

7. Rogan, 11 January–12 February 1864; Richard Lodor to Johnson, 25 March 1864, RG 249, Letters Sent, NA.

8. Prison Fund Account, January and February 1864; *Union,* 2 February 1864; Hoffman to Stanton, 14 July 1864, RG 249, Letters Sent, NA. The citizen's name is variously given as Winkless and Wenkless.

9. Rogan, 23 April 1864; Johnson to Hoffman, 16 May 1864, RG 249, Register of Letters Received, NA.

10. Rush to Hoffman, 25 November 1863, RG 249, Letters Received, NA; *Argus,* 25 January 1864.

11. Register of Prisoners Confined at Rock Island Barracks, Ill., RG 109, Volume 394, NA (hereafter cited as Prison Register); *Union,* 3 March 1864; *Argus,* 27 February 1864; Johnson to Hoffman, 23 April 1864, RG 249, Letters Received, NA.

12. Rogan, 25 February, 17 March 1864.

13. Post Orders No. 63, 14 March 1864, and No. 66, 17 March 1864, RG 393, NA.

14. *Argus,* 21, 26 March 1864; Descriptive, Letter Endorsement, and Order Book, 4th VRC, RG 94, Entry 113, NA.

15. Post Orders No. 75, 4 May 1864, RG 393, NA.

16. Gaebel to Johnson, 20 May 1864, RG 94, Letter Book, 4th VRC, NA.

17. Post Orders No. 97, 23 May 1864, RG 393, NA; Johnson to Fuller,

5 May 1864, RG 393, Register of Letters Received, NA.

18. Harriet Stevens, ed., *The Graybeards: The Family of Major Lyman Allen during the American Civil War* (Iowa City, Iowa: Press of the Camp Pope Bookshop, 1998), 44.

19. Johnson to Hoffman, 13 August 1864, RG 249, Letters Received, NA; Perry-Mosher, "History of Rock Island, Illinois"; Nancy Ann Duke Buford to Susan Buford, n.d. [1864], Charles Buford Papers, LC.

20. Perry-Mosher, "History of Rock Island, Illinois."

21. P. P. Pullen, "A Kentucky Hero," *Confederate Veteran* (August 1923): 287.

22. Wright, "Rock Island Prison," 283; John Bateson, "Testimony of a Federal Soldier," Southern Historical Society, *Papers* (April 1876): 293; *Union*, 22 June 1864; W. J. Bohon, "Rock Island Prison," *Confederate Veteran* (July 1908): 346; Johnson to Hoffman, 13 August 1864, RG 249, Letters Received, NA.

23. W. T. Norton, "Reminiscences of a Private Soldier of the Confederate Prison at Rock Island, Ill.," *Union*, 3 October 1915.

24. *Union*, 3 February 1864; Rogan, 3 April 1864; Nancy Ann Duke Buford to Dear Susan [Buford], n.d. [1864], Charles Buford Papers, LC.

25. *Union*, 9 May 1864; *Massachusetts in the Army and Navy during the War of 1861–65* (Boston: Wright and Potter Printing Co., 1895), 2:208; Unnumbered order, 22 September 1863, RG 110, Entry 306, Orders and Circulars of the Provost Marshal General, Vols. 1 and 2; Special Orders No. 78, Orders Received, NA; Muster Rolls, 4th VRC, NA.

26. Gracey, *Annals of the Sixth Pennsylvania Cavalry*, 214, 315; Rogan, 22 April 1864; *Argus*, 19 May 1864.

27. *Argus*, 29 January 1864; Augustus Adamson, Diary, 14 August 1864, now published as A. P. Adamson, *Sojourns of a Patriot: The Field and Prison Papers of an Unreconstructed Rebel*, ed. Richard Bender Abell and Fay Adamson Gecik (Murfreesboro, Tenn.: Southern Heritage Press, 1998); Reynolds to "General," RG 92, Consolidated Correspondence, NA; *Union*, 21 September 1864; Minutes, Post Council of Administration, RG 393, Part IV, Entry 1087, Proceedings and Accounts of Post Council of Administration, Rock Island Barracks, NA.

28. Rogan, 15 April, 9 May 1864; Dillon, 17 May 1864. Although Grant was indeed defeated at the Wilderness, he did not, as his predecessors had done, retreat toward Washington. Instead, he began a series of sidesteps around Lee's army, forcing Lee ever closer to Richmond.

29. Rogan, various dates in June and July 1864.

30. Rogan, 15 February, 16 April 1864; Dillon, 15 July 1864. It is a mistaken notion that Grant stopped the exchanges. He merely confirmed a state of affairs that had endured since the spring of 1863.

31. Wright, "Rock Island Prison," 283; Dillon, 9 June 1864; Rogan, 29, 30 December 1864.

32. Dillon, 17 March 1864.

33. *Union,* 5 October 1864.

34. Minnich, "Comment on Rock Island Prison"; James B. Drake to My Dear Aunt, 21 August 1864, RIA; Cantrell, "Vivid Experiences in Prison"; Rogan, 29 April 1864.

35. Dillon, 2 April 1864; Minnich, *Inside of Rock Island Prison from December, 1863 to June, 1865* (Nashville, Tenn.: Publishing House of the M. E. Church, South, 1908), 17.

36. Minnich, *Inside of Rock Island Prison,* 17. Minnich has misidentified Graham; the true identity of this lieutenant cannot be determined.

37. Ibid., 16–17.

38. Rogan, 13, 22 August 1864; Cantrell, "Vivid Experiences in Prison."

39. Interview, W. S. Howard; Rogan, 6 August 1864.

40. Special Orders No. 8, n.d. [late November 1863], RG 393, NA; Gaston to Parents, 20 January, 21 July 1864, RIA.

41. Everett to Wife, 17 April 1864, Hall to Father and Mother Brothers and Sisters, 24 October 1864, Gaston to Parents, 6, 27 September 1864, all RIA.

42. Everett to Wife, 17 April 1864, RIA; Death Register, RG 109, vol. 395, NA; *Argus,* 12 March 1864.

43. Gaston to Parents, n.d. [probably April 1864], Hall to Father and Mother Brothers and Sisters, 9 August, 24 October 1864, Gaston to Parents, 21 July 1864, all RIA; Rogan, 2 February, 23 March 1864.

44. *Democrat,* 31 December 1863.

45. *Union,* 16 March 1864.

46. Johnson to Hoffman, 23 February 1864, RG 393, Letters Sent, NA; *Union,* 2 March 1864; Guard Report, 28 November 1864, RG 393, NA.

47. Special Orders No. 8, n.d. [late November 1863], RG 393, NA.

48. Thomas to Reynolds, 11 September 1863, RG 94, Miscellaneous Letters, NA; Johnson to Hoffman, 5 August 1864, RG 393, Letters Sent, NA; Guard Reports, 11–14 January 1864, RG 393, NA.

49. Post Orders No. 124, 5 November 1864, RG 393, NA; General Orders No. 19, 6 May 1864, RG 393, NA.

50. B. M. Hord, "Forty Hours in a Dungeon at Rock Island," *Confederate Veteran* (August 1904): 386 (Hord was the nephew of Confederate General Ben McCulloch); Minnich, *Inside of Rock Island Prison,* 22–23.

51. *Revised Regulations,* 107; *OR,* ser. 2, 3:604; Circular, 20 April 1864, Office of the Commissary General of Prisoners, RG 249, Letters Sent, NA.

52. *OR,* ser. 2, 5:140, 6:778–800.

53. Ibid., 5:138, 605, 6:1081, 4:180, 758–59.

54. Prison Fund Account; Minnich, *Inside of Rock Island Prison,* 5; Wright, "Rock Island Prison"; E. Polk Johnson, "Some Prison Experiences," *Confederate Veteran* (January 1919): 82; Interview, David Sears, Hauberg Interviews, RICHS.

NOTES TO PAGES 96–104   229

55. *OR*, ser. 2, 6:660, 5:139, 247; *Revised Regulations*, 35.

56. *Argus*, 19 August, 5 December 1863; A. J. Johnson endorsement on Hoffman to Johnson, 1 January 1865, RG 393, Letters Sent, NA; *OR*, ser. 2, 6:523–24.

57. *OR*, ser. 2, 6:523, 535.

58. Ibid., 6:531, 570–71.

59. Ibid., 625; Proceedings and Accounts of Post Council, RG 393, NA.

60. *OR*, ser. 2, 6:774, 1014, 1036; Hoffman to Stanton, 23 February 1864, RG 107, Letters Received, NA.

61. Hoffman to Stanton, 23 February 1864, RG 107, Letters Received, NA; Minnich, *Inside of Rock Island Prison*, 6.

62. *Argus*, 13, 26 March, 1 April 1864.

63. Ibid., 11, 21, 23 April 1864.

64. Ibid., 13, 20 April 1864; *Union*, 27 April 1864.

4: "SUCH RECKLESS CONDUCT"

1. Hoffman to Stanton, 7 January 1864, RG 107, Letters Received, NA; Circular, Office of the Commissary General of Prisoners, 20 April 1864, RG 249, Letters Sent, NA.

2. Prison Fund Account, January through March 1864,

3. Ibid., March 1864.

4. Johnson to Hoffman, 9 July 1864, RG 94, General Information Index, NA; *OR*, ser. 2, 7:60, 133.

5. Hoffman's files contain two sets of such scratchings; neither is labeled, but the figures suggest that at least one set is for the construction of the prison on Johnson's Island. The second appears to be calculations for the hospitals on Rock Island. *OR*, ser. 2, 7:196; Johnson to Hoffman, 9 July 1864, RG 249, Letters Received, NA; Prison Fund Account.

6. Hoffman to Johnson, 6 May 1864, RG 249, Letters Sent, NA; *OR*, ser. 1, 32 (pt. 2):608–9.

7. Report of the Joint Committee on the Conduct and Expenditures of the War, 38th Congress, 1st Session, Rep. Com. No. 63, 4–5; Brian Steel Wills, *A Battle from the Start: The Life of Nathan Bedford Forrest* (New York: HarperCollins, 1992), 196; *OR*, ser. 2, 7:113. It is possible that the "extraordinary vigilance" would be required because of ration cuts earlier instituted; however, the timing of the correspondence makes it much more likely that Hoffman feared trouble as a result of the proposed retaliation for Forrest's actions.

8. Rogan, 15 April 1864; Johnson to Hoffman, 30 May 1864, RG 249, Register of Letters Received, NA.

9. Dillon, 2 April 1864; *Democrat*, 6 June 1864.

10. Hoffman to Stanton, 23 July 1864, RG 249, Letters Sent, NA.

11. Rogan, 8, 16 May 1864; *Argus*, 16 May 1864.

12. Adjutant General, Illinois, *Report of the Adjutant General of the State of Illinois, Containing Reports for the Years 1861–66*, 8 vols. (Springfield, Ill.: H. W. Borker, 1886), 1:181; James W. Geary, *We Need Men: The Union Draft in the Civil War* (DeKalb: Northern Illinois University Press, 1991), 133.

13. Johnson to Hoffman, 30 May 1864, RG 249, Letters Received, NA; *Argus*, 6 June 1864.

14. Phillips to Longworth, 12 June 1864, Phillips to Mattocks, 7 June 1864, both in Regimental Descriptive, Letter, and Order Book, 133rd Illinois Infantry, RG 94, Entry 114, NA.

15. Muster Rolls, 133rd Illinois, ISA; *Report of the Adjutant General*, 7:34; Norton cited from *Union*, 15 October 1915; *Argus*, 30 May 1864; Death Register, RG 109, vol. 395, NA.

16. *Argus*, 14 June 1864; Death Register, RG 109, vol. 395, NA; Dillon, 9 June 1864; Rogan, 22 June 1864; Wright, "Rock Island Prison," 285.

17. *Argus*, 27 June 1864; Hospital Registers, RG 74, Entry 544, NA. There is some confusion about the date. According to Danforth, Barnes reported the incident the day before it happened. The story probably appeared in the *Union* on 25 June, a Saturday, and Danforth misreported the date.

18. Kingsbury to Johnson, 10 June 1864, RG 156, Letters Sent, NA; *Argus*, 11 June 1864.

19. *Argus*, 3 August 1864; Strength Returns, Administrative Files, 133rd Illinois, ISA.

20. Phillips to Watson, 3 July 1864, Phillips to Johnson, 22 August 1864, both in RG 94, Letter Book, 133rd Illinois, NA; Regimental Files, 133rd Illinois, ISA.

21. Special Orders No. 11, 14 June 1864, No. 32, 27 July 1864, and No. 36, 1 August 1864, RG 393, NA.

22. Summers to Fuller, 25 July 1864, Administrative Files, 133rd Illinois, ISA.

23. Frederick H. Dyer, *A Compendium of the War of the Rebellion* (Des Moines, Iowa: Dyer Publishing Co., 1908), 3:1624; Samuel Bates, *History of the Pennsylvania Volunteers, 1861–5*, 5 vols. (Harrisburg, Pa.: B. Singerly, 1869), 5:450–63; *Roster and Record of Iowa Soldiers*, 1543; Waldschmidt to Baker, 11 August 1864, Correspondence, 48th Iowa, ISHS; Special Orders, various numbers and dates July–September 1864, RG 393, NA; Circular, 10 September 1864, and Circular, 3 August 1864, both in Order and Letter Book, 48th Iowa, ISHS.

24. R. Buckley to Dear Wife and Mother, 5 October 1864, Buckley Papers, VP; General Orders No. 111, 1 July 1864, RG 393, NA.

25. A. W. McPheeters to R. P. McPheeters, 26 January 1863 [1864], McPheeters Papers, USAMHI; General Orders No. 3, 29 July 1864, RG 94, Letter Book, 133rd Illinois, NA; Stevens, *Graybeards*, 47.

26. *OR*, ser. 2, 6:144; *Report of the Joint Committee on the Conduct and Expenditures of the War, No. 63*, 38th Congress, 1st Session (Washington,

D.C.: Government Printing Office, 1864), 5. These were special exchanges of only the sick—outside the cartel, which still did not operate.

27. *Report of Joint Committee No. 63,* 3–4.

28. U.S. Sanitary Commission, *Narrative of the Privations and Sufferings of United States Officers and Soldiers While Prisoners of War in the Hands of the Rebel Authorities* (Philadelphia: U.S. Sanitary Commission, 1864), 80–84.

29. Ibid., 142–43, 150–51.

30. Circular, 1 June 1864, RG 249, Letters Sent, NA; Skinner cited from *OR,* ser. 2, 7:143.

31. *OR,* ser. 2. 6:948; Clark to Johnson, 6 February 1864, Clark to Hoffman, 6, 10 February 1864, RG 107, Letters Received, NA; *Argus,* 31 August 1863.

32. *OR,* ser. 2, 6:1002–3; *Union,* 27 April 1864; *Argus,* 19 March 1864.

33. *OR,* ser. 2, 6:1002–3.

34. Ibid., 3:32, 4:238; General Orders No. 100, 24 April 1863, *General Orders;* George Levy, *To Die in Chicago: Confederate Prisoners at Camp Douglas, 1862–1865* (Evanston, Ill.: Evanston Publishing Company, 1994), 163.

35. Minnich, *Inside of Rock Island Prison,* 19–20.

36. *OR,* ser. 2, 6:589.

37. Ibid., 632, 863–64.

38. Ibid., 870.

39. Ibid., 893–94.

40. Johnson to Hoffman, 10 August 1864, RG 249, Register of Letters Received, NA; Reynolds to Johnson, 30 May 1864, RG 249, Letters Received, NA.

41. *OR,* ser. 2, 7:154; A. M. Keiley, *In Vinculis; or, The Prisoner of War . . .* (Petersburg, Va.: Daily Index, 1866), 114.

42. *OR,* ser. 2, 7:180–81, 366–67; Lewis and Mewha, *Utilization of Prisoners of War,* 39, 42.

43. Hospital Registers, RG 74, Entry 544, NA; Death Register, RG 109, vol. 395, NA.

44. *OR,* ser. 2, 7:415; Johnson to Hoffman, RG 393, Letters Sent, NA; Jamey to Mrs. McMahon [?], n.d. [June 1864], Civil War Miscellaneous Collection, 133rd Illinois, USAMHI. That one escapee drowned has been reported as true by every modern account of the prison save Bryan England's. Johnson originally reported the death, but in July he corrected himself in another letter. This letter, however, was not included in the *Official Records* and has largely been overlooked.

45. Johnson to Hoffman, RG 393, Letters Sent, NA.

46. *OR,* ser. 2, 7:25–29, 65; War Department Special Orders No. 177, 14 May 1864, and No. 207, 14 June 1864, RG 393, Orders Received, NA.

47. *Argus,* 15, 18 June, 13, 15, 18 July 1864.

48. Ibid., 6 June, 3, 5, 15 July, 8 August, 5 September 1864.

49. *Argus,* 27 June, 23 August 1864; Death Register, RG 109, vol. 395, NA.

50. *Argus,* 25 July 1864.

51. Guard Report, 30 May 1864, RG 393, NA; Rogan, 14 June 1864.

52. Charles Smart, ed., *The Medical and Surgical History of the War of the Rebellion,* 3 vols. (Washington, D.C.: Government Printing Office, 1870), Medical Volume, Second Part, 50.

53. Ibid., 52.

54. Ibid., 53–54.

55. Ibid., 54–61.

56. George Worthington Adams, *Doctors in Blue: The Medical History of the Union Army in the Civil War* (New York: H. Schuman, 1952), 226.

57. *Argus,* 1 August 1864; Hospital Registers, RG 74, Entry 544, NA; Death Register, RG 109, vol. 395, NA; *Union,* 24 August 1864; Dillon, 13 August 1864; Smart, *Medical and Surgical History,* Medical Volume, Second Part, 107–14.

58. Johnson to Hoffman, 11 July 1864, RG 249, Letters Received, NA; *OR,* ser. 2, vols. 7 and 8.

59. Johnson to Hoffman, 7 July 1864, RG 393, Letters Sent, NA; Hoffman to Johnson, 26 July 1864, RG 249, Letters Sent, NA.

60. Blagden to Johnson, 1 August 1864, RG 249, Letters Sent, NA.

61. Hoffman to Stanton, 23 July 1864, RG 249, Letters Sent, NA; *OR,* ser. 2, 7:537.

62. *OR,* ser. 2, 7:528, 530.

63. Ibid., 531, 573–74.

5: "The Glare of Wolfish Hunger"

1. Proceedings and Accounts of Post Council, RG 393, NA; Johnson to Hoffman, 14 September 1864, RG 393, Letters Sent, NA; *Argus,* 27 June 1864.

2. Hoffman to Johnson, 6 September 1864, RG 249, Telegrams Sent, NA; Blagden to Johnson, 6 September 1864, RG 249, Entry 8, Letters Sent Relating to Prison Funds, NA; Johnson to Hoffman, 14 September 1864, RG 393, Letters Sent, NA.

3. Prison Fund Account.

4. James G. Hollandsworth, Jr., *The Louisiana Native Guards: The Black Military Experience during the Civil War* (Baton Rouge: Louisiana State University Press, 1995), 6–10; Butler cited from *OR,* ser. 1, 15:548–49, 559.

5. *OR,* ser. 2, 6:31, 186, 240–42, 808, 1034, 1090; ser. 3, 3:722, 1203.

6. Geary, *We Need Men,* 145; "More War History," *Pittsburgh* (?) *Weekly Tribune-Republican,* 15 December, no year [after 1884].

7. "More War History"; Executive Order, 1 September 1864, RG 107, Letters Received, NA.

8. "More War History"; James Fry, "Lincoln at his Best," *New York Tribune,* 28 June 1885; Benjamin P. Thomas and Harold M. Hyman, *Stanton:*

The Life and Times of Lincoln's Secretary of War (New York: Alfred A. Knopf, 1962), 387–88; Roy P. Basler, ed., *The Collected Works of Abraham Lincoln*, 9 vols. (New Brunswick, N.J.: Rutgers University Press, 1955), 7:530–31.

9. Pettis to Lincoln, 20 September 1864, quoted in Basler, ed., *Collected Works of Abraham Lincoln*, 7:14.

10. Ibid.; Dillon, 12 September 1864; Johnson to Hoffman, 27 October 1864, RG 393, Letters Sent, NA.

11. Dillon, 15 October 1864; Minnich, *Inside of Rock Island Prison.*, 30–31, *Argus*, 21 November 1864.

12. Hord, "Forty Hours in a Dungeon," 385; Bohon, "Rock Island Prison," 346; "C 7 K," *Confederate Veteran* (September 1904): 455; Thomas F. Berry, *Four Years with Morgan and Forrest* (Oklahoma City: Harlow-Ratliff Company, 1914), frontispiece, 298.

13. Rogan, 30 September 1864; Dillon, 15 October 1864.

14. Geary, *We Need Men*, 52; Thomas and Hyman, *Stanton*, 234–36; Thomas Wentworth Higginson, *Army Life in a Black Regiment* ([East Lansing]: Michigan State University Press, 1960), 12, 211; *OR*, ser. 3, 2:295, 311–12.

15. Theodore J. Karamanski, *Rally 'round the Flag: Chicago and the Civil War* (Chicago: Nelson-Hall Publishers, 1993), 181–82; Mary Ashton Rice Livermore, *My Story of the War: A Woman's Narrative . . .* (1889; rpt., New York: Da Capo Press, 1995), 351; Ford Douglas, Service Record; Edward A. Miller, *The Black Civil War Soldiers of Illinois: The Story of the Twenty-ninth U.S. Colored Infantry* (Columbia: University of South Carolina Press, 1998), 4–5.

16. *OR*, ser. 2, 6:595–96. According to Hitchcock, the issue of black prisoners led to the breakdown of the exchange cartel. It has been suggested that the Federal administration used the blacks as a pawn in the exchange game, their treatment by the Confederacy serving as excuse to refuse exchange not for reasons of humanity but for more practical reasons: refusing exchange allowed the North to keep Confederate prisoners, weakening Southern armies.

17. Ibid., 2; *Report of the Adjutant General*, 4:445, 462; Heitman, *Historical Register*, 1:220.

18. Bishop to Johnson, 17 October 1864, RG 94, Entry 114, Regimental Letter and Endorsement Book, 108th USCT, NA (hereinafter Letter Book, 108th USCT); Nathan Shirley and Louis Troutman, Pension Files; *Portrait and Biographical Album of Rock Island County, Illinois . . .* (Chicago: Biographical Publishing Company, 1885), 742; *Argus*, 24 September 1864.

19. Isaac McMerkin, Service Record; Descriptive Book, 108th USCT, RG 94, Entry 114, NA; Trimonthly Returns, 108th USCT, RG 94, Entry 115, NA.

20. Hord, "Forty Hours in a Dungeon," 387.

21. William Boyd, Service Record; Guard Reports, various dates in 1864 and 1865, RG 393, NA; Hord, "Forty Hours in a Dungeon," 387.

22. Pearl Martin, certificate attached to Tuttle to Neal, 27 April 1865; Tuttle to Thomas, May 1865, both found in Boyd, Service Record.

23. Hord, "Forty Hours in a Dungeon," 388.

24. Sears, Hauberg Interviews, RICHS; Rogan, 25 September–3 October 1864.

25. Minnich, *Inside of Rock Island Prison*, 30.

26. Ibid., 36; Wright, "Rock Island Prison," 286; Kollock cited from Guard Report, 27 September 1864, RG 393, NA.

27. Guard Report, 26 July–5 August 1864, RG 393, NA.

28. Prison Fund Account; E. Polk Johnson, "Some Prison Experiences"; Wright, "Rock Island Prison," 82; Hord, "Forty Hours in a Dungeon," 385.

29. "Perils of Escape from Prison," *Confederate Veteran* (May 1907): 2; Dillon, 25 November 1864; Wright, "Rock Island Prison," 82; Minnich, *Inside of Rock Island Prison*, 7–8.

30. U.S. Sanitary Commission, *Narrative of Privations*, 52, 106.

31. Death Register, RG 109, vol. 395, NA; Minnich, *Inside of Rock Island Prison*, 8; Gustavus W. Dyer and John Trotwood Moore, comps., *The Tennessee Civil War Veterans Questionnaires*, 5 vols. (Easley, S.C.: Southern Historical Press, 1985), 3:1300.

32. Minnich, *Inside of Rock Island Prison*, 8; Bateson, "Testimony of a Federal Soldier," 293; Dillon, 25 November 1864; Hord, "Forty Hours in a Dungeon."

33. Hord, "Forty Hours in a Dungeon," 386.

34. Dillon, 25 November 1864. The accusation of intentional starvation is the greatest charge leveled against the Federal administration. That there was great hunger in the camps, including Rock Island, is beyond dispute. There is some doubt, however, about how many men hunger actually killed, at least at Rock Island.

35. Minnich, *Inside of Rock Island Prison*, 23; Wright, "Rock Island Prison."

36. *OR*, ser. 2, 8:996–99.

37. Ibid., 998–99; Johnson to Hoffman, 5 November 1864, RG 393, Letters Sent, NA.

38. Hord, "Forty Hours in a Dungeon," 386–87; Guard Report, 7 November 1864, RG 393, NA.

39. Rogan, 7 October 1864; Johnson to Hoffman, 5 November 1864, RG 393, Letters Sent, NA.

40. Guard Report, 26 September 1864, RG 393, NA; Prison Register; Johnson to Hoffman, 5 October 1864, RG 249, Letters Received, NA.

41. Dillon, 4 November 1864; Minnich, *Inside of Rock Island Prison*, 27.

42. J. W. Minnich, "Tunnels to Release Prisoners," *Confederate Veteran* (November 1909): 554; Johnson, "Some Prison Experiences."

43. Joshua Brown, "C. C. Hemming and His Bequest," *Confederate Veteran* (May 1896): 148.

44. Hoffman to Johnson, 29 January 1864, RG 249, Letters Sent, NA;

Prison Fund Account, various dates in 1864; Rogan, 6 June 1864.

45. Prison Fund Account, November 1864; Johnson to Hoffman, 18 December 1864, RG 249, Letters Received, NA; Johnson, "Some Prison Experiences."

46. "The Northwest Conspiracy," *Southern Bivouac* 2 (1887): 442–43.

47. *OR,* ser. 2, 7:8, 241, 1089.

48. Ibid., 260–76.

49. *Union,* 2 September 1863.

50. "The Northwest Conspiracy," 506–8, 566; *OR,* ser. 2, 8:688.

51. "The Northwest Conspiracy," 566–74; Special Orders No. 2, 20 August 1864, RG 393, Orders Received, NA.

52. *OR,* ser. 2, 8:502; Eddy, *Patriotism of Illinois,* 2:515–17.

53. *Argus,* 9, 15 November 1864; Morning Reports, 108th USCT, RG 94, Entry 115, NA; Johnson to Hoffman, 15 November 1864, RG 393, Letters Sent, NA.

54. "C 7 K," *Confederate Veteran* (August 1904): 595; Minnich, *Inside of Rock Island Prison,* 29.

55. *Union,* 19 October 1864.

56. "Reminiscences of Fighting Joe Hooker," *National Tribune* (Washington, D.C.), 7 May 1885; "General Hooker, A Visit to Rock Island Prison," *National Tribune,* 8 February 1883.

57. Hoffman to Johnson, 6 June 1864, RG 393, Register of Letters Received, NA; Minnich, *Inside of Rock Island Prison,* 27.

58. *OR,* ser. 2, 8:993–98.

59. Johnson to Hoffman, 27 October 1864; Circular, Rock Island Barracks, 10 September 1864, RG 107, Letters Received, NA.

60. Johnson to Hoffman, 2 November 1864, RG 249, Letters Received, NA.

6: "HAD I THE POWER"

1. *Argus,* 28, 31 October 1864.

2. Ibid., 21 November 1864.

3. Ibid., 25 November 1864.

4. Ibid.

5. Ibid.

6. Ibid.

7. Ibid.

8. Johnson to Fry, 18 November 1864, RG 393, Letters Sent, NA.

9. Johnson to Hoffman, 10 November 1864, RG 249, Letters Received, NA.

10. Johnson to Smith, 26 December 1864, RG 393, Letters Sent, NA; Special Orders No. 247, 27 October 1864, RG 393, NA.

11. Guard Reports, various dates in December 1864 and January 1865,

RG 393, NA; Hospital Registers, RG 74, Entry 544, NA; Death Register, RG 109, vol. 395, NA; Burial records, Rock Island Arsenal National Cemetery.

12. *Argus,* 28 January, 6 February 1865; R. R. Cable to B. F. Reno, 20 August 1864, RG 94, General Information Index, NA.

13. Johnson to Hamis, 26 November 1864, RG 393, Letters Sent, NA.

14. Dillon, 25 December 1864; Rogan, 25 December 1864.

15. Minnich, *Inside of Rock Island Prison,* 10–11; Dillon, 21, 23 December 1864; Prison Fund Account.

16. Endorsement, Johnson to Danforth, 4 December 1864, RG 393, Register of Letters Received, NA.

17. *OR,* ser. 2, vols. 7 and 8, various entries; *Argus,* 25 January 1864.

18. *OR,* ser. 2, 7:574.

19. Ibid., 575, 837, 926–31.

20. Ibid., 1071, 1080, 1149, 1165, 1195.

21. Hoffman to Johnson, 14 February 1865, RG 249, Telegrams Sent, NA; *Argus,* 5 December 1864.

22. Johnson to Wessels, 24 December 1864, RG 393, Letters Sent, NA; McDermid to Wessels, 23 December 1864, RG 249, Letters Sent, NA.

23. General Orders No. 1, Office of the Commissary General of Prisoners, 15 November 1864, RG 249, Entry 25, Orders and Circulars, Office of the Commissary General of Prisoners, November 1864–August 1865, NA; *OR,* ser. 2, 8:999; Hoffman, Pension File.

24. General Orders No. 9, 13 February 1865, No. 6, 31 January 1865, No. 7, 2 February 1865, RG 393, NA.

25. General Orders No. 6, 31 January 1865, No. 8, 9 February 1865, No. 10, 11 February 1865, RG 393, NA; Morning Reports, 108th USCT, RG 94, NA.

26. Higgs to Capt. M. W., 24 February 1865, Bishop to Higgs, 21 November 1864, both in Letter Book, 108th USCT; Morning Reports, 108th USCT, RG 94, NA.

27. *Argus,* 18 November 1864; *Gazette,* 10 January 1865.

28. *Democrat,* 10 January 1865.

29. *Gazette,* 10 January 1865; Guard Report, 9 January 1865, RG 393, NA; Cargill to Bishop, 27 January 1865, Letter Book, 108th USCT.

30. Regimental Orders No. 5, Letter Book, 108th USCT.

31. Kollock to Johnson, 25 October 1864, Peter Cowherd, Pension File; General Orders No. 6, 29 November 1864, RG 393, NA; Morning Reports, 108th USCT, RG 94, NA; *Democrat,* 3 January 1865.

32. Johnson to Wessels, 6, 24, 25 December 1864, RG 393, Letters Sent, NA.

33. Johnson to Wessels, 12, 25 January 1865, ibid.

34. Johnson to Provost Marshal, 27 January 1865, ibid.

35. Johnson to Wessels, 9 December 1864, Johnson to Hoffman, 11 March 1865, ibid.; Prison Fund Statement.

36. *OR,* ser. 2, 7:578–79.

37. Ibid., 689, 793, 988.

38. Ibid., 8:86, 97–98, 206.

39. Ibid., 7:1298; Dillon, 15, 16 January 1865; Hoffman to Johnson, 6 February 1865, RG 249, Letters Received, NA.

40. Bennett to Johnson, 16 February 1865, RG 249, Letters Received, NA.

41. Lawrence to Johnson, 19 March 1865, ibid.

42. Dillon, 4, 6 February 1865; *OR,* ser. 2, 8:82; Johnson to Hoffman, 28 February 1865, RG 249, Letters Received, NA.

43. Hospital Registers, RG 74, Entry 544, NA.

44. Johnson to Hoffman, 28 February 1865, RG 249, Letters Received, NA.

45. Johnson to Smith, 23 March 1865, RG 393, Letters Sent, NA.

46. Lucy Ann Duke Buford to My Dear Sue, n.d. [late 1864 or early 1865], Buford Papers, LC; *Union,* 15 February 1865; *Argus,* 19 September 1864, 15 April 1865.

47. *Argus,* 15 March 1865; *OR,* ser. 2, 8:15.

48. *OR,* ser. 2, 7:1284–85, 8:33–37.

49. *Gazette,* clipped in *Union,* 15 March 1865; *Argus,* 25, 27 January, 28 February 1865; *OR,* ser. 3, 4:1203.

50. *Argus,* 18 February 1865; *Democrat,* 1 March 1865.

51. Special Orders No. 39, 28 February 1865, RG 393, NA; *Argus,* 25 February 1865.

7: "ALL OF THE PRISONERS HAVE LEFT THIS ISLAND"

1. Circulars Nos. 2 and 3, 13 and 28 February 1865, RG 249, Orders and Circulars, NA; Dillon, 27 January 1865; *OR,* ser. 2, 8:994–95.

2. Endorsement, A. F. Higgs, 3 March 1865, Letter Book, 108th USCT.

3. *Argus,* 5 March 1864; Guard Reports, March 1865, RG 393, NA; Bishop to Higgs, 24 March 1865, Letter Book, 108th USCT.

4. Circular, 11 May 1865, Post Orders, RG 393, NA; General Orders No. 20, 13 May 1865, RG 393, NA.

5. Ewell to Sheffey, 14 March 1865, ISHL; *Argus,* 4 April 1865.

6. Smith to Johnson, 5 April 1865, RG 393, Telegrams Received, NA; Johnson to Smith, 5 April 1865, RG 393, Telegrams Sent, NA.

7. *Argus,* 14 April 1865.

8. Death Register, RG 109, vol. 395, NA.

9. Minnich, *Inside of Rock Island Prison,* 33–34.

10. *Argus,* 20 April 1865.

11. Johnson to Hoffman, 28 February 1865, RG 249, Letters Received, Johnson to Hoffman, 14 May 1865, RG 393, Telegrams Sent, Hoffman to Johnson, 15 May 1865, RG 393, Telegrams Received, Johnson to Hoffman,

19 May 1865, RG 393, Telegrams Sent, Hoffman to Johnson, 22 May 1865, RG 393, Telegrams Received, Hoffman to Johnson, 2 June 1865, RG 249, Telegrams Sent. All in NA.

12. *Argus,* 23 May 1865.

13. Mathew Marx, Pension File; List of Officers Accepting Appointments in the VRC, RG 110, pt. I, Entry 321, NA.

14. Mathew Marx, Service Record; *Argus,* 5 May 1865; Johnson to Marx, 14 July, 23 October 1864, RG 393, Letters Sent, NA; General Orders No. 25, Headquarters, Northern Department, 31 March 1865, in Marx, Pension File.

15. Johnson to Potter, 6 March 1865, RG 393, Letters Sent, NA.

16. Ibid.; Endorsement, Johnson to Satter, 5 March 1865, RG 393, Register of Letters Received, NA.

17. *Argus,* 5 May 1865.

18. Endorsement on Kollock to Bishop, 20 May 1865; Kollock to Bishop, 26 May 1865, both in Letter Book, 108th USCT; *OR,* ser. 2, 8:654. Kollock was correct in the matter of bounties: his men did not get them, because they were not entitled to them. Any bounties due were paid to their former owners.

19. Prison Fund Account. It should be noted that this was half the "full" ration—that is, half the amount issued to Federal troops in the field. See Appendix.

20. *OR,* ser. 2, 8:1001; Johnson to Hoffman, 1 April 1865, RG 393, Letters Sent, NA; Prison Fund Account; Johnson to Hoffman, 15 May, 13 June 1865, RG 393, Letters Sent, NA.

21. General Orders No. 23, 6 June 1865, RG 393, NA.

22. Trimonthly Returns, 108th USCT, RG 94, NA; General Orders No. 14, 5 April 1865, and No. 15, 10 April 1865, RG 393, NA; *OR,* ser. 2, 8:1002.

23. Kingsbury to Johnson, 14 February 1865, Kingsbury to Adjutant General, Northern Department, 16 and 17 February 1865, RG 156, Letters Sent; Endorsement, 3 April 1865, on Kingsbury to Adjutant General, Northern Department, 17 February 1865, RG 393, Register of Letters Received. All in NA.

24. Kingsbury to Dyer, 1 March 1865, RG 156, Letters Sent, NA.

25. Kingsbury to Dyer, 14, 25 March 1865, ibid.

26. Johnson to Nichols, 23 May 1865, RG 393, Kingsbury to Dyer, 10 March 1865, RG 156, ibid.

27. *OR,* ser. 2, 8:538, 585; Johnson to Hoffman, 16, 17, 18 May, RG 249, Telegrams Received, NA.

28. *OR,* ser. 2, 8:537.

29. Johnson to Hoffman, 25, 26, 29 May, RG 249, Telegrams Received, NA; *Argus,* 27 March 1865; Morning Report, 29 February, 12 March 1864, RG 94, Entry 316, Morning Reports, Rock Island Barracks, NA.

30. *Argus,* 14, 15 May, 2 June 1865; Guard Report, 7 June 1865, RG

393, NA; Johnson to Hoffman, 15 May 1865, RG 393, Letters Sent, NA; Higgs to Bishop, 28 May 1865, RG 393, Letters Sent, NA.

31. *Argus,* 27 May 1865; *Democrat,* 29 May 1865.

32. *Democrat,* 31 May 1865.

33. Johnson to Hoffman, 21, 22 June 1865, RG 249, Telegrams Received, NA; *Argus,* 20 June 1865.

34. Johnson to Hoffman, 24 June 1865, RG 249, Letters Received, NA.

35. Guard Report, 24 August 1865, RG 393, NA; Hoffman to Johnson, 29 June 1865, RG 393, Letters Sent, NA; Johnson to Hoffman, 15 July 1865, RG 393, Telegrams Sent, NA; *Democrat,* 28 June 1865.

36. *Argus,* 6, 23 June 1865.

37. Ibid., 26 June 1865.

38. Ibid.

39. Ibid., 14 August 1865.

40. Ibid; John Gitterman, Service Record.

41. *Argus,* 2 December 1865.

42. Ibid.

43. Kress to Dyer, 11 July 1865, RG 156, Letters Sent, NA.

44. *OR,* ser. 2, 6:668.

45. Hord, "Forty Hours in a Dungeon," 385; Minnich, *Inside of Rock Island Prison,* 23.

NOTE ON SOURCES

History has deprived us of a great deal of information on Rock Island. Some of the prison's records have been lost over the years. Accidents of marriage have also deprived the historian of correspondence that would have been invaluable. Hoffman was a widower during the war; Danforth's wife had deserted him; Johnson and Kingsbury, as well as most of the Greybeard officers, had their wives with them while they were on the Island. The prisoners' correspondence also leaves a great deal to be desired. The prison authorities censored their letters. Inmates could say little or nothing of conditions inside the prison. Although prisoners evaded the censors by smuggling letters out of the prison, no example of such a letter has yet come to light.

For the Federal viewpoint, there remain a number of letter books and similar records at national and various state archives. These, coupled with contemporary newspapers and such correspondence as is available, form the bulk of the Federal source material. For the Confederate point of view, two diaries have proved priceless both as unvarnished illustrations of conditions in the Barracks and as corroboration of other sources. One was left by Lafayette Rogan. Although it is generally a record of events Rogan thought worth noting, often without comment, Rogan wrote consistently. Rogan's diary is now in the Illinois State Historical Library in Springfield. Without question, however, William Sylvester Dillon's diary, in the possession of his descendent Helen Ormsby, is the most valuable of any Confederate record of Rock Island. It is straightforward, generally objective, and accurate. It is a shame Dillon wrote no more than he did. Dillon kept his diary throughout the war. Its publication would be a valuable addition to the literature. A third diary, that of Augustus Adamson, has recently been published as *Sojourns of a Patriot*. Whereas both Rogan and Dillon were perceptive observers of their surroundings, Adamson's diary concerns itself primarily with weather, religion, and his inner thoughts; it adds little, and its editors' comments perpetuate the same mistakes other Rock Island sources contain.

Numerous prisoners wrote postwar accounts, many of which appeared in *Confederate Veteran*. Distorted by time and imagination, these accounts nevertheless fill in many blanks. Captain Thomas Berry wrote a memoir of his service, which includes a chapter on Rock Island. Berry's main contribution to history is the emblem of the 7 C K. Much of what Berry wrote is fanciful, to use no harsher term. Far more valuable is the memoir of J. W. Minnich, published in 1905. Minnich had an axe to grind but is usually reliable, if bitter.

Secondary sources for Rock Island are woefully inadequate and, where they exist, woefully in error. For example, *Portals to Hell*, the massive history of Civil War prisons, identifies Johnson as "Andrew" rather than "Adolphus," insists (in concert with several other sources) that one of the escapees during the great June escape drowned in the slough, and states unequivocally that there "were never more than two stoves in a barracks building." All these things, as well as others, are incorrect. T. R. Walker, who worked at the Arsenal Museum in the 1960s, produced an article on the prison and it, too, suffers errors. Because of the plethora of inaccuracies, these and other secondary works on Rock Island were found wanting and have not been cited.

Standing apart from these works and deserving notice is Otis Bryan England's "A Short History of Rock Island Barracks." Mr. England's work is accurate; however, it suffers by its brevity. Because his sources were some of the same ones used by this writer, he is not noted below. His work, however, saved me much consternation.

For topics not bearing directly on life at the Barracks, secondary sources have been consulted. William Hesseltine's *Civil War Prisons: A Study in War Psychology* suffers a decided pro-Confederate bias. Despite this it remains invaluable, especially for discussion of the exchange question. So far, no one has better traced the childish bickering over exchange. Hesseltine's thesis that the North suffered a war psychosis that led to unwarranted retaliation against the prisoners has in recent years been questioned, and at all events lies outside the scope of this book. (A new introduction to a recent reprint of Hesseltine's book and William Marvel in his own introduction to *Andersonville: The Last Depot* both call for a fresh examination of the exchange problem—a call to which I add my own small voice.) For the North's manpower needs and schemes to meet those needs, James Geary's *We Need Men: The Union Draft in the Civil War* provides a wealth of detail on the draft, including some information on the Veteran Reserve Corps, the United States Colored Troops, and the Galvanized Yankees. For the last, Dee Brown's *Galvanized Yankees*, while paying but slight attention to the recruiting at Rock Island, is an excellent history of the regiments that went west to fight Indians.

An overview of Hoffman's prison system can be found in Leslie Hunter's 1971 doctoral dissertation, "Warden for the Union: General William Hoffman (1807–1884)." The research is meticulous, and it gratified this writer that he independently reached the same conclusions about Hoffman's character as did Hunter.

PRIMARY SOURCES

Manuscript and Archival Collections

Illinois State Archives, Springfield
> Administrative Files, 51st Illinois Infantry.
> Administrative Files, 133rd Illinois Infantry.
> Muster Rolls, 133rd Illinois Infantry.

Illinois State Historical Library, Springfield
> Ewell Letter.
> Grierson Papers.
> Marsh Papers.
> "National Armory: An Appeal to Congress by the Citizens of Rock Island and Moline, Illinois," 1861.
> Rogan, Lafayette, Diary, 1864.

Iowa State Historical Society, Des Moines
> Adjutant General's Papers.
>> Correspondence, 37th Iowa.
>> Correspondence, 48th Iowa.
>> Monthly Returns, 37th Iowa.
>> Order and Letter Book, 48th Iowa.
>> Returns for Alterations, 37th Iowa.

Library of Congress, Washington, D.C.
> Charles Buford Papers.

Mississippi State Archives, Jackson
> Reeves, James, Service Record.

National Archives, Washington, D.C.
> Record Group 92, Records of the Office of the Quarter Master General
>> Consolidated Correspondence, Entry 225.
>> Miscellaneous Letters Sent, Entry 14.
>> Registers of Letters Received, Entry 19.

Record Group 94, Office of the Adjutant General
    Compiled Service Records, Volunteer Soldiers:
        Boyd, William, Pension File and Service Record.
        Caraher, Andrew P., Pension File and Service Record.
        Cowherd, Peter, Pension File.
        Galloway, Fletcher, Pension File and Service Record.
        Gitterman, John, Service Record.
        Hoffman, William, Pension File.
        Johnson, Adolphus J., Pension File and Service Record.
        Kincaid, George, Pension File and Service Record.
        Marx, Mathew, Pension File and Service Record.
        Troutman, Louis, Pension File and Service Record.
        Wolfe, Reuben, Pension File and Service Record.
    Descriptive, Letter, Endorsement, and Order Book, 4th VRC,
        Entry 113.
    General Information Index, Entry 289.
    Morning Reports, 108th USCT, Entry 115.
    Morning Reports, Rock Island Barracks, Entry 316.
    Muster Rolls, 4th VRC, Entry 114.
    Regimental Letter, Order, and Endorsement Book, 108th USCT,
        Entry 113.
    Register of Sick and Wounded, Prison Hospitals, Rock Island,
        Illinois, Entry 544, vols. 178–81.
    Trimonthly Returns, 108th USCT, Entry 115.
Record Group 107, Records of the Office of the Secretary of War
    Letters Received by the Secretary of War, Unregistered Series,
        1789–1861, Entry 19.
    Letters Received by the War Department from the Commissary
        General of Prisoners, Entry 32.
Record Group 109, War Department Collection of Confederate
    Records
    Record of Prisoners Who Have Died at Rock Island Barracks,
        Illinois, Volume 395. Microform.
    Register of Prisoners Confined at Rock Island Barracks, Illinois,
        Volume 394. Microform.
Record Group 110, Provost Marshal General's Bureau
    General Information Index, Rock Island, Illinois, Entry 289.
    List of Officers Accepting Appointments in the VRC, Entry 321.
    Orders and Circulars of the Provost Marshal General, Entry 306,
        vols. 1 and 2.
Record Group 156, Records of the Chief of Ordnance
    Burr, Lt. Col. George W., "History of the Rock Island Arsenal,
        1862–1913."
    Letters Sent, Chief of Ordnance, Miscellaneous, August 6, 1863,

to January 30, 1866 (includes letters sent from Rock Island Arsenal).

Register of Letters Received, Rock Island Arsenal.

Record Group 249, Records of the Office of the Commissary General of Prisoners

Ledger of Disbursements Made on Account of the Prison Fund, 1864–1866, Entry 97.

Letters Received, Entry 11.

Letters Sent, Entry 3.

Letters Sent Relating to the Prison Fund, Entry 8.

Papers of General Hoffman, Entry 16.

Register of Letters Received, Entry 10.

Telegrams Received, Entry 22.

Telegrams Sent, Entry 21.

Record Group 393, Records of the United States Army Continental Commands (all entries Part IV)

Endorsements Sent, Rock Island Barracks, Entry 1079.

General Orders, Rock Island Barracks, Entry 1083.

Guard Reports and List of Prisoners, Rock Island Barracks, Entry 1088.

Letters Sent, Rock Island Barracks, Entry 1078.

Orders Received, Rock Island Barracks, Entry 1086.

Post Orders and Circulars, Rock Island Barracks, Entry 1085.

Records of Post Council of Administration, Rock Island Barracks, Entry 1087.

Register of Letters Received, Rock Island Barracks, Entry 1081.

Special Orders, Rock Island Barracks, Entry 1084.

Telegrams Received, Rock Island Barracks, Entry 1082.

Telegrams Sent, Rock Island Barracks, Entry 1080.

Rock Island Arsenal Historical Office, Rock Island, Illinois

Everett Letters (photostats).

Gaston Letters (photostats).

Hall Letters (photostats).

Perry-Mosher, Kate. "History of Rock Island, Illinois, 1863." Paper read before the Henrietta Hunt Morgan Chapter, United Daughters of the Confederacy, [1901].

Rock Island Arsenal Museum, Rock Island, Illinois

Drake Letter.

Rock Island County Historical Society, Rock Island, Illinois

Hauberg Interviews

Sears, David.

Military Records of Rock Island County.

United States Military Academy Archives, West Point, New York
   Annual Reunion of the Graduates of the United States Military
      Academy, June 17, 1880.
   Annual Reunion of the Graduates of the United States Military
      Academy, June 12, 1885.
   Cadets Arranged in Order of Merit in Their Respective Classes,
      as Determined at the General Examination in June 1829.
   Cullum, Bvt. Major General George W., Biographical Register of
      the Officers and Graduates of the U.S. Military Academy at
      West Point, N.Y., From Its Establishment, in 1802, to 1890.
   Special Collections
      Hoffman, William.
      Kingsbury, Charles P.

Virginia Polytechnic Institute and State University, Blacksburg
   Buckley Papers.

Unpublished Sources in Private Possession

Bardelabeu Letter. Author's collection.
Beardsley Letters. Barbara Appleby, Apopka, Florida.
Dillon, William Sylvester, Diary. Helen Ormsby, Eagle Pass, Alaska.
Paschal Letters. Maggie Burmeister, St. Charles, Illinois.
Yates et al. to Abraham Lincoln (2 letters, no dates), and memoran-
   dum, 16 January 1865, from A. Lincoln, unaddressed but to either
   Stanton or Hoffman. Owner prefers to remain anonymous.

PUBLISHED LETTERS AND COLLECTIONS

Adamson, A. P. *Sojourns of a Patriot: The Field and Prison Papers of an Unrecon-
   structed Rebel*. Edited by Richard Bender Abell and Fay Adamson
   Gecik. Murfreesboro, Tenn.: Southern Heritage Press, 1998.
Basler, Roy P., ed. *The Collected Works of Abraham Lincoln*. 9 vols. New
   Brunswick, N.J.: Rutgers University Press, 1955.
Brumgardt, John R., ed. *Civil War Nurse: The Diary and Letters of Hanna
   Ropes*. Knoxville: University of Tennessee Press, 1980.
Higginson, Thomas Wentworth. *Army Life in a Black Regiment*. [East Lan-
   sing]: Michigan State University Press, 1960.
Stevens, Harriet, ed. *The Graybeards: The Family of Major Lyman Allen during
   the American Civil War*. Iowa City: Press of the Camp Pope Bookshop,
   1998.
Williams, Alpheus S. *From The Cannon's Mouth: The Civil War Letters of Gen-
   eral Alpheus S. Williams*. Lincoln: University of Nebraska Press, 1995.

Published Memoirs

Berry, Thomas F. *Four Years with Morgan and Forrest.* Oklahoma City: Harlow-Ratliff Company, 1914.

Billings, John. *Hardtack and Coffee; or, The Unwritten Story of Army Life.* 1887; rpt., Lincoln: University of Nebraska Press, 1993.

Frost, Griffin. *Camp and Prison Journal.* 1867; rpt., Iowa City: Press of the Camp Pope Bookshop, 1994.

Gracey, Samuel L. *Annals of the Sixth Pennsylvania Cavalry.* Philadelphia: E. H. Butler & Co., 1868.

Jackson, Donald, ed. *Black Hawk: An Autobiography.* Urbana: University of Illinois Press, 1955.

Keiley, A. M. *In Vinculis; or, The Prisoner of War . . .* Petersburg, Va.: Daily Index, 1866.

Livermore, Mary Ashton Rice. *My Story of the War: A Woman's Narrative . . .* 1889; rpt., New York: Da Capo Press, 1995.

Minnich, J. W. *Inside of Rock Island Prison from December, 1863 to June, 1865.* Nashville: Publishing House of the M. E. Church, South, 1908.

Quaife, Milo Milton, ed. *The Early Days of Rock Island and Davenport: The Narratives of J. W. Spencer and J. M. D. Burrows.* Chicago: Lakeside Press, 1942.

U.S. Sanitary Commission. *Narrative of the Privations and Sufferings of United States Officers and Soldiers While Prisoners of War in the Hands of the Rebel Authorities . . .* Philadelphia: U.S. Sanitary Commission, 1864.

Newspapers

Chicago Tribune
Davenport Democrat
Davenport Gazette
Harper's Weekly
National Tribune (Washington, D.C.)
Newark Daily Advertiser
New York Times
Rock Island Argus
Rock Island Argus and Islander
Rock Island Republican
Rock Island Union
Weekly Times Republican (Troy, N.Y.)

Government Documents

Adjutant General, Illinois. *Report of the Adjutant General of the State of Illinois: Containing Reports for the Years 1861–66.* 8 vols. Springfield, Ill.: H. W. Borker, 1886.

Baker, Nathaniel B. *Report of Brig.-Gen. Nathaniel B. Baker, Adjutant General*. Des Moines, Iowa: F. W. Palmer, 1867.

Bates, Samuel. *History of the Pennsylvania Volunteers, 1861–5*. 5 vols. Harrisburg, Pa.: B. Singerly, 1869.

General Orders Affecting the Volunteer Force, 1861–1863. Washington, D.C.: Government Printing Office, 1864.

Heitman, Francis. *Historical Register and Dictionary of the United States Army, from Its Organization, September 29, 1789, to March 2, 1903*. 2 vols. Washington, D.C.: Government Printing Office, 1903.

Massachusetts in the Army and Navy during the War of 1861–65. Boston: Wright & Potter Printing Co, 1895.

Report of the Joint Committee on the Conduct and Expenditures of the War, No. 63. Washington, D.C.: Government Printing Office, 1864.

Report of the Joint Committee on the Conduct and Expenditures of the War, No. 68. Washington, D.C.: Government Printing Office, 1864.

Revised Regulations for the Army of the United States. Washington, D.C.: Government Printing Office, 1861.

Roster and Record of Iowa Soldiers in the War of the Rebellion. Des Moines, Iowa: Emory H. English, 1911.

Smart, Charles, ed. *The Medical and Surgical History of the War of the Rebellion*. 3 vols. Washington, D.C.: Government Printing Office, 1870.

The War of the Rebellion: A Compilation of the Official Records of the Union and Confederate Armies. 128 vols. Washington, D.C.: Government Printing Office, 1880–1901.

Articles

Baird, Rupert. "In Camp and Prison." *Confederate Veteran* (February 1917): 95.

Bateson, John. "Testimony of a Federal Soldier." Southern Historical Society, *Papers* (April 1876): 292–94.

Bohon, W. J. "Rock Island Prison." *Confederate Veteran* (July 1908): 346–47.

Brown, Joshua. "C.C. Hemmings and His Bequest." *Confederate Veteran* (May 1896): 48–49.

"C 7 K." *Confederate Veteran* (September 1904): 455.

Cantrell, A. J. "Vivid Experiences in Prison." *Confederate Veteran* (May 1908): 216.

Damon, H. G. "Perils of Escape from Prison." *Confederate Veteran* (May 1907): 223–26.

Dodson, W. C. "Stories of Prison Life." *Confederate Veteran* (March 1900): 121–22.

Duke, Basil, and Thomas Hines, eds. "The Northwest Conspiracy." *Southern Bivouac* 2 (1887): 436–42, 501-10, 567–74, 699–704.

Hord, B. M. "Forty Hours in a Dungeon at Rock Island." *Confederate Veteran* (August 1904): 385–89.

Johnson, E. Polk. "Some Prison Experiences." *Confederate Veteran* (January 1919): 81–82.

Minnich, J. W. "Comment on Rock Island Prison." *Confederate Veteran* (August 1908): 394.

———. "Tunnels to Release Prisoners." *Confederate Veteran* (November 1909): 554.

Pullen, P. P. "A Kentucky Hero." *Confederate Veteran* (August 1923): 287–88.

"7 C K." *Confederate Veteran* (August 1904) 594–95.

Wright, Charles. "Rock Island Prison, 1864–5." Southern Historical Society, *Papers,* April 1876.

SECONDARY SOURCES

Books

Adams, George Worthington. *Doctors in Blue: The Medical History of the Union Army in the Civil War.* New York: H. Schuman, 1952.

Berkow, Robert M., ed. *The Merck Manual of Diagnosis and Therapy.* 13th ed. Rahway, N.J.: Merck, Sharpe, and Dohme Research Laboratories, 1977.

Byers, S. H. M. *Iowa In War Times.* Des Moines, Iowa: W. D. Condit & Co., 1888.

Cole, Arthur Charles. *The Era of the Civil War, 1848–1870.* Springfield: Illinois Centennial Commission, 1919.

Cunningham, H. H. *Doctors in Gray: The Confederate Medical Service.* Baton Rouge: Louisiana State University Press, 1960.

Dean, Eric T. *Shook over Hell: Post-Traumatic Stress, Vietnam, and the Civil War.* Cambridge, Mass.: Harvard University Press, 1997.

Dyer, Frederick H. *Compendium of the War of the Rebellion.* Des Moines, Iowa: Dyer Publishing Co., 1908.

Dyer, Gustavus W., and John Trotwood Moore, comps. *The Tennessee Civil War Veterans Questionnaires.* 5 vols. Easley, S.C.: Southern Historical Press, 1985.

Eddy, T. E. *Patriotism of Illinois: A Record of the Civil and Military History of the State in the War for the Union.* 2 vols. Chicago: Clarke & Co., 1865.

Geary, James W. *We Need Men: The Union Draft in the Civil War.* DeKalb: Northern Illinois University Press, 1991.

Gleeson, Ed. *Illinois Rebels: A Civil War Unit History of G Company . . .* Carmel, Ind.: Guild Press of Indiana, 1996.

Gordon, Richard. *The Alarming History of Medicine.* New York: St. Martin's Press, 1994.

Guernsey, Alfred H., and Henry M. Alden. *Harper's Pictorial History of the Civil War.* New York: Harper and Brothers, 1866.

Hayes, William Edward. *The Iron Road to Empire: The History of 100 Years of *the Progress and Achievements of the Rock Island Line.* New York: Simons-Bordman, 1953.

Historical Encyclopedia of Illinois and History of Rock Island County. 2 vols. Chicago: Munsell Publishing Co., 1914.

Hollandsworth, James G., Jr. *The Louisiana Native Guards: The Black Military Experience during the Civil War.* Baton Rouge: Louisiana State University Press, 1995.

Johannsen, Robert. *Stephen A. Douglas.* Urbana: University of Illinois Press, 1997.

Karamanski, Theodore. *Rally 'round the Flag: Chicago and the Civil War.* Chicago: Nelson-Hall Publishers, 1993.

Levy, George. *To Die in Chicago: Confederate Prisoners at Camp Douglas, 1862–1865.* Evanston, Ill.: Evanston Publishing Company, 1994.

Lewis, George G., and John Mewha. *History of Prisoner of War Utilization by the United States Army, 1776–1945.* Washington, D.C.: Department of the Army, 1955.

Marvel, William. *Andersonville: The Last Depot.* Chapel Hill: University of North Carolina Press, 1995.

Meyer, Paul. *Iowa Valor: A Compilation of Civil War Combat Experiences . . .* Garrison, Iowa: Meyer Publishing, 1994.

Miller, Edward A. *The Black Civil War Soldiers of Illinois: The Story of the Twenty-ninth U.S. Colored Infantry.* Columbia: University of South Carolina Press, 1998.

Mullins, Michael. *The Fremont Rifles: A History of the 37th Illinois Veteran Volunteer Infantry.* Wilmington, N.C.: Broadfoot Publishing Company, 1990.

Newton, William Monroe. *History of Barnard, Vermont, with Family Genealogies, 1761–1927.* [Montpelier]: Vermont Historical Society, [1928].

The Past and Present of Rock Island County, Illinois. . . Chicago: H. F. Kett & Co., 1877.

Portrait and Biographical Album of Rock Island County, Illinois . . . Chicago: Biographical Publishing Co., 1885.

Thomas, Benjamin P., and Harold M. Hyman. *Stanton: The Life and Times of Lincoln's Secretary of War.* New York: Alfred A. Knopf, 1962.

War's Greatest Workshop: Rock Island Arsenal. [Rock Island, Ill.]: Arsenal Publishing Co., 1922.

Weigley, Frank. *Quartermaster General of the Union Army: A Biography of M. C. Meigs.* New York: Columbia University Press, 1959.

Wiley, Bell Irvin. *The Life of Johnny Reb: The Common Soldier of the Confederacy.* Baton Rouge: Louisiana State University Press, 1972.

Wills, Brian Steel. *A Battle from the Start: The Life of Nathan Bedford Forrest.* New York: HarperCollins, 1992.

Wilson, James. *Biographical Sketches of Illinois Officers Engaged in the War against the Rebellion in 1861.* Chicago: J. Barnet, 1862.

Interviews by the Author

Howard, W. S. Descendent of William Bennefield.
Krippner, Ralph. Archivist, Rock Island Arsenal Historical Office.
Ormsby, Helen. Descendent of William Dillon.